Origami Symphony No. 1

The Elephant's Trumpet Call

Books by John Montroll
www.johnmontroll.com

General Origami

DC Super Heroes Origami
Origami Worldwide
Teach Yourself Origami: Second Revised Edition
Christmas Origami
Storytime Origami
Origami Inside-Out: Third Edition

Animal Origami

Dogs in Origami
Perfect Pets Origami
Dragons and Other Fantastic Creatures in Origami
Bugs in Origami
Horses in Origami
Origami Birds
Origami Gone Wild
Dinosaur Origami
Origami Dinosaurs for Beginners
Prehistoric Origami: Dinosaurs and other Creatures: Third Edition
Mythological Creatures and the Chinese Zodiac Origami
Origami Under the Sea
Sea Creatures in Origami
Origami Sea Life: Third Edition
Bringing Origami to Life
Bugs and Birds in Origami
Origami Sculptures: Fourth Edition
African Animals in Origami: Third Edition
North American Animals in Origami: Third Edition

Geometric Origami

Origami Stars
Galaxy of Origami Stars: Second Edition
Origami and Math: Simple to Complex
Origami & Geometry
3D Origami Platonic Solids & More: Second Edition
3D Origami Diamonds
3D Origami Antidiamonds
3D Origami Pyramids
A Plethora of Polyhedra in Origami: Third Edition
Classic Polyhedra Origami
A Constellation of Origami Polyhedra
Origami Polyhedra Design

Dollar Bill Origami

Dollar Origami Treasures: Second Edition
Dollar Bill Animals in Origami: Second Revised Edition
Dollar Bill Origami
Easy Dollar Bill Origami

Simple Origami

Fun and Simple Origami: 101 Easy-to-Fold Projects: Second Edition
Super Simple Origami
Easy Dollar Bill Origami
Easy Origami Animals
Easy Origami Polar Animals
Easy Origami Ocean Animals
Easy Origami Woodland Animals
Easy Origami Jungle Animals
Meditative Origami

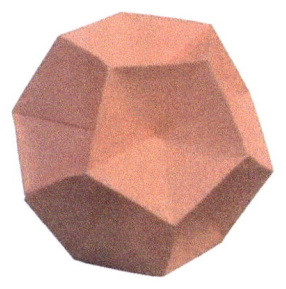  

Origami Symphony No. 1

The Elephant's Trumpet Call

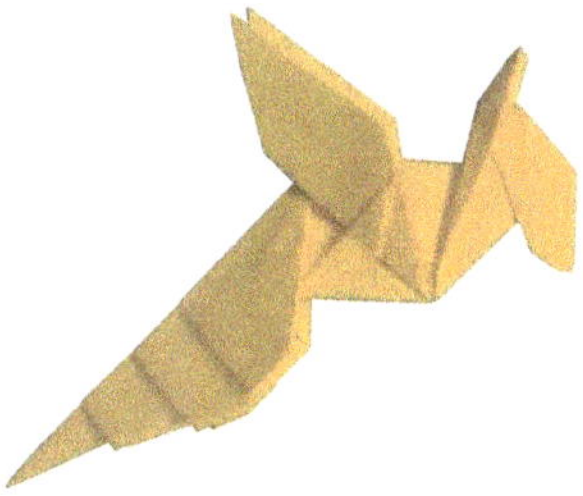

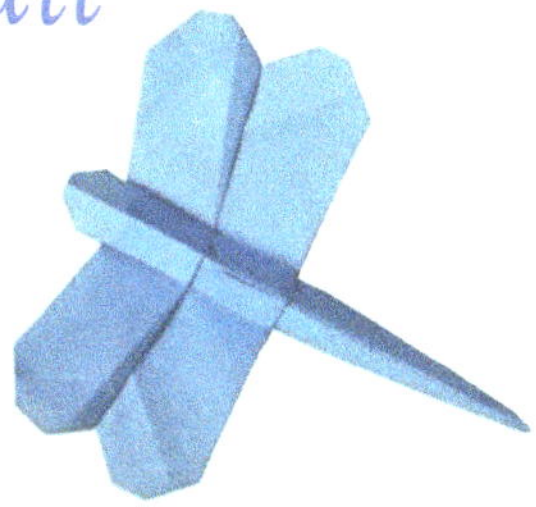

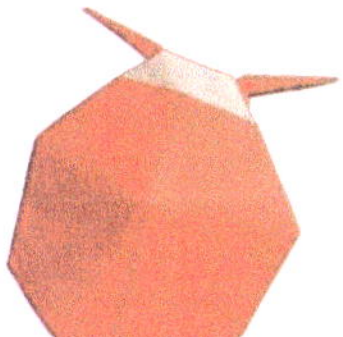

John Montroll

Antroll Publishing Company

To Robert and Yojna

Origami Symphony No. 1: *The Elephant's Trumpet Call*

Copyright © 2019 by John Montroll. All rights reserved.
No part of this publication may be copied or reproduced by any means without the express written permission of the author.

ISBN-10: 1-877656-45-3
ISBN-13: 978-1-877656-45-3

Antroll Publishing Company

Introduction

Welcome to the world premier of the first Origami Symphony! A musical symphony is an elaborate composition that typically has four movements, each with various musical expressions and forms. When first developed, the symphony brought music to a new level. This origami symphony is also an elaborate composition with four movements of varying themes from simple to complex, depicting the richness of origami.

My vision of origami is that it is fun to fold, that standard origami paper is all that is required, and that the models are pleasing and hold together well when completed. An elegant folding method using fewer steps is better than a cumbersome method requiring lots of steps to achieve the same look. While many like to judge a model by its finished look, the folding experience is also important. I look for hidden structures to allow the model to have good proportions, with minimal thickness of layers so it does not spread. This way, it gives models a life-force. All models in this symphony are folded from a single uncut square.

In music, every time the performer plays a composition, he improves. The same is true with origami. While it is fun to fold a model and then move on to the next, it would also be a good practice to fold it a few more times, making it easier to fold, perhaps foldable by memory, making one's own improvements on the model in the process, ultimately making the folding experience more enjoyable.

This symphony has four movements depicting various life forms and more abstract qualities of the Earth. The first movement, Allegro, is theme and variation on the traditional crane. The symphony begins by taking a classic work and expanding upon it, showing new directions in origami. The crane symbolizes peace and is a favorite model to fold and to teach the beginner. The variations include a Sandhill Crane, a Whooping Crane, a Crowned Crane, and a Black-Necked Crane. The second movement, Andante, captures simple crawling bugs. While much has been done recently to depict insects in full detail with all the legs and appendages, it is also important to find an easy way to depict them. The third movement is a minuet of the Platonic Solids with a trio of Sunken Solids. The Platonic Solids symbolize Fire, Earth, Air, Water, and the Universe. Unusual folding methods are used so the models are fun to fold in as few steps as possible, and hold together well when completed. The symphony concludes with the fourth movement, The March of the Large African Animals. You can hear the Elephant's trumpet call and the Lion's roar.

The diagrams are drawn in the internationally approved Randlett-Yoshizawa style. You can use any kind of square paper for these models, but the best results will be achieved with standard origami paper, which is colored on one side and white on the other (in the diagrams in this book, the shading represents the colored side). Large sheets, such as nine inches squared, are easier to use than small ones.

Please follow me on Instagram @montrollorigami to see posts of my origami.

I thank Antoni Wellisz, Ian Patzman-Rivard, and Jay Sella for the photography. I thank my editor, Charley Montroll. I also thank Himanshu Agrawal and Brian Webb for their continued support of this project.

John Montroll
www.johnmontroll.com

Contents

Symbols 9
Appreciating Symphonies and Origami 9
Origami Symphony No. 1 10
First Movement 11
Second Movement 40
Third Movement 71
Fourth Movement 99

★ Simple
★★ Intermediate
★★★ Complex
★★★★ Very Complex

First Movement
Allegro: Theme and Variation on the Classic Crane

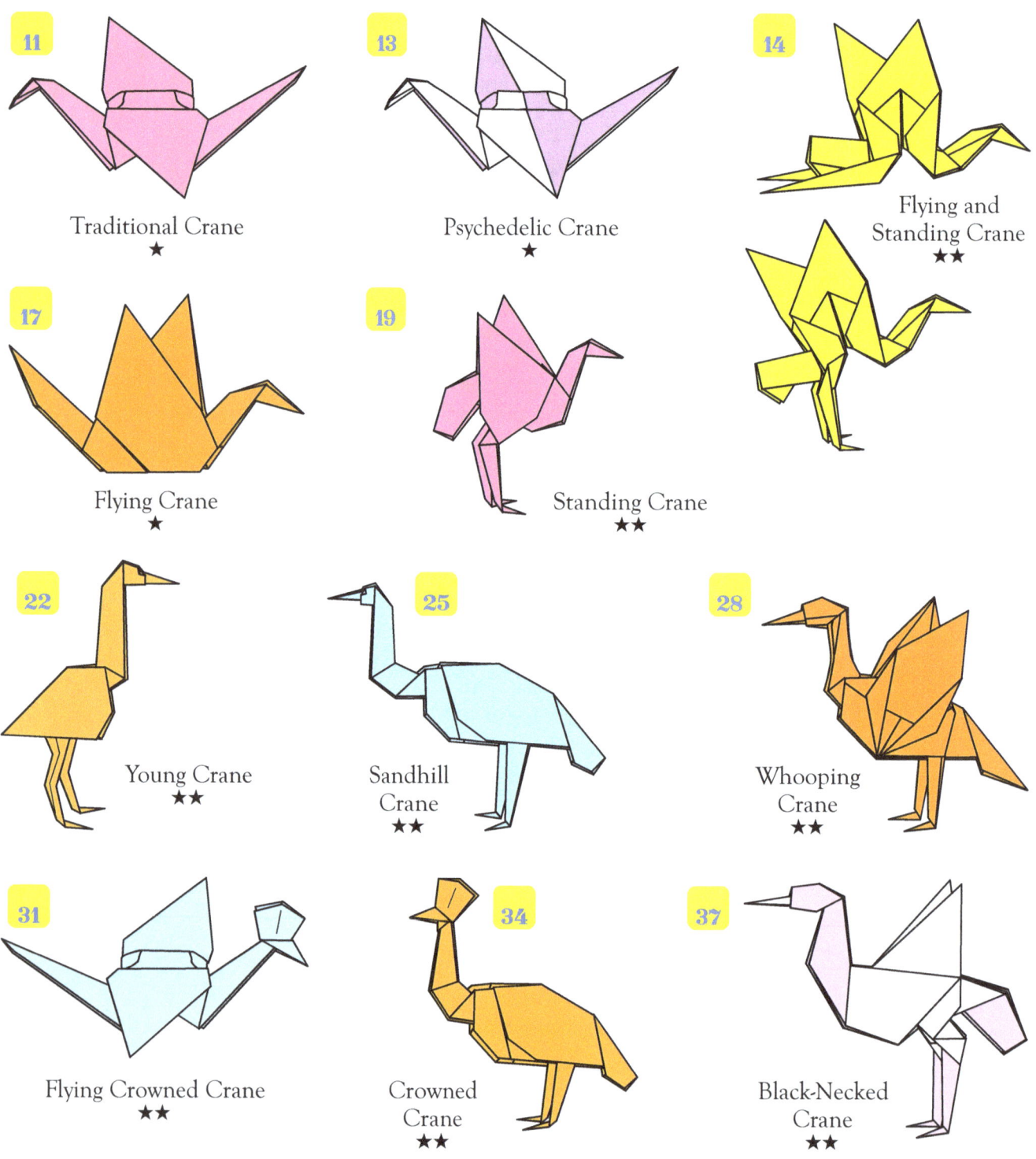

11 Traditional Crane ★

13 Psychedelic Crane ★

14 Flying and Standing Crane ★★

17 Flying Crane ★

19 Standing Crane ★★

22 Young Crane ★★

25 Sandhill Crane ★★

28 Whooping Crane ★★

31 Flying Crowned Crane ★★

34 Crowned Crane ★★

37 Black-Necked Crane ★★

6 *Origami Symphony No. 1*

Third Movement
Minuet of Platonic Solids with a Trio of Sunken Solids

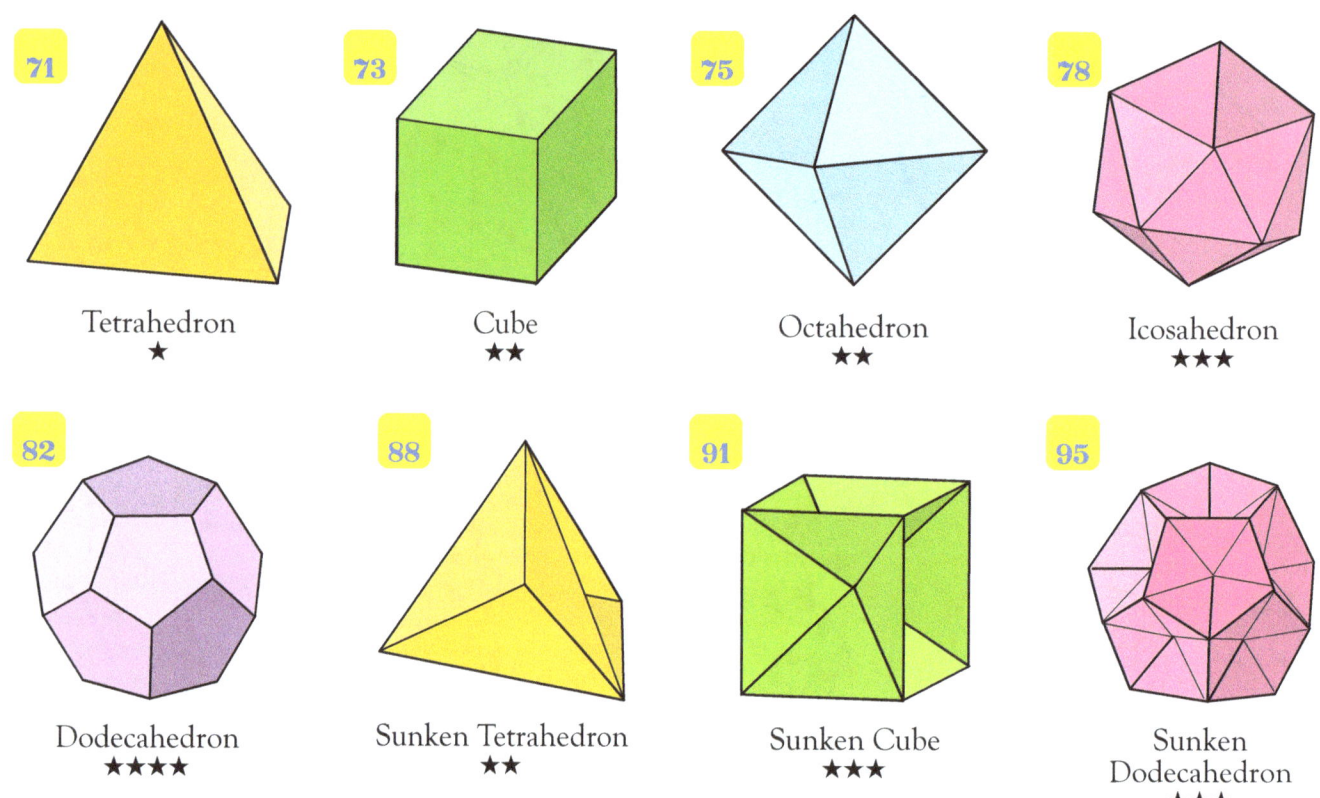

Fourth Movement
March of the Large African Animals

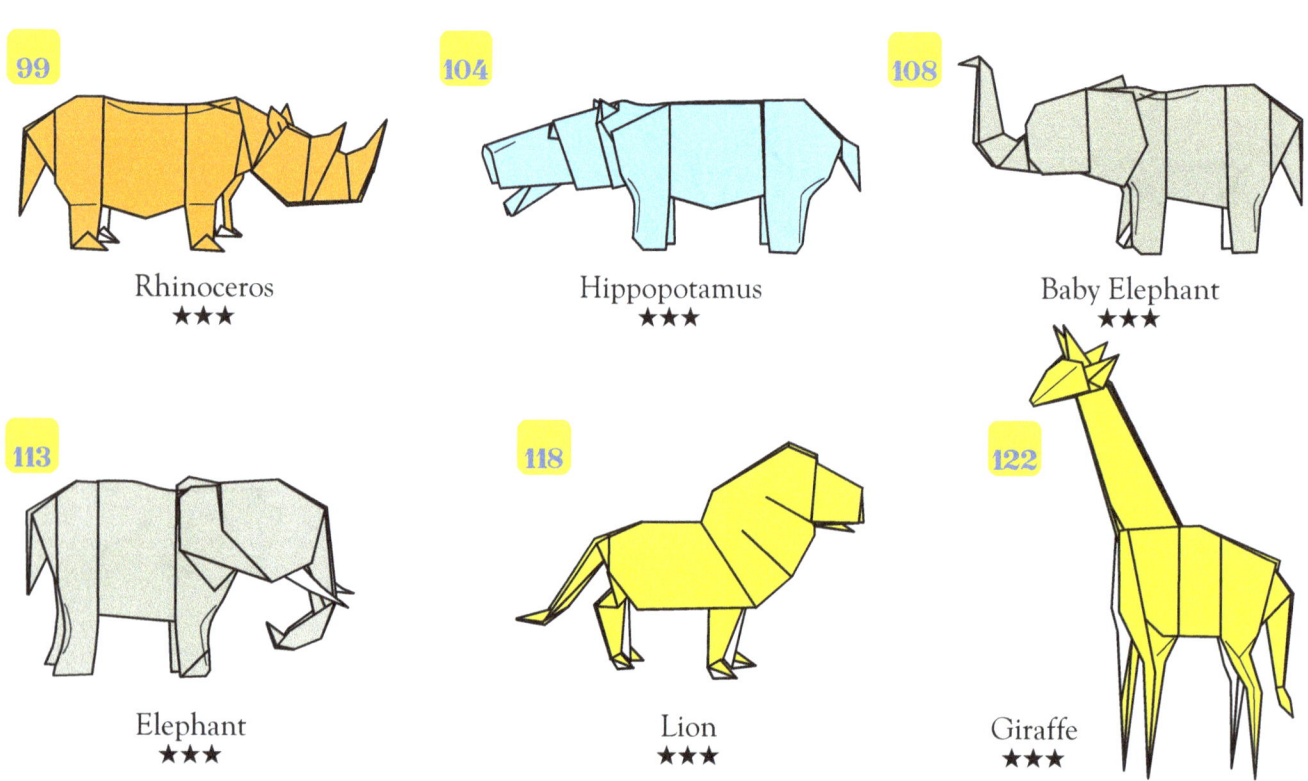

Origami Symphony No. 1

Symbols

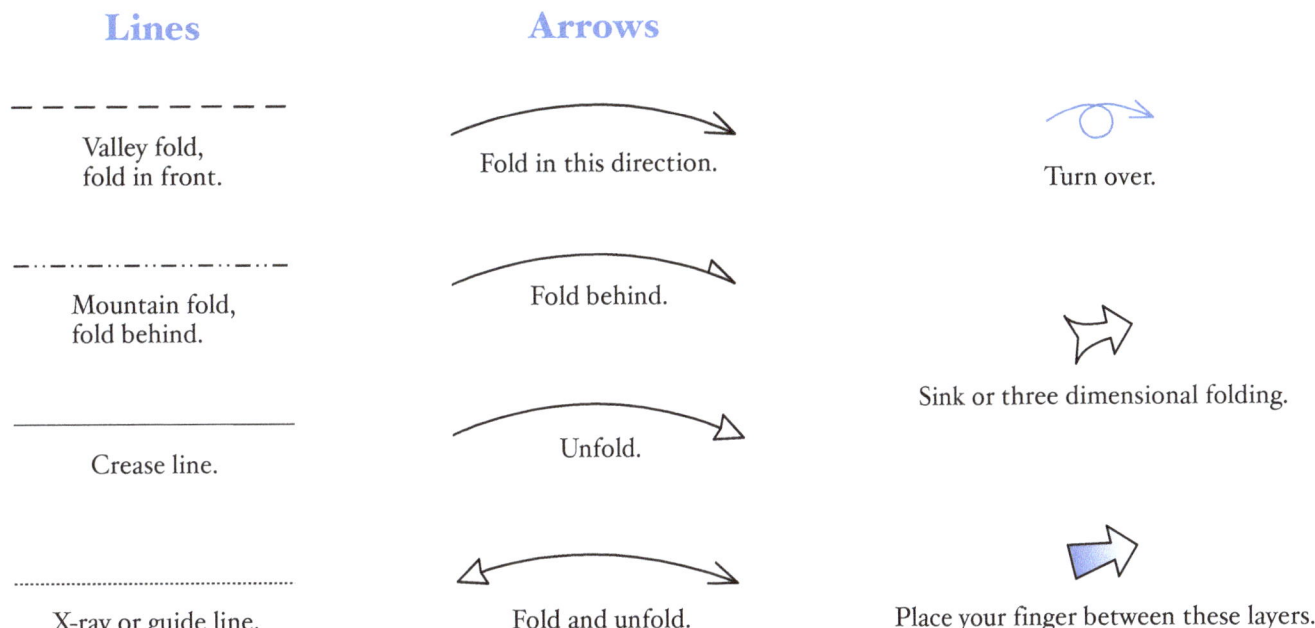

Appreciating Symphonies and Origami

Symphonies were invented in Europe around the 18th century during the Classical Period of musical history, approximately 1740 to 1820. Composers put deep thought into musical expression to be performed by an orchestra under a conductor's guidance in a grand concert hall for an appreciative audience. An unimaginable amount of work went into the development of the instruments, effective and acoustically balanced concert halls, the skill of the performers, along with music theory and the composers' evolving thoughts as music changed throughout the centuries. As a result, each instrument in the orchestra has a rich history. All of this represents and celebrates the highest of human achievement, as art is the concrete and sharable expression of human thought, emotion and creativity.

A typical symphony is structured in four movements. The first and last movements are often in Sonata form, introducing themes, developing them, bringing them back, and ending. When listeners understand the Sonata form, they can follow the progression of the symphony. After a complex first movement, the second movement is often slow and gentle. The third is a fast-paced Minuet or Scherzo, with a Trio in the middle, and can be dance-like. The last movement is often once again in Sonata form with rich and complex themes. Any of the movements can also take other forms, such as theme and variation.

Music composers throughout the past several centuries have written a variety of work for different skill levels. Do all composers perform their own work? Some composers are also violinists or play other instruments, so they might. However, most composers are not experts at playing all the instruments, yet understand them very well. Much of music is playable by a performer with a certain skill, yet there are difficult pieces that only a few can perform. So the composer thinks of not only the musical expression, but its ability to be playable by a large group of performers or a specific performer.

As an origami composer, I am searching for the simplest way to achieve the complex. That is where the magic is. I strive to make my work foldable by the mainstream folder, hold well using standard origami paper, use the fewest folds for the highest level of detail and effect, and be enjoyable to fold. This brings origami to a higher level and gives each model its own life-force. I am always looking for ways to improve origami design through taking related and varied subjects and putting them together to create a common context in the form of full scenes, where both individual models and groups of models can tell their story.

Origami Symphony No. 1

Cranes, Bugs, Geometric Shapes, and Mammals are all united in this Symphony. Elegant folding methods make the models fun to fold with a minimal number of steps for their detail.

The first movement opens the Symphony with a theme and variation on the traditional Crane, which is a symbol of peace. For several of the Cranes, legs are added, and others have crowns and color changes. The first variations use elements from the traditional Crane, and then develop into new forms. The folding methods for the Cranes are all kept at an intermediate level, all under 30 steps.

The slow and relaxing second movement, Andante, presents over a dozen simple crawling Bugs. Other small creatures such as a snail are included because the Japanese character for Bugs includes other small creatures. While it is fun and challenging to fold insects with legs and full detail, it is also fun to capture their essence. Specific colors can make a display of these insects more life-like, such as a Red Ladybug, Blue Dragonfly, Green Grasshopper, Yellow Wasp, Orange Butterfly, and a Black Fly.

The third movement is a Minuet of Platonic Solids with a trio of Sunken Solids. These geometric shapes represent the Elements of Fire, Earth, Air, Water, and the Universe. Folding three dimensional models that hold and lock together requires a special way of folding; the folding methods for the five Platonic Solids shows a wide range of folding techniques and a range of skill levels from simple to very complex. The Trio shows three models built on Sunken Triangles, Squares, and Pentagons. While these shapes are fun to fold and exhibit, they are also stunning with Origami animals placed around them.

The fourth movement, March of the Large African Animals, concludes the symphony with more complex work. You can hear the Elephant's trumpet call, the Lion's roar, the Hippo making bubbles in the water, and the galloping of Giraffes. Exhibits can be made with mother and baby Elephant, along with Rhinos, Lions, Hippos, and Giraffes.

This symphony, then, captures several themes, folding styles, and levels of skill, and making colorful scenes of models from the different movements shows the diversity of Origami.

First Movement

Allegro: Theme and Variation on the Classic Crane

The symphony opens with the Traditional Crane, a symbol of peace. Variations are at first adapted from the Traditional Crane, and then develop into new forms. Models are simple and intermediate in skill level. Spread your wings and soar with the cranes.

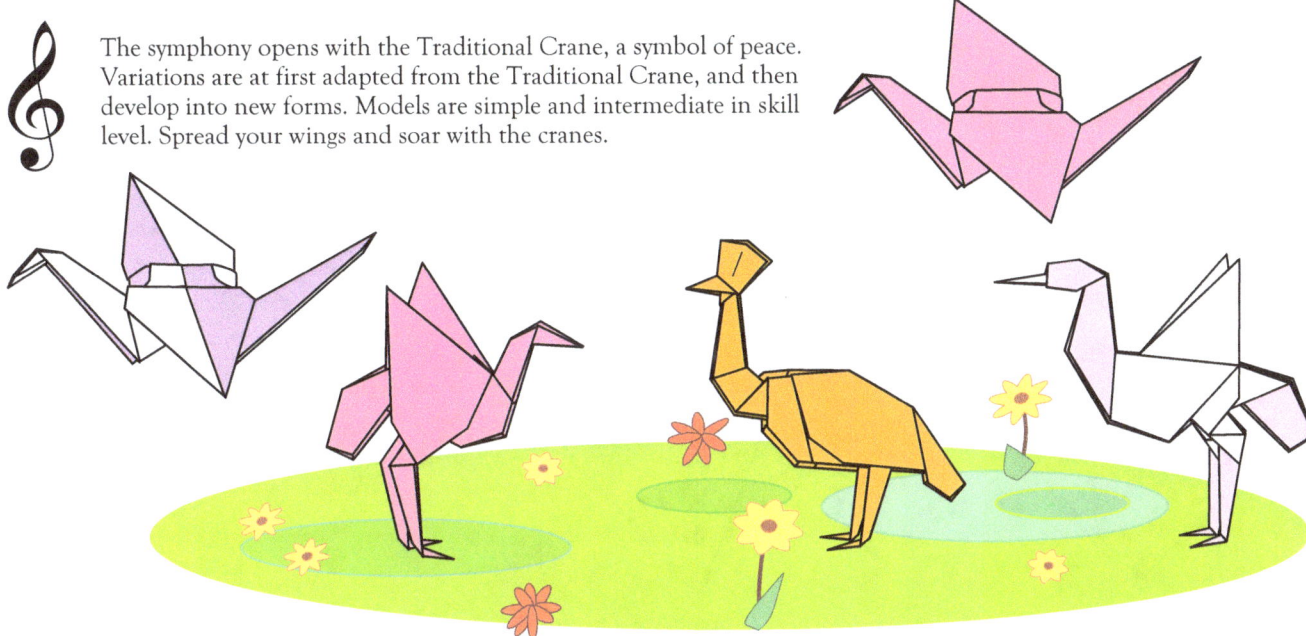

Traditional Crane

This is perhaps the most famous model in all of origami. The crane symbolizes peace and hope; a thousand cranes, often strung together, are folded for many occasions. Many Japanese children know this model. Being able to fold it is a milestone.

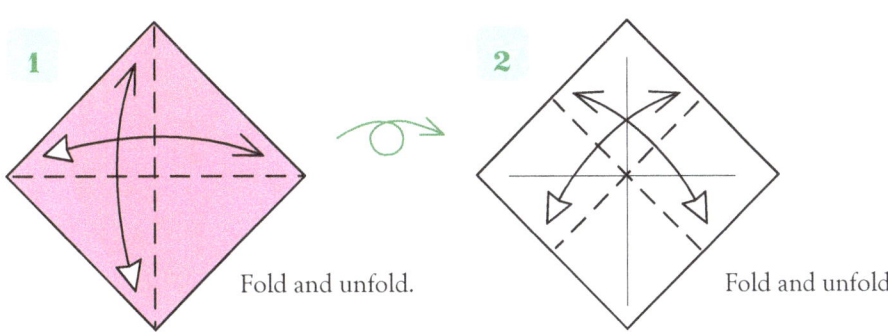

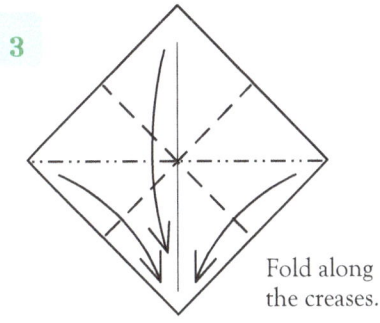

1. Fold and unfold.
2. Fold and unfold.
3. Fold along the creases.

Traditional Crane **11**

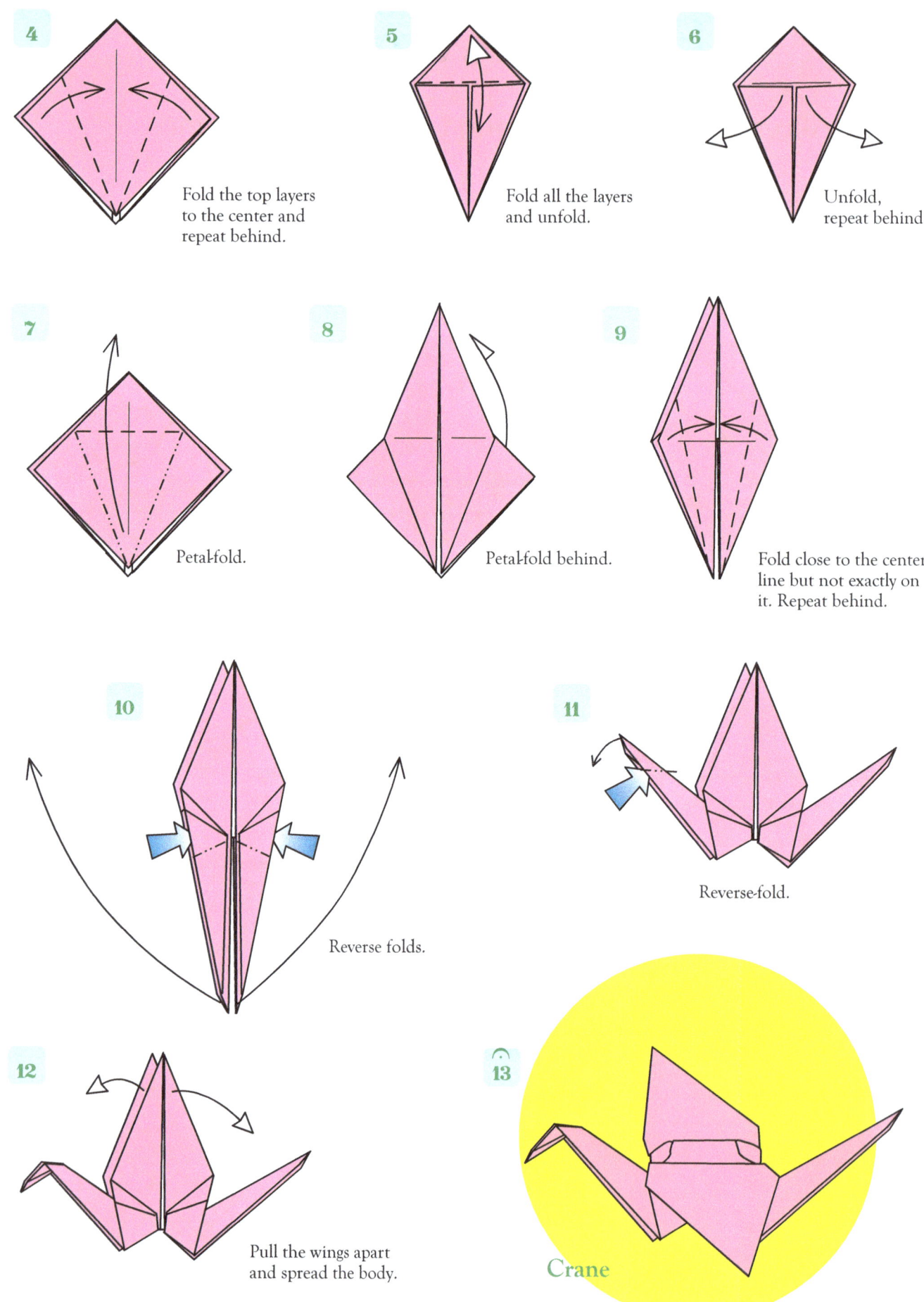

Psychedelic Crane

An interesting technique for creating more points is to blintz the paper. For the blintz-fold, the four corners of the square are folded to the center. This results in a smaller square with more layers and points to make more complex models. For this crane, opposite corners are folded to the center, forming a new square with color changes. By folding the traditional crane from it, a new crane is formed with stunning color changes.

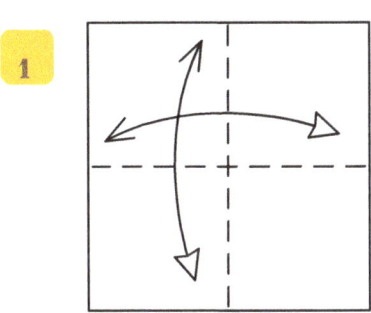

1. Fold and unfold.

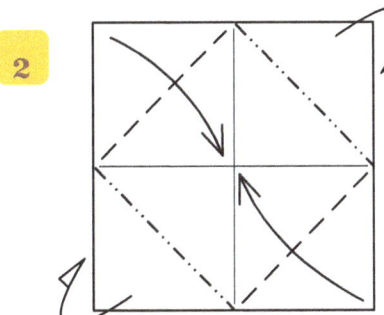

2. Fold opposite corners to the center in front and behind.

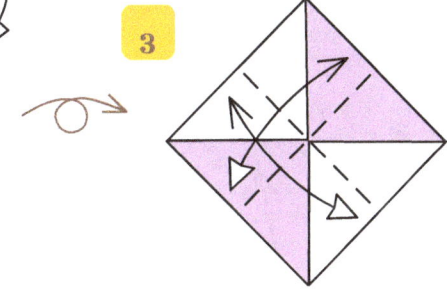

3. Fold and unfold.

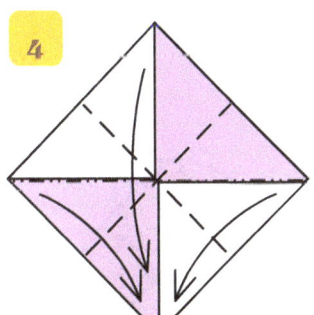

4. Fold along the creases.

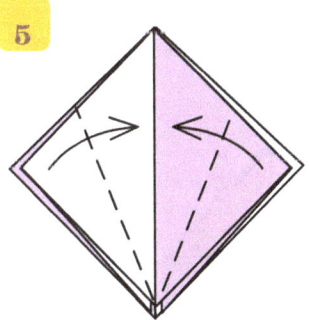

5. Continue with steps 4 through the end of the Traditional Crane.

6. Psychedelic Crane

Psychedelic Crane

Flying and Standing Crane

Let's take the traditional crane and add long legs. It can be in several positions including flying and standing. Many of the folds are the same as in the traditional crane.

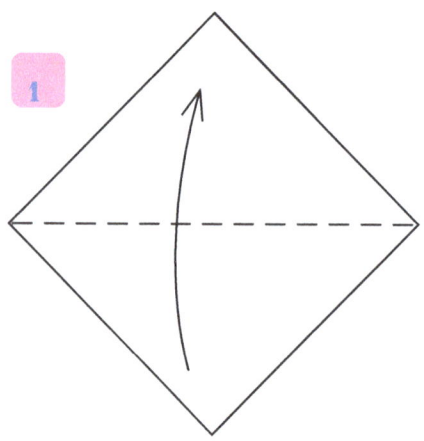

1

2

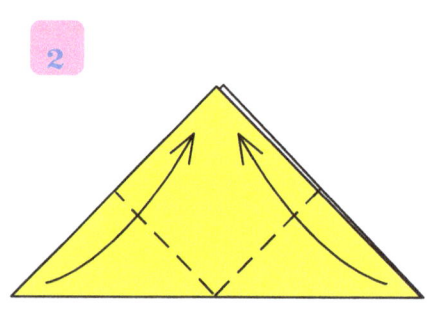

3

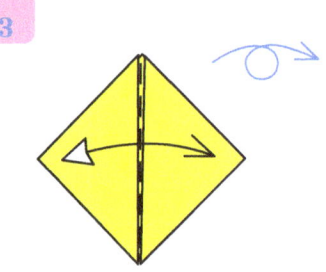

Fold and unfold.

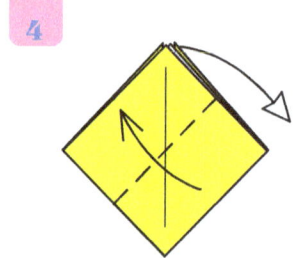

4

Fold in half and swing out from behind.

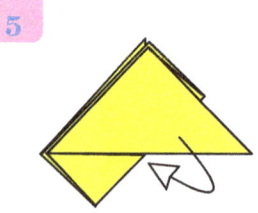

5

Unfold back to step 4.

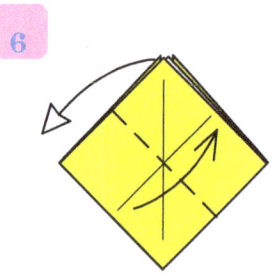

6

Repeat steps 4–5 in the opposite direction. Rotate 90°.

14 *Origami Symphony No. 1*

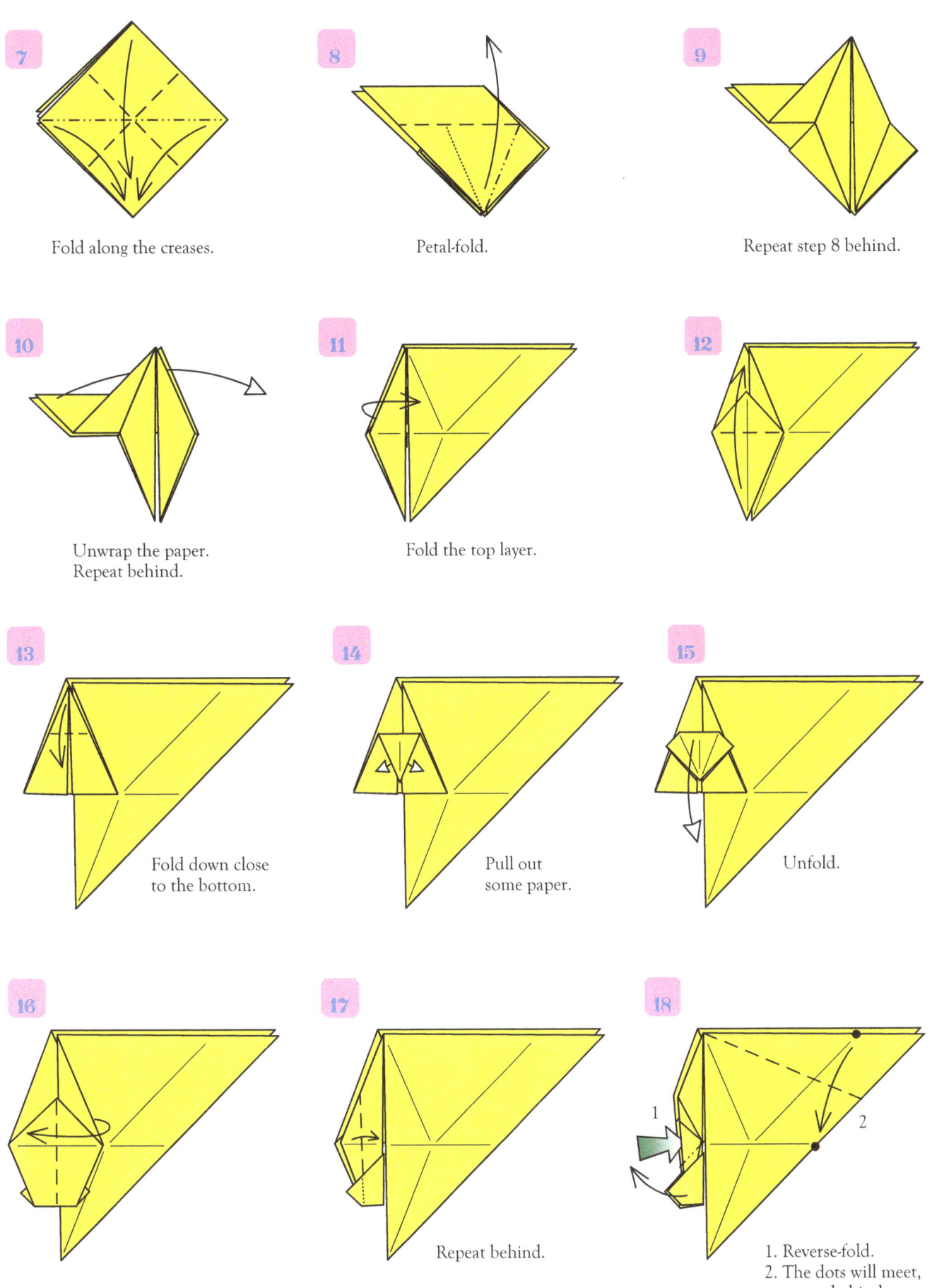

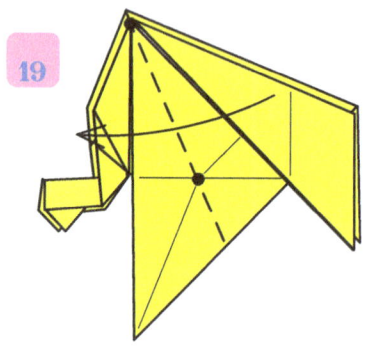

Fold along the crease between the dots. Repeat behind.

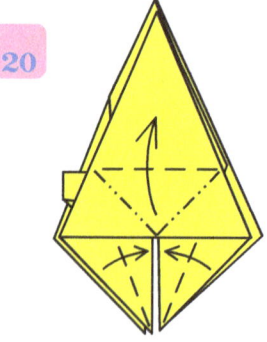

Petal-fold, repeat behind.

1. Fold to the center.
2. Leave some space at the bottom.
Repeat behind.

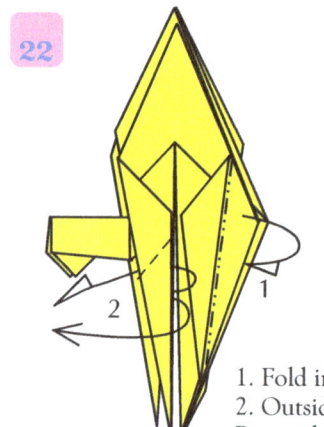

1. Fold inside.
2. Outside-reverse-fold.
Repeat behind.

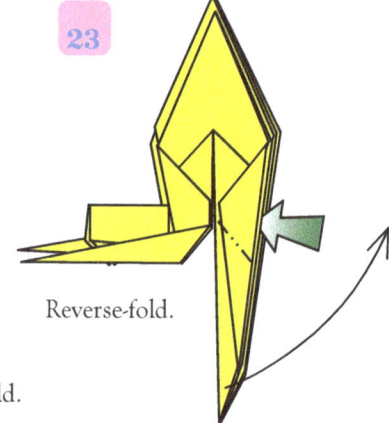

Reverse-fold.

Crimp-fold.

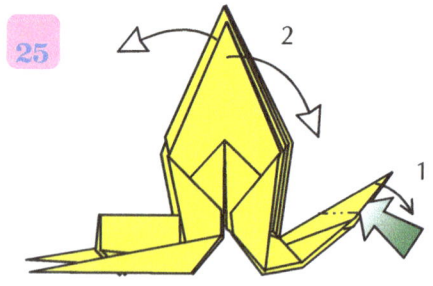

1. Reverse-fold.
2. Pull the wings apart and spread the body.

Flying Crane

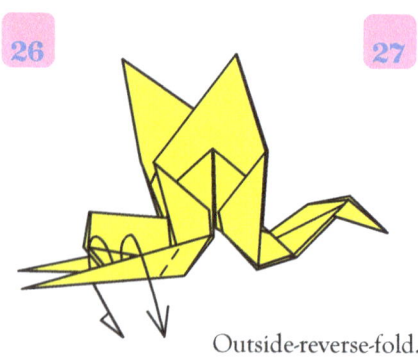

Outside-reverse-fold. Repeat behind.

Reverse-fold. Repeat behind. The crane can balance on its legs.

Standing Crane

16 *Origami Symphony No. 1*

Flying Crane

This variation resembles the traditional crane though it is folded without the the bird base or use of petal folds. This model is related to the next one, the Standing Crane, which looks similar but includes long legs.

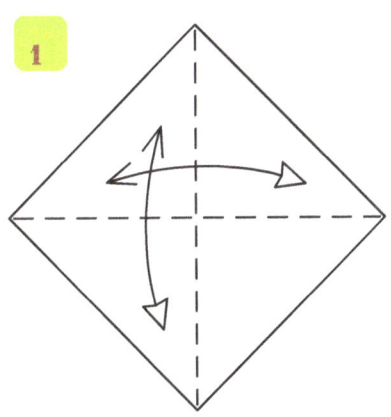

1

Fold and unfold.

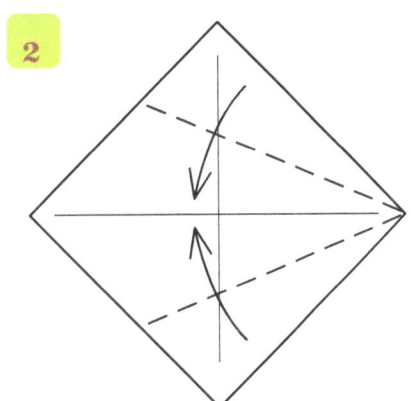

2

Fold to the center.

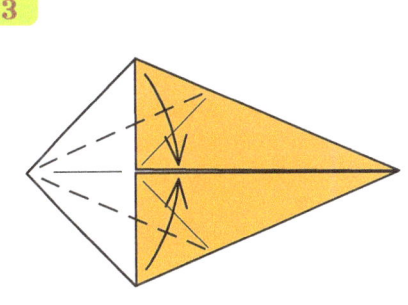

3

Fold to the center.

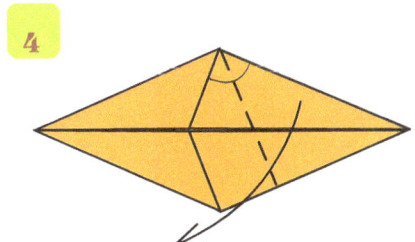

4

5

The dots will meet.

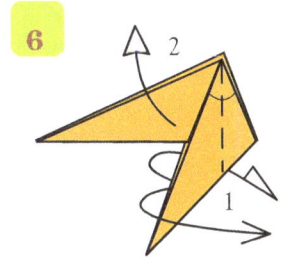

6

1. Outside-reverse-fold.
2. Unfold, repeat behind.

Flying Crane **17**

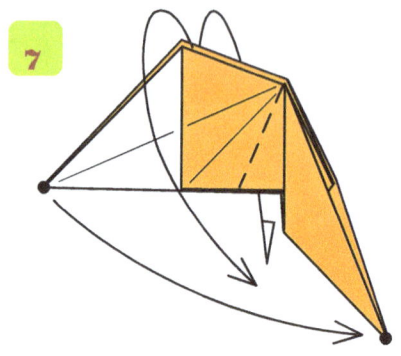

Outside-reverse-fold.
The dots will meet.

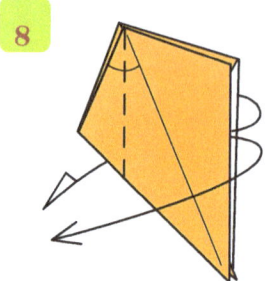

Outside-reverse-fold.

Squash-fold and repeat behind.

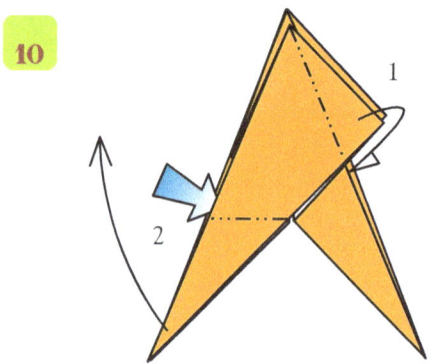

1. Fold between the layers. Repeat behind.
2. Reverse-fold.

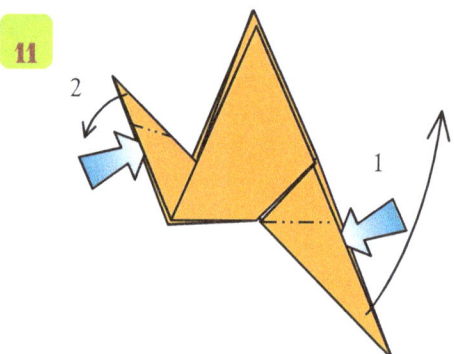

Make reverse folds.

1. Fold inside.
2. Fold inside.
3. Spread the wings. Repeat behind.

Flying Crane

18 *Origami Symphony No. 1*

Standing Crane

This crane builds upon the previous flying crane and has a similar look. The pair goes well together in a display.

Cranes are the world's largest flying birds with long legs and long necks. They range in height from 3 to over 6 feet and have a lifespan of 30 to 40 years. They feed on small animals, grains, and berries. Cranes form monogamous couples and families. They have special dances for courtship and have a vocabulary with a rich variety of sounds.

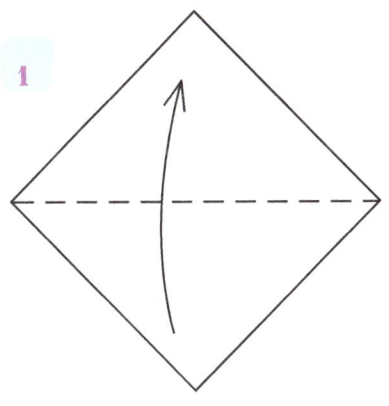

1.

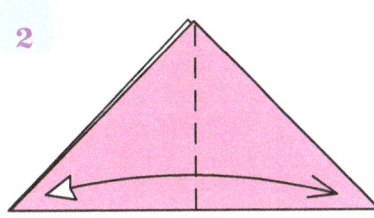

2. Fold and unfold.

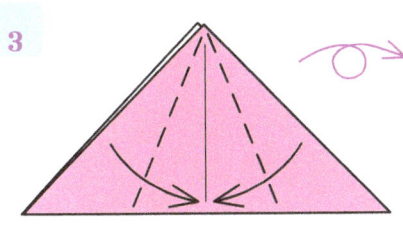

3. Fold to the center.

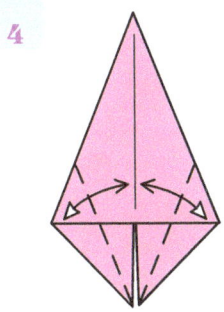

4. Fold to the center and unfold.

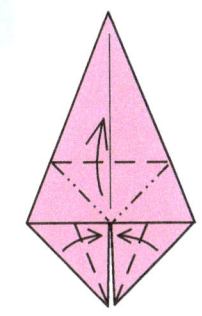

5. Petal-fold.

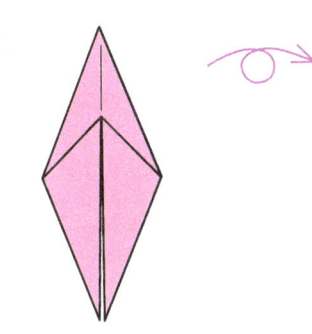

6.

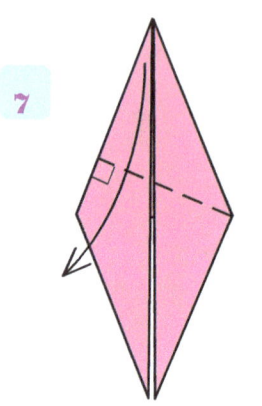

Fold at 90° from the edge.

Unfold.

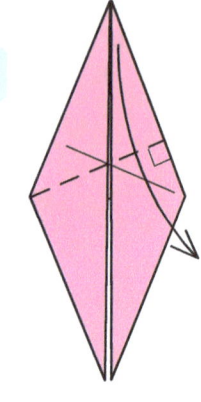

Repeat steps 7–8 on the right.

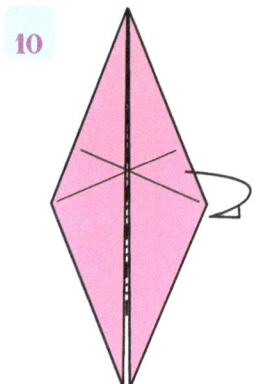

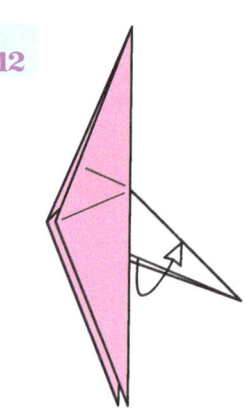

Outside-reverse-fold the inner white flap along the creases.

Wrap the inside layers around. Repeat behind.

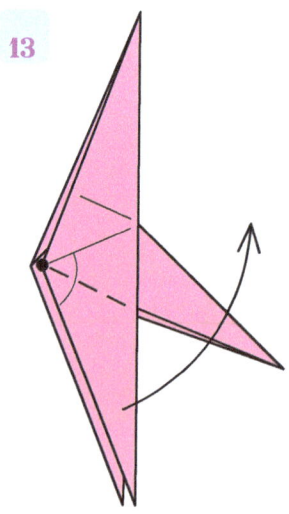

Repeat behind. Rotate the dot to the top.

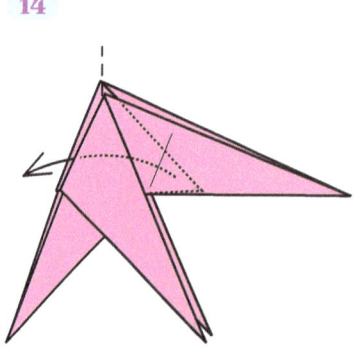

Reverse-fold the inner flap.

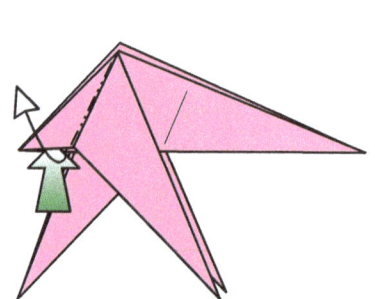

Unlock the paper. Repeat behind.

20 Origami Symphony No. 1

16

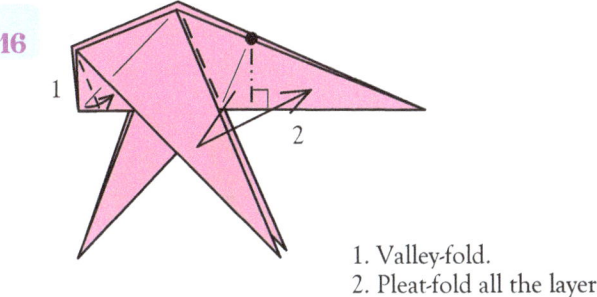

1. Valley-fold.
2. Pleat-fold all the layers.

17

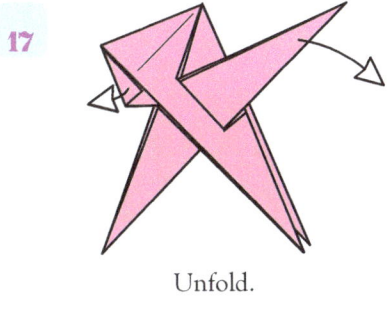

Unfold.

18

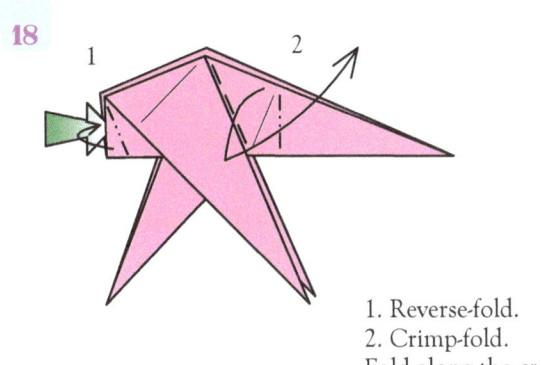

1. Reverse-fold.
2. Crimp-fold.
Fold along the creases.

19

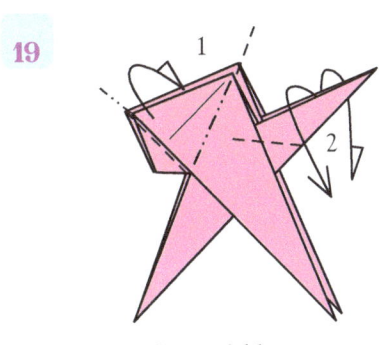

1. Crimp-fold.
2. Outside-reverse-fold.

20

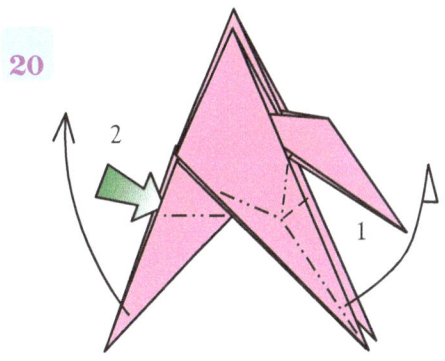

1. Rabbit-ear, repeat behind.
2. Reverse-fold.

21

1. Reverse-fold.
2. Repeat behind.

22

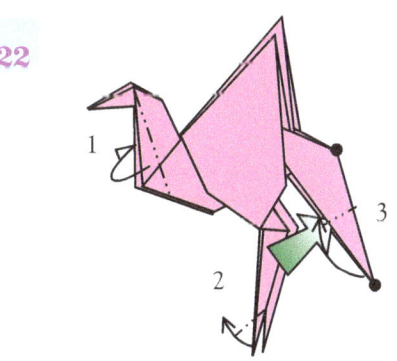

1. Fold inside, repeat behind.
2. Reverse-fold, repeat behind.
3. Reverse-fold so the dots meet.

23

Standing Crane

Young Crane

While the earlier cranes were modeled after the traditional crane, this crane begins a new series. The young crane fits in well with an exhibit of cranes. Cranes live in families that take care of the young and teach them how to eat.

1

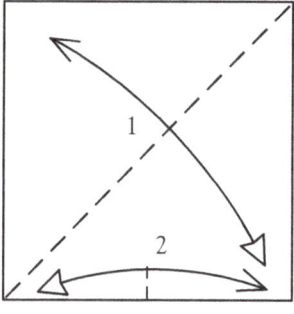

1. Fold and unfold.
2. Fold and unfold at the bottom.

2

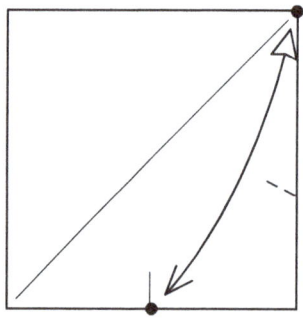

Fold and unfold on the right.

3

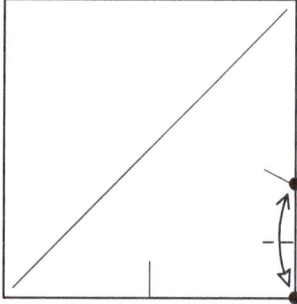

Fold and unfold on the right.

4

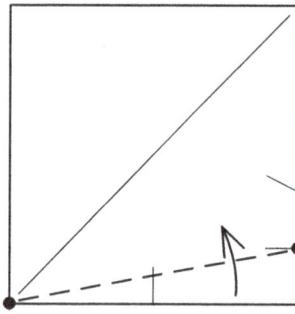

5

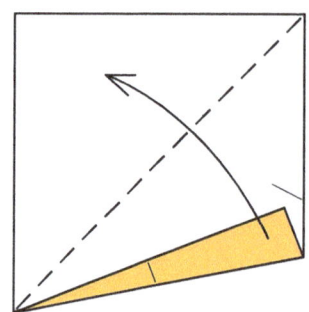

6

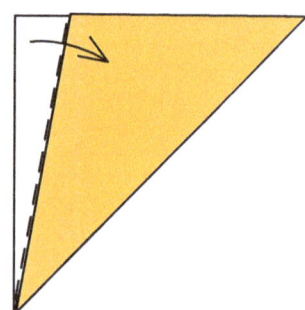

22 Origami Symphony No. 1

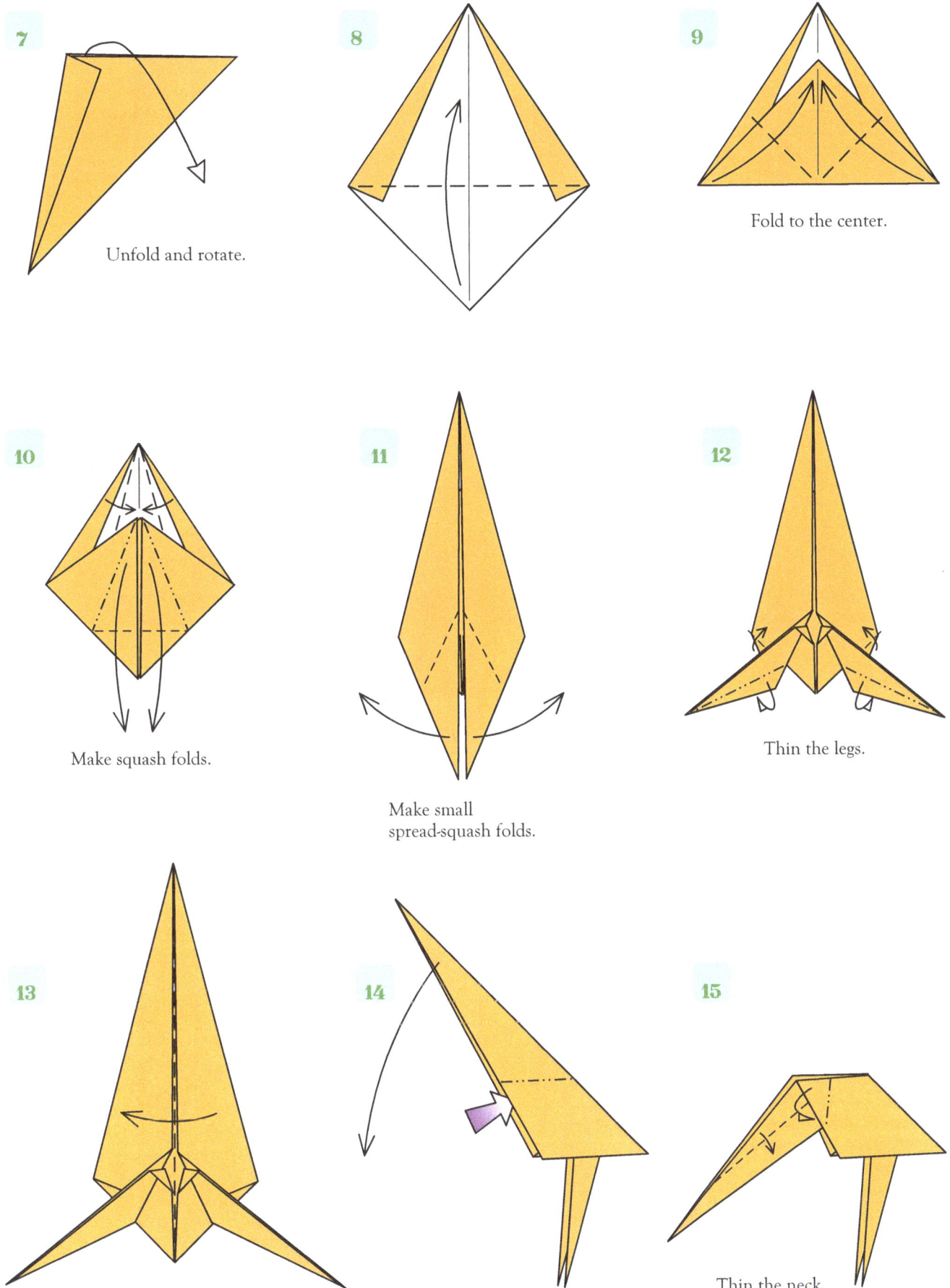

Young Crane

16

Reverse-fold.

17

Reverse-fold.

18

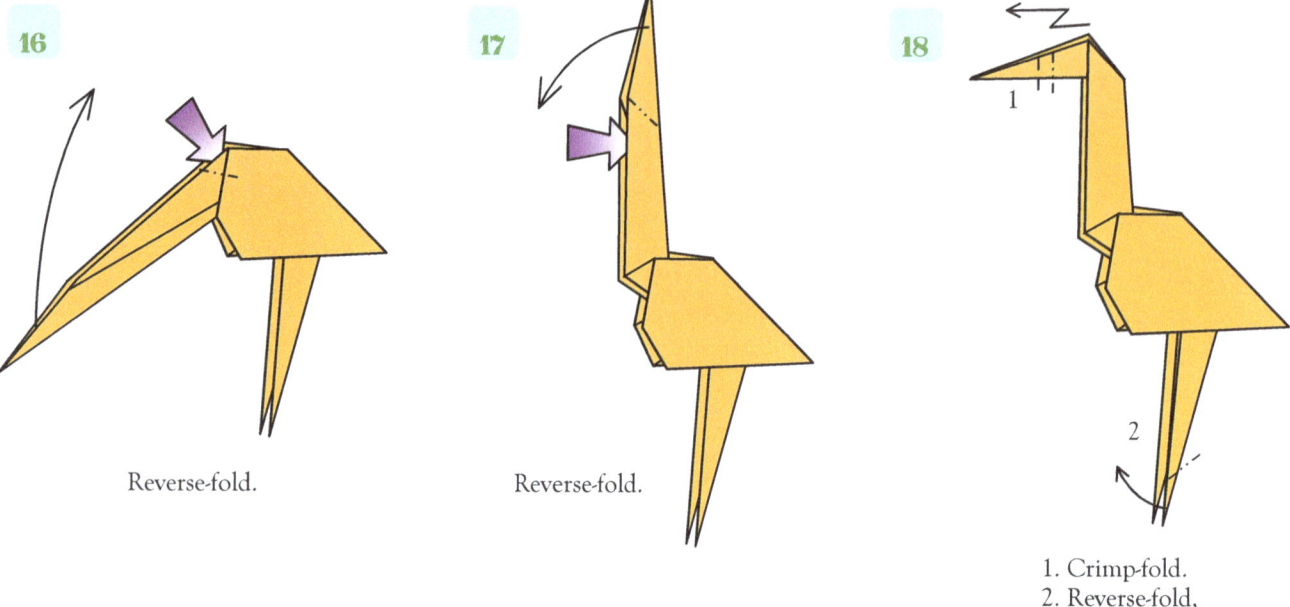

1. Crimp-fold.
2. Reverse-fold, repeat behind.

19

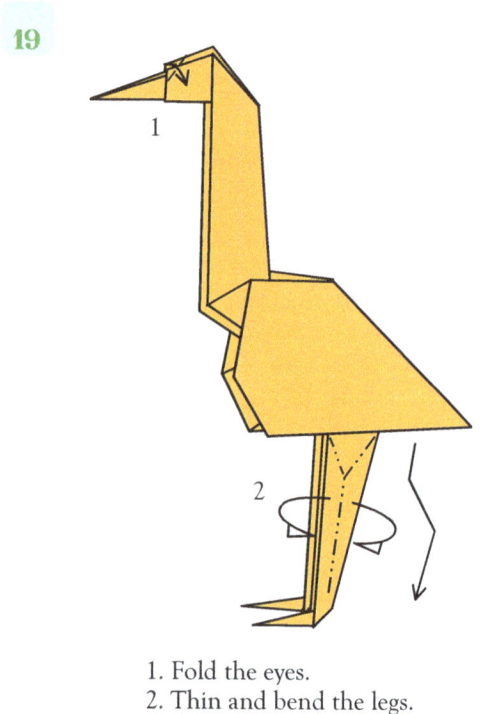

1. Fold the eyes.
2. Thin and bend the legs. Repeat behind. The crane can stand.

20

Young Crane

24 *Origami Symphony No. 1*

Sandhill Crane

Rather large birds, Sandhill Cranes are gray with tan feathers and have a crimson-capped head. They sing a loud trilling bugle call, honk, and snoring sounds. Their long windpipe produces lower pitches with richer sounds. Mainly found in marshlands and other wet areas from North America to Siberia, they have long, thin necks and bulky bodies.

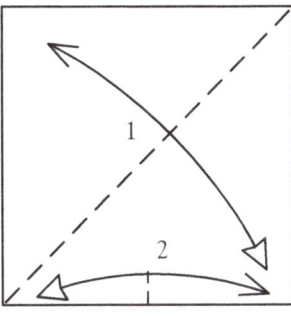

1. Fold and unfold.
2. Fold and unfold at the bottom.

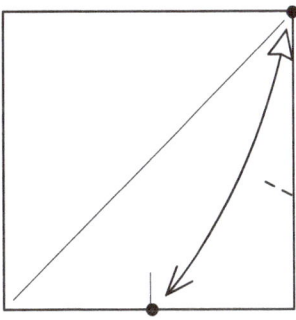

Fold and unfold on the right.

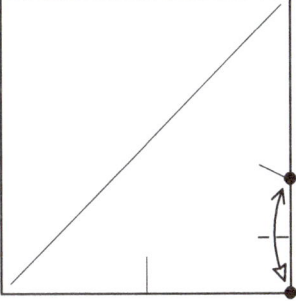

Fold and unfold on the right.

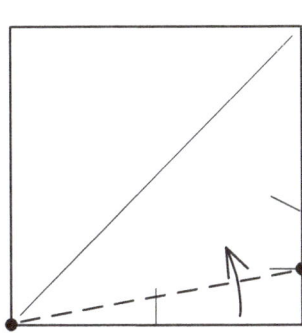

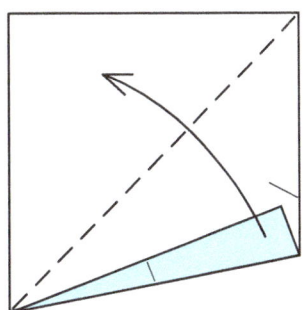

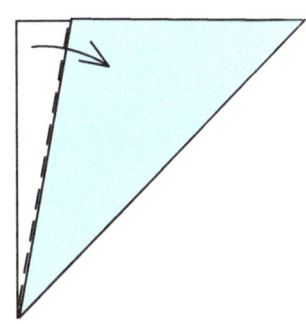

Sandhill Crane

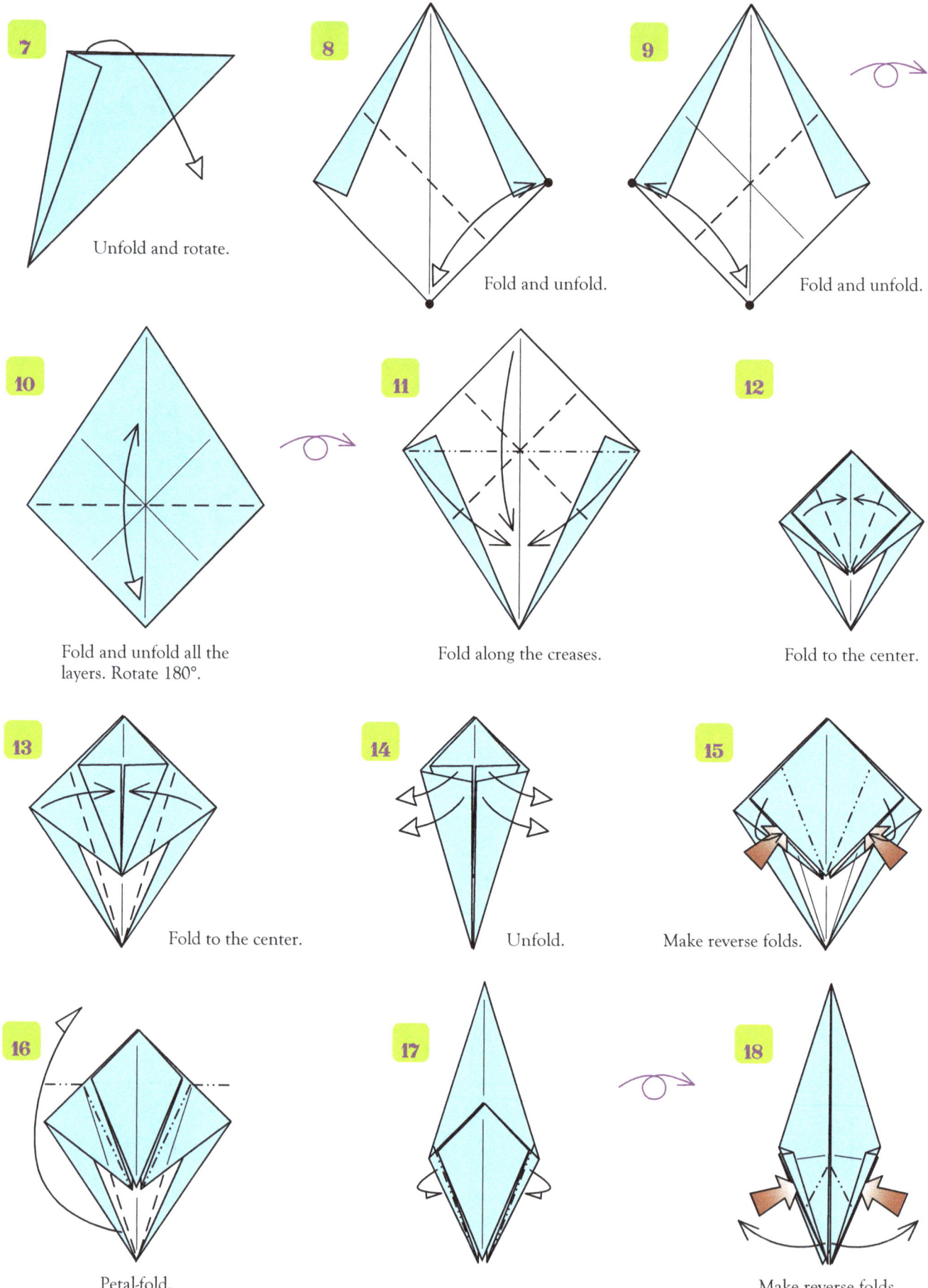

26 *Origami Symphony No. 1*

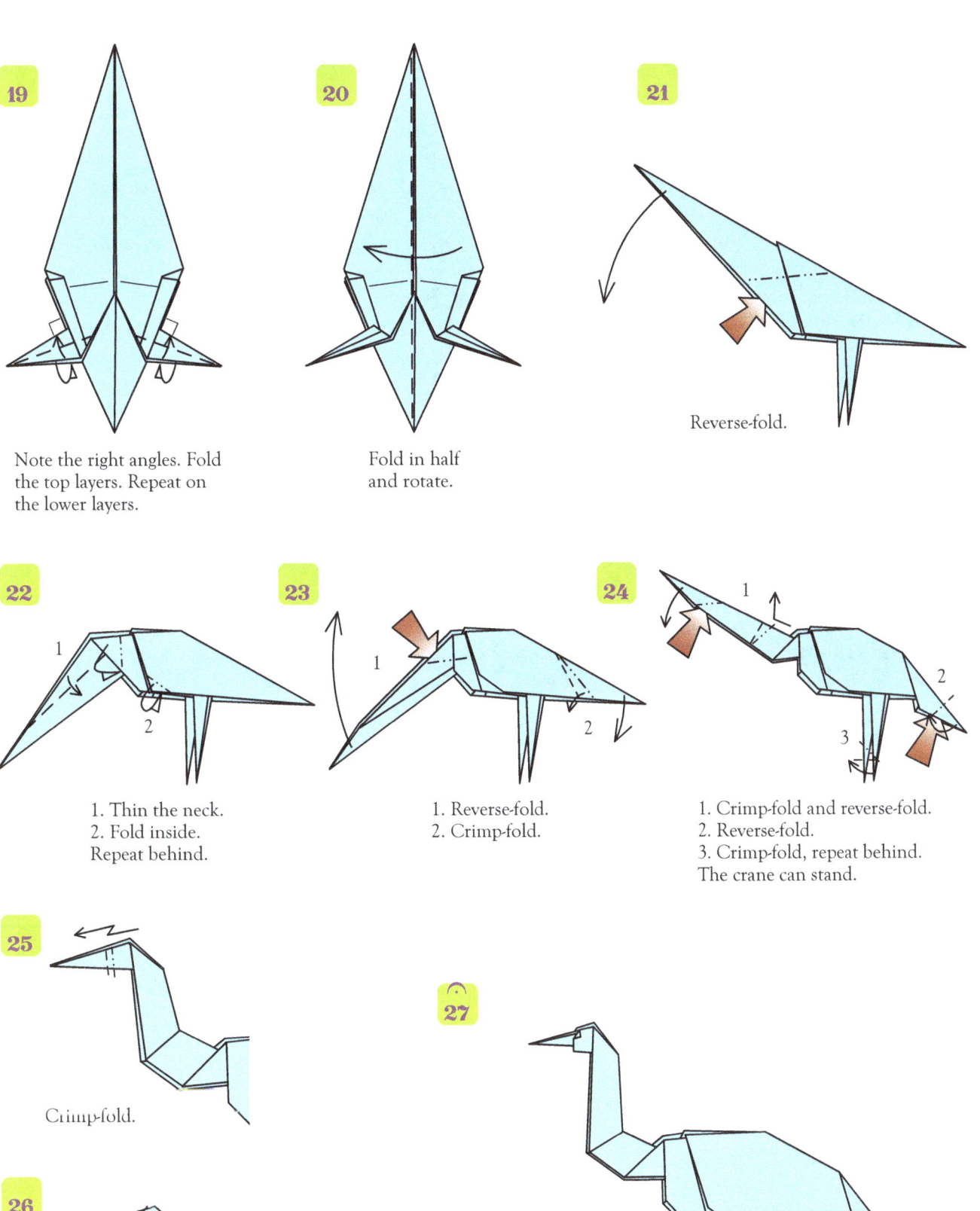

Sandhill Crane

Whooping Crane

With a strong, high-pitched burst of sound, Whooping Cranes join the Sandhill Cranes as the only two varieties of the Crane that make their home in North America. They form smaller flocks and are an endangered species. They are white with a red crown and stripe by the beak. In flight, their black wingtips can be seen.

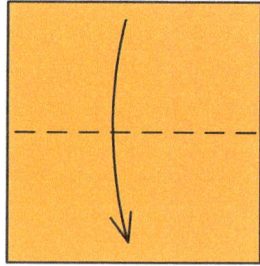

1

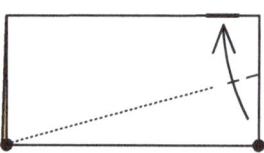

2

Bring the right dot to the top. Crease on the right.

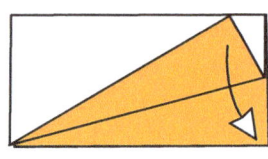

3

Unfold.

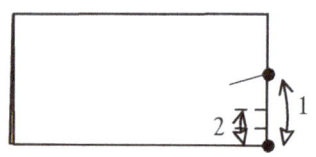

4

Fold and unfold the top layer on the right.

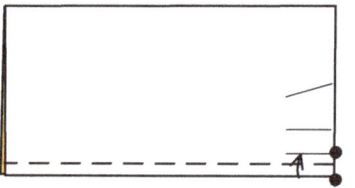

5

Repeat behind.

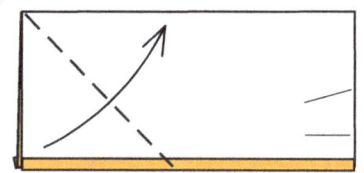

6

Repeat behind.

Origami Symphony No. 1

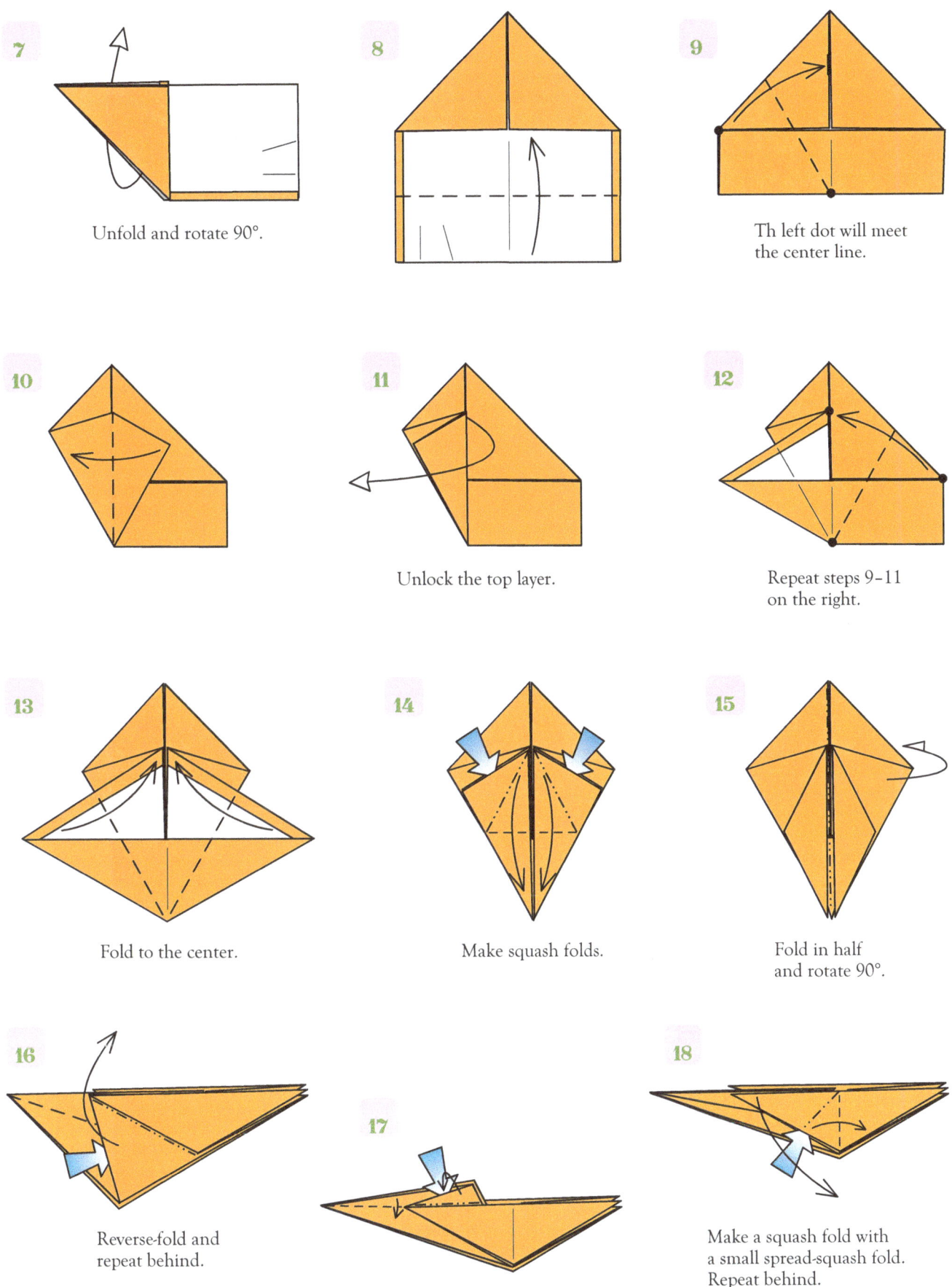

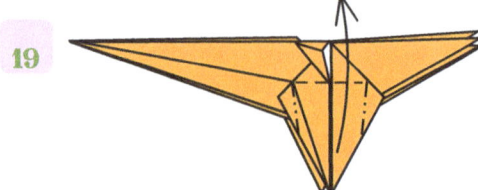

Petal-fold and repeat behind.

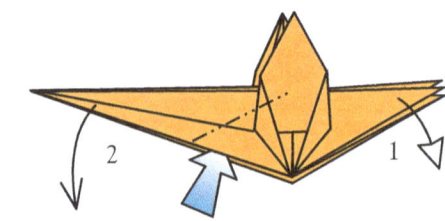

1. Unlock and slide the leg, repeat behind.
2. Reverse-fold.

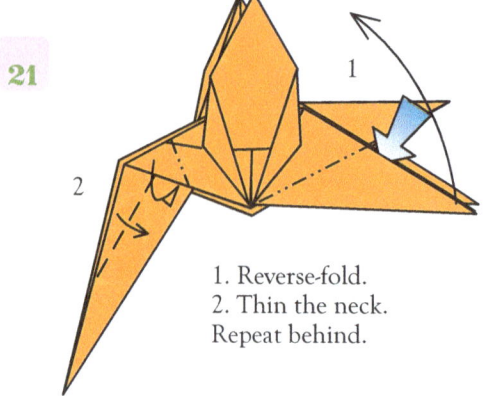

1. Reverse-fold.
2. Thin the neck.
Repeat behind.

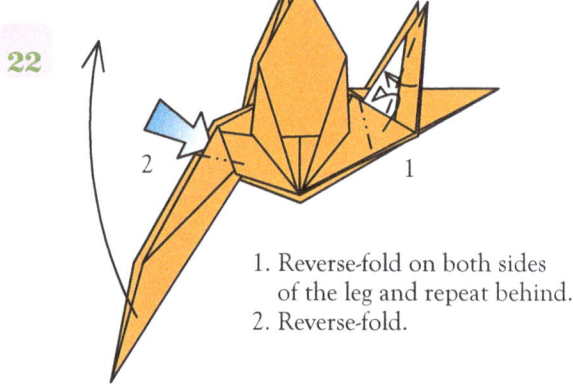

1. Reverse-fold on both sides of the leg and repeat behind.
2. Reverse-fold.

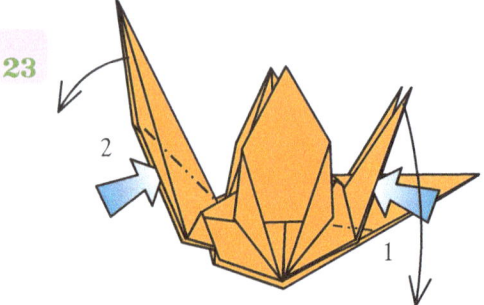

1. Reverse-fold and repeat behind.
2. Reverse-fold at an angle.
Rotate slightly.

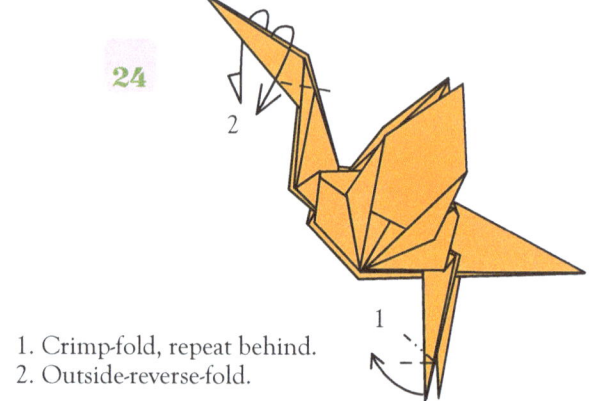

1. Crimp-fold, repeat behind.
2. Outside-reverse-fold.

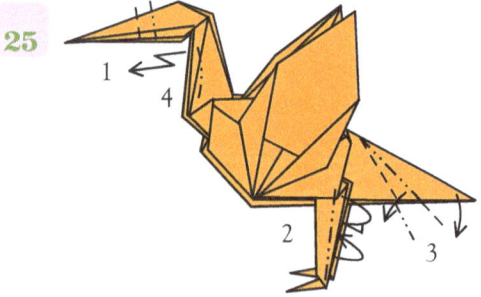

1. Crimp-fold.
2. Fold inside on both sides, repeat behind.
3. Crimp-fold.
4. Shape the neck.
The crane can stand.

Whooping Crane

Flying Crowned Crane

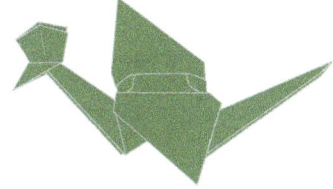

This model is designed as a variation of the classic crane. Crowned Cranes fly in flocks of 30 to 130 cranes, making loud honks.

1. 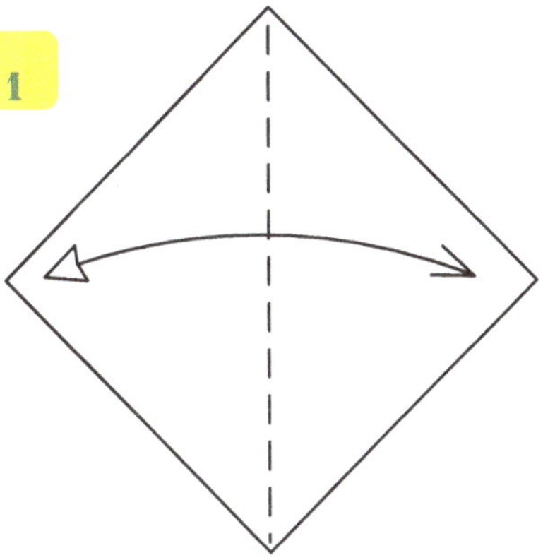 Fold and unfold.

2. Fold to the center and unfold.

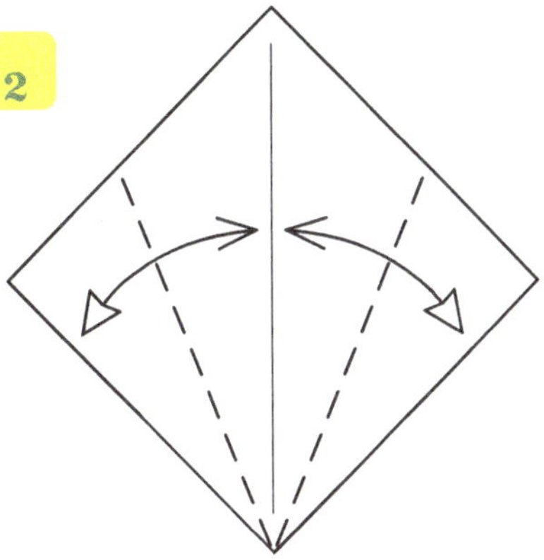

3.

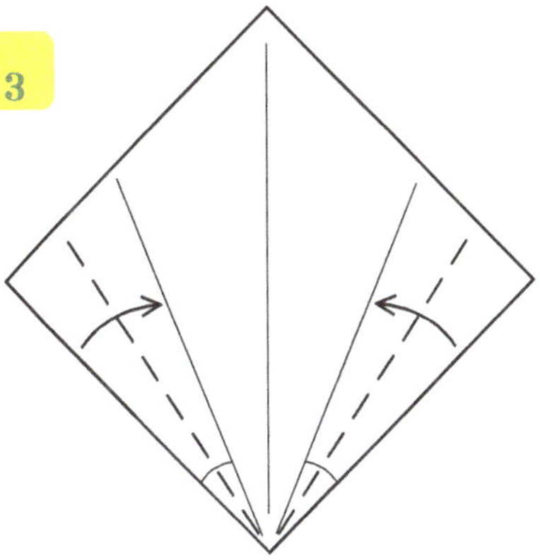

4. 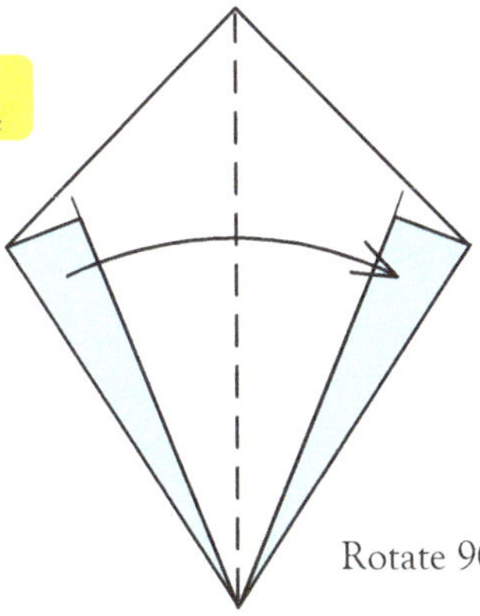 Rotate 90°.

5.

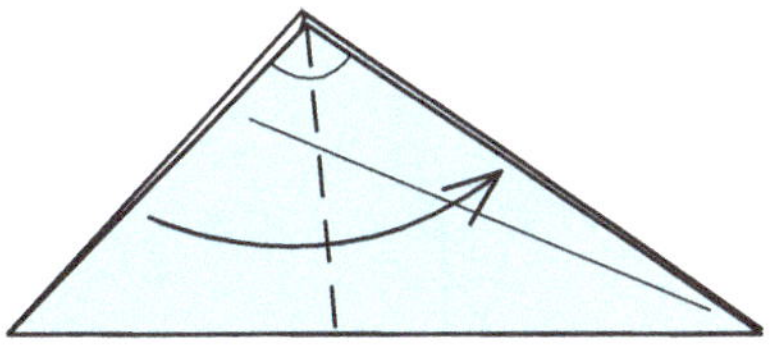

6.  Unfold.

Flying Crowned Crane **31**

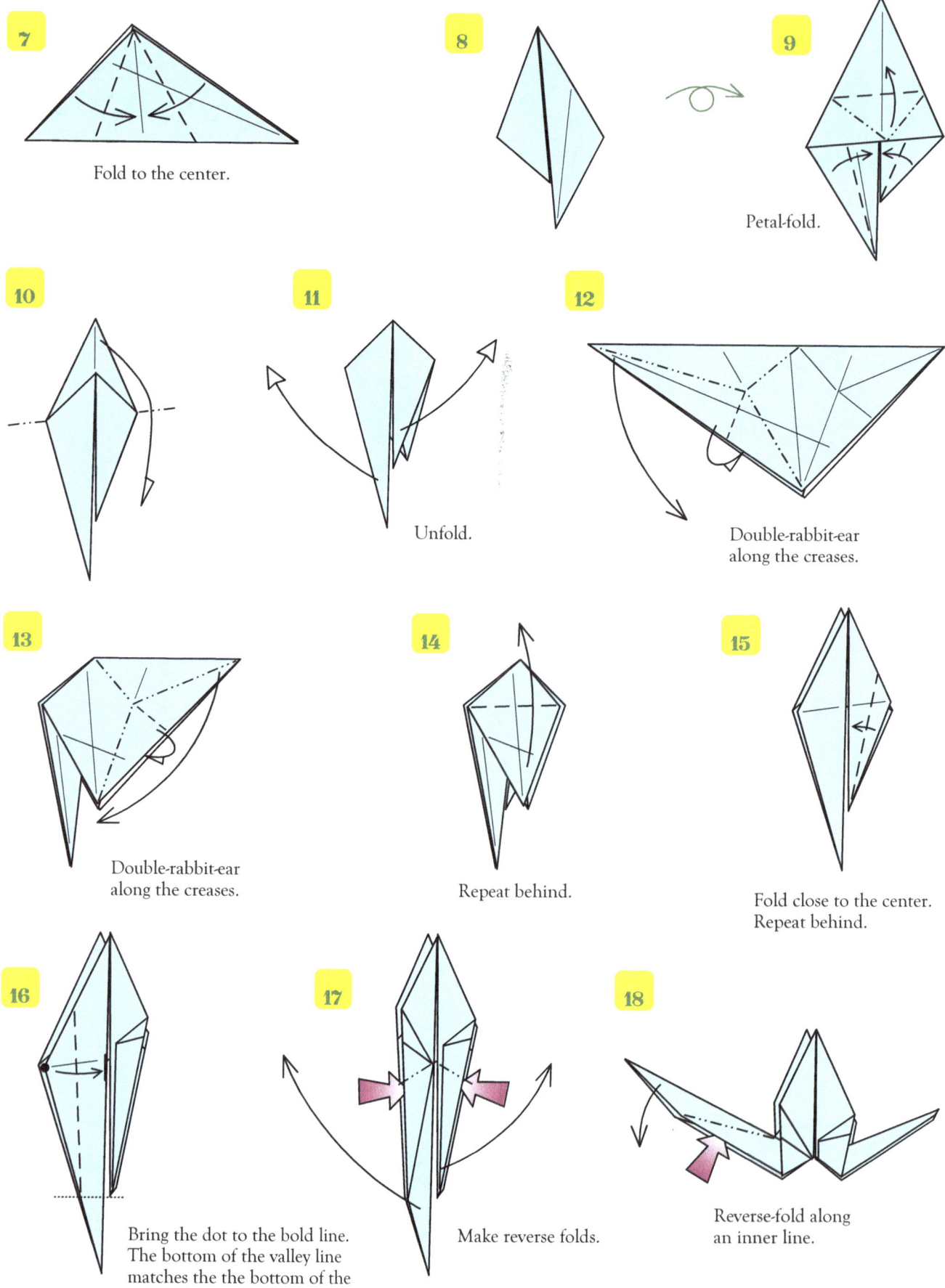

Spread at the head.

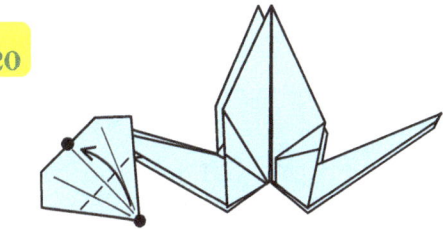

The head is 3D.

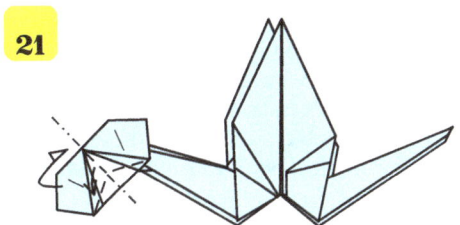

Begin with a rabbit ear, then fold half the crown behind.

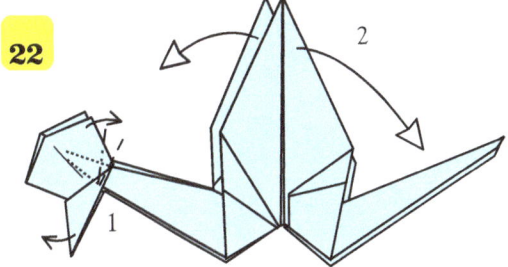

1. Crimp-fold to pivot the head.
2. Pull the wings apart and spread the body.

Flying Crowned Crane

Crowned Crane

A number of varieties of Crane are known as Crowned Cranes, including the Grey Crowned Crane, which is the national bird of Uganda, and the Black Crowned Crane, which is found in the African savannah. They are smaller than most cranes. They are the only cranes that can grasp branches and roost in trees.

1. 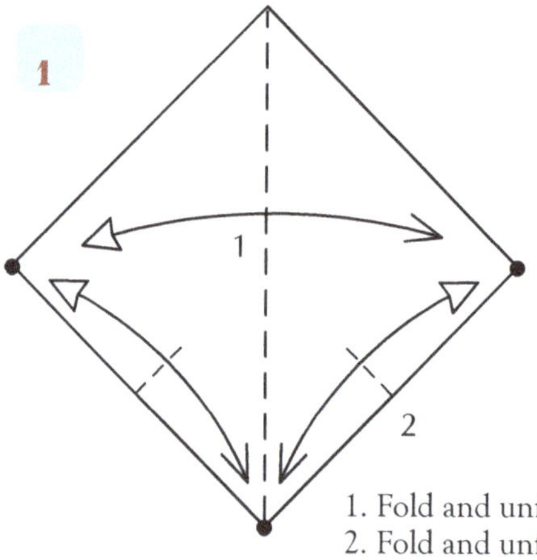
1. Fold and unfold.
2. Fold and unfold on the edge.

2. Bring the corners to the lines.

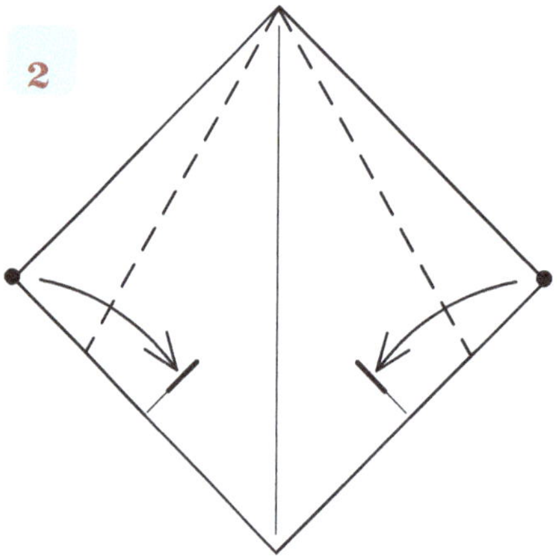

3. Fold and unfold.

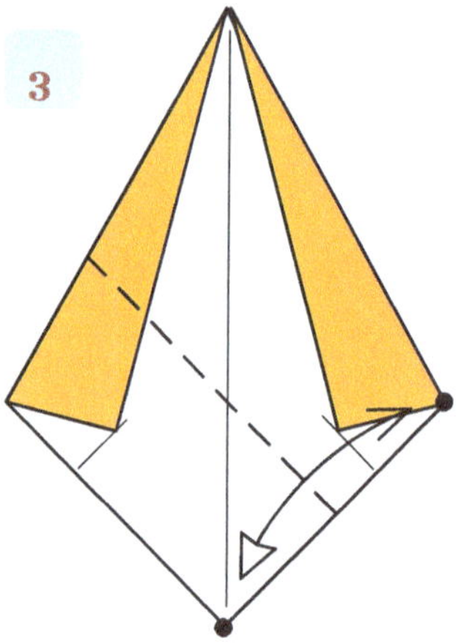

4. Fold and unfold.

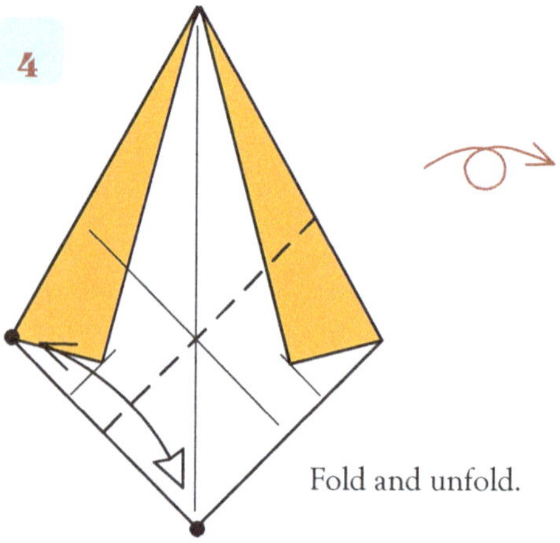

5. Fold and unfold all the layers. Rotate 180°.

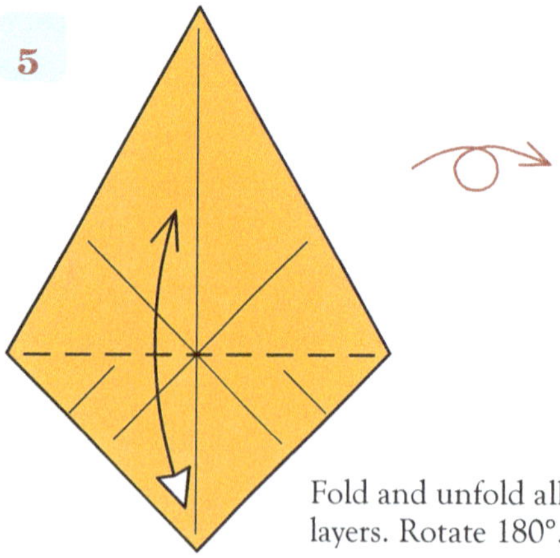

6. Fold along the creases.

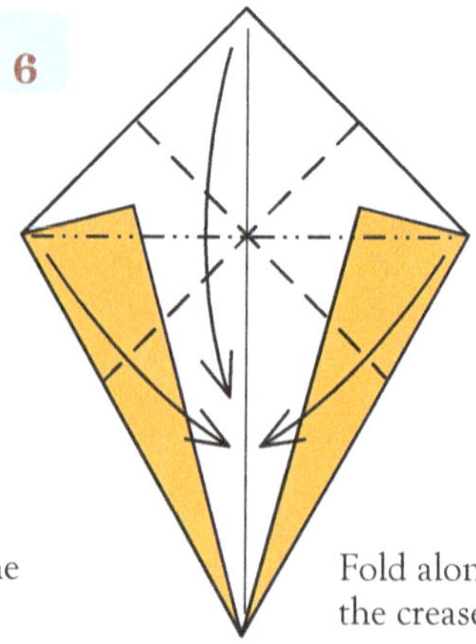

34 Origami Symphony No. 1

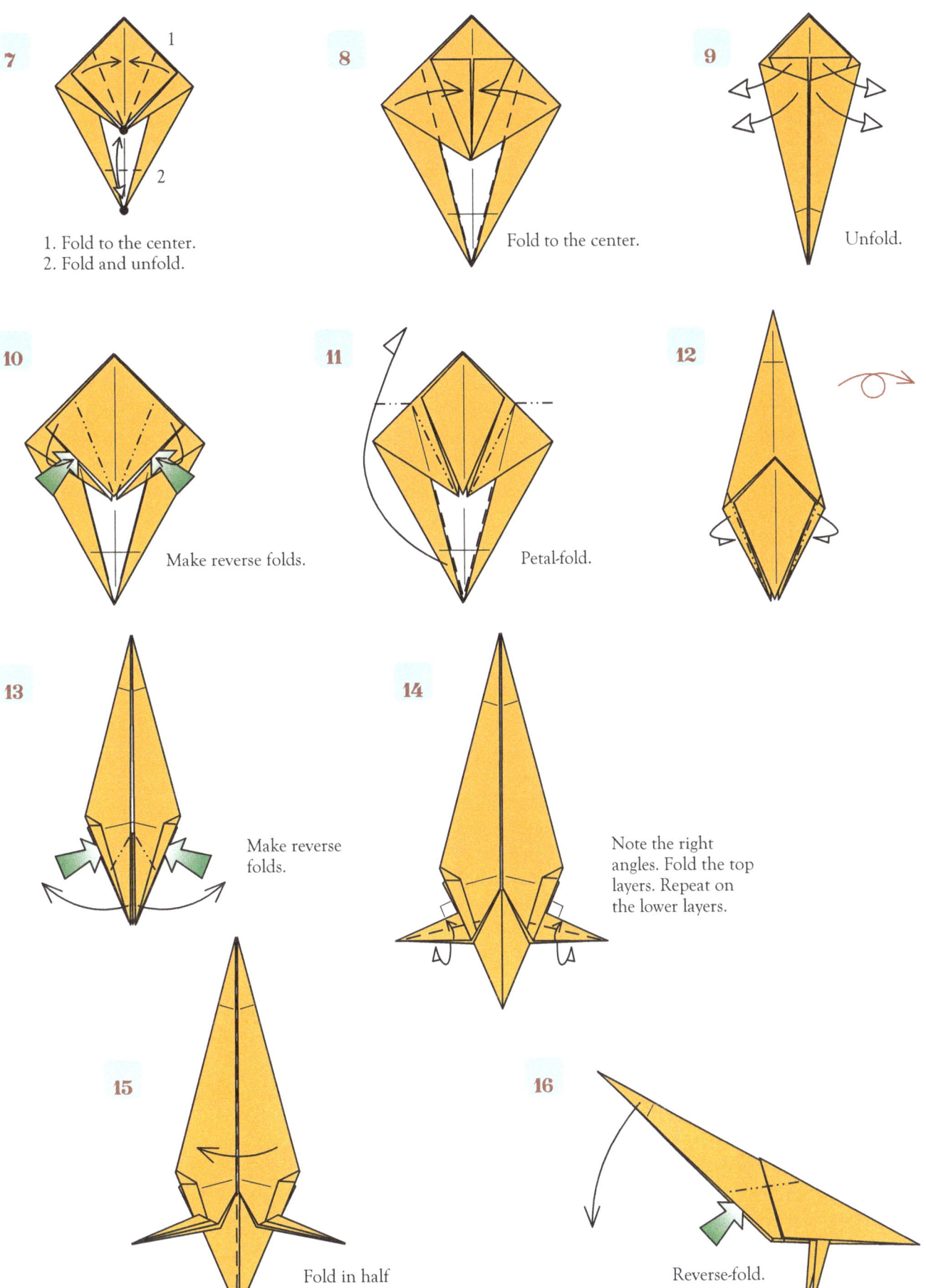

Crowned Crane

17

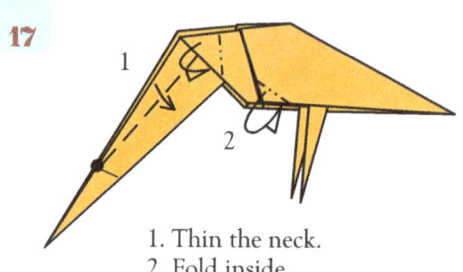

1. Thin the neck.
2. Fold inside.
Repet behind.

18

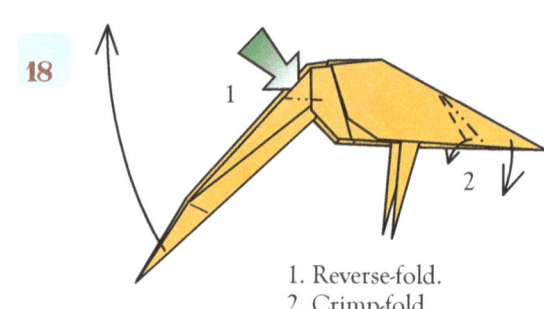

1. Reverse-fold.
2. Crimp-fold.

19

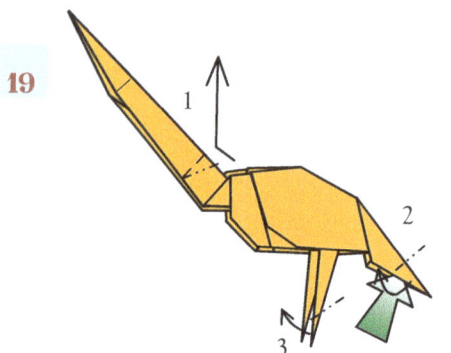

1. Crimp-fold.
2. Reverse-fold.
3. Reverse-fold, repeat behind.
The crane can stand.

20

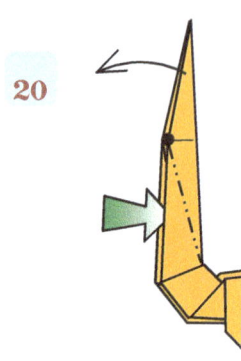

Reverse-fold.

21

Spread at the top.

22

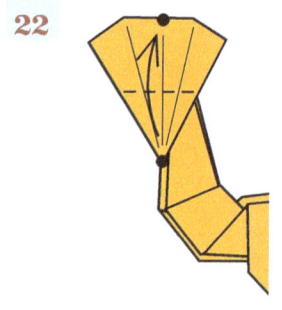

23

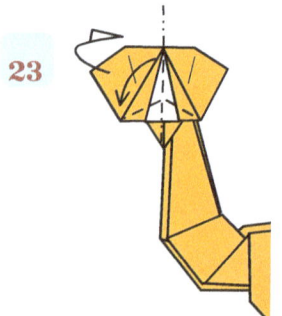

Begin with a rabbit ear, then fold half the crown behind.

24

Crowned Crane

36 *Origami Symphony No. 1*

Black-Necked Crane

Black-necked Cranes can be found in Tibet, where they have their breeding grounds, as well as in India, Vietnam and Bhutan. They have been long revered as a symbol of Peace, and Bhutan hosts a yearly festival to honor these birds. They are the only cranes that live in the mountains.

1. Fold and unfold.
2. Fold to the center.
3. Fold and unfold.
4. Tuck inside.
5. Fold and unfold.
6. Fold and unfold.
7. Reverse-fold along the crease.

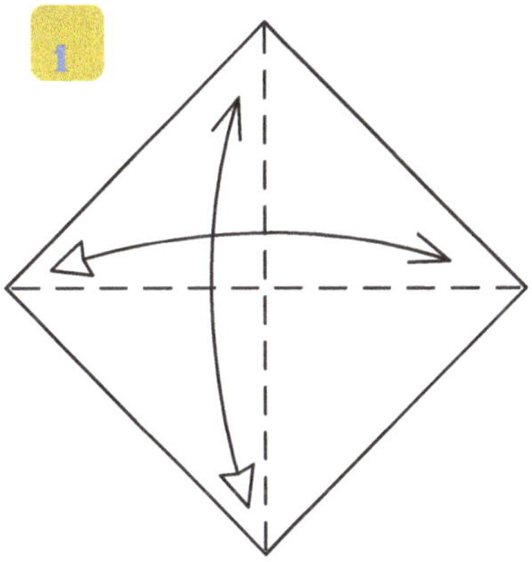

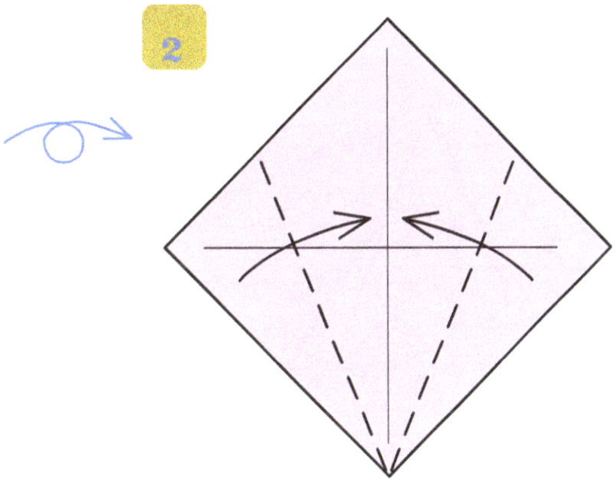

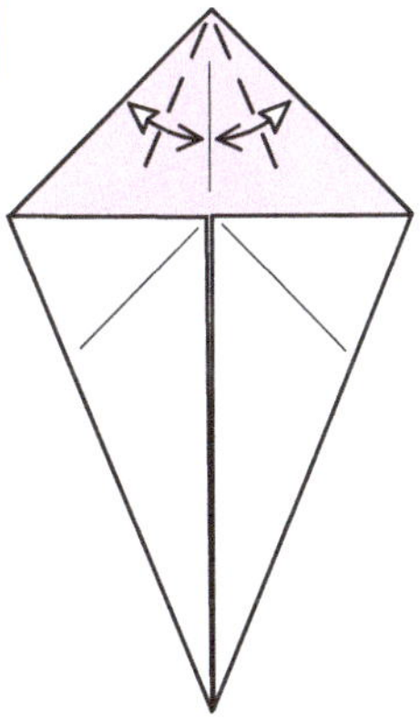

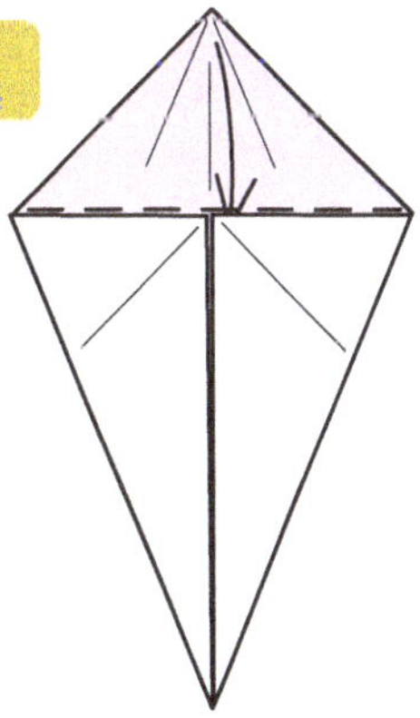

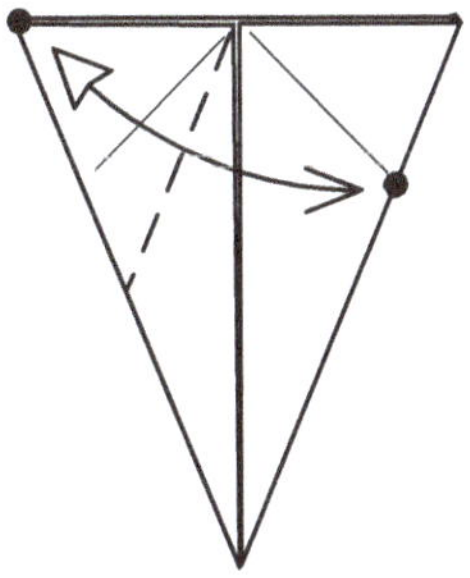

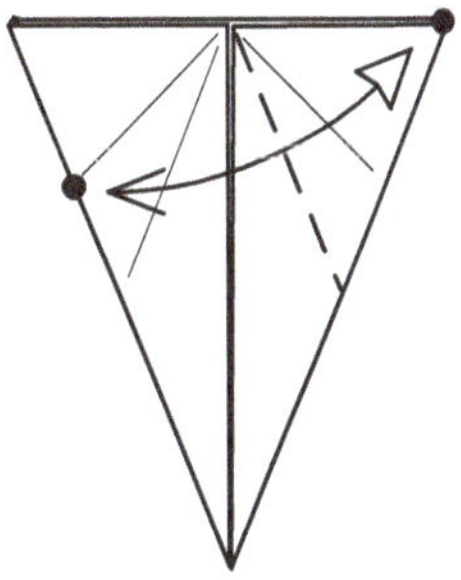

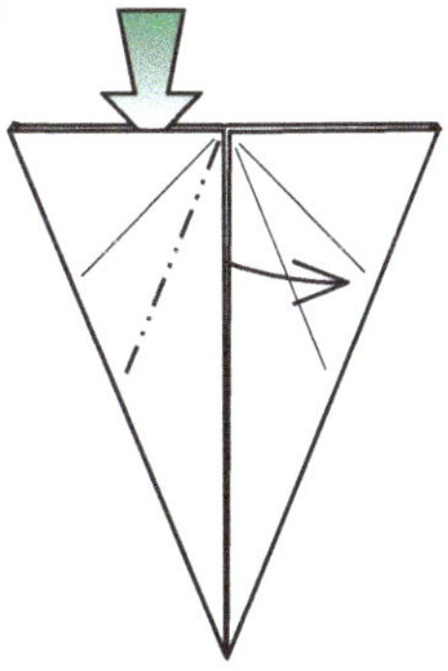

Black-Necked Crane 37

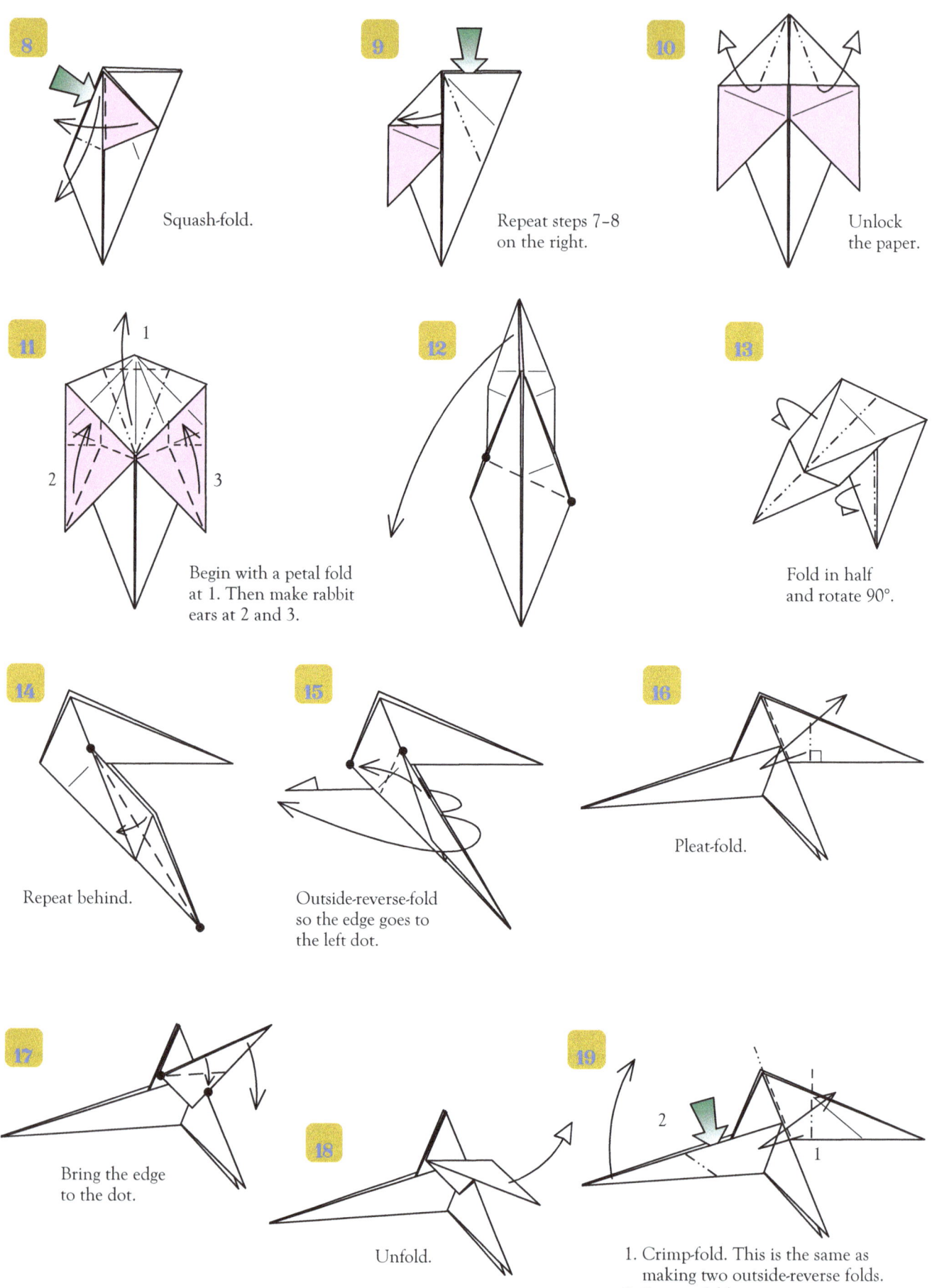

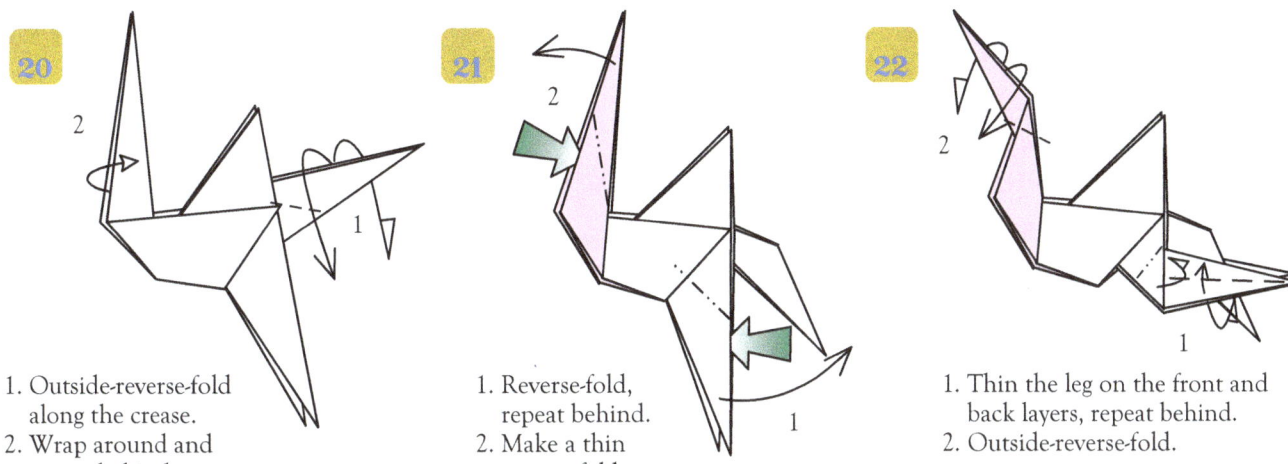

1. Outside-reverse-fold along the crease.
2. Wrap around and repeat behind.

1. Reverse-fold, repeat behind.
2. Make a thin reverse-fold.

1. Thin the leg on the front and back layers, repeat behind.
2. Outside-reverse-fold.

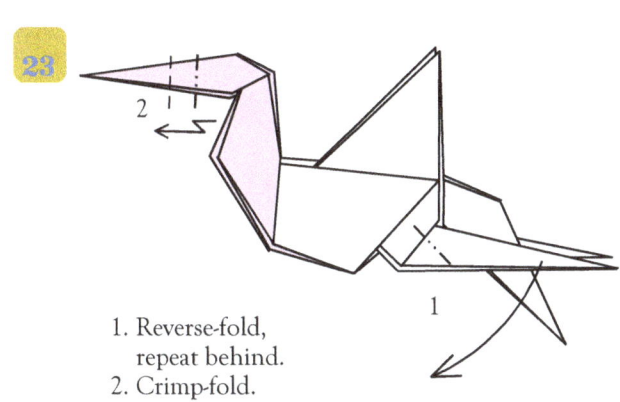

1. Reverse-fold, repeat behind.
2. Crimp-fold.

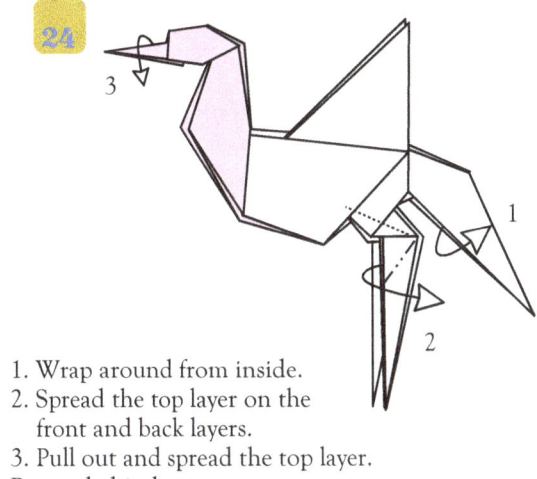

1. Wrap around from inside.
2. Spread the top layer on the front and back layers.
3. Pull out and spread the top layer. Repeat behind.

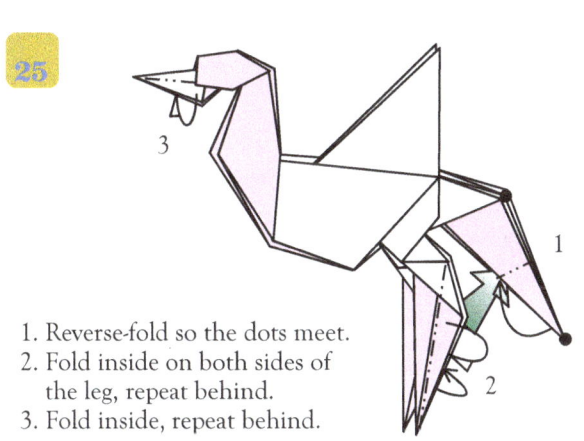

1. Reverse-fold so the dots meet.
2. Fold inside on both sides of the leg, repeat behind.
3. Fold inside, repeat behind.

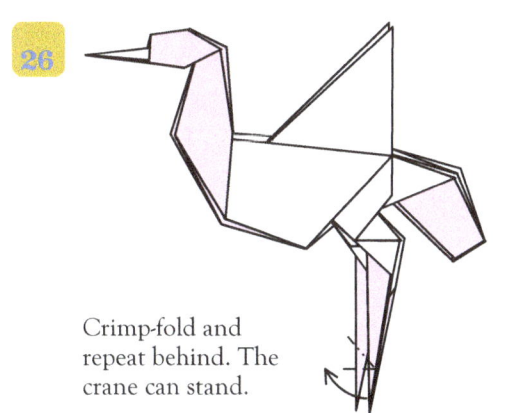

Crimp-fold and repeat behind. The crane can stand.

Black-Necked Crane

Black-Necked Crane **39**

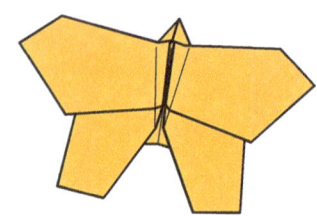

Second Movement

Andante: Simple Crawling Bugs

The slow and relaxing second movement presents simple bugs. The Japanese word for bug also includes other small creatures such as a snail. Models are simple and intermediate in skill level. Sit back, relax, and enjoy these little creatures.

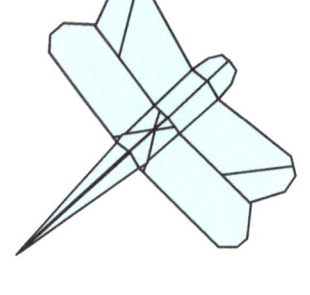

Ladybug

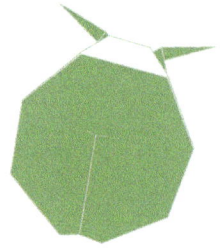

Also called Ladybirds, Ladybugs are in fact not bugs, but are members of the Beetle family, and many scientists refer to them as Lady Beetles. Ladybugs protect our gardens from plant-damaging pests, and some cultures believe they bring good fortune. There are over 4,000 varieties of Ladybugs.

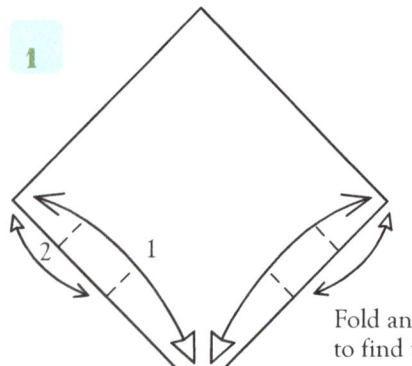

1. Fold and unfold to find the quarter marks.

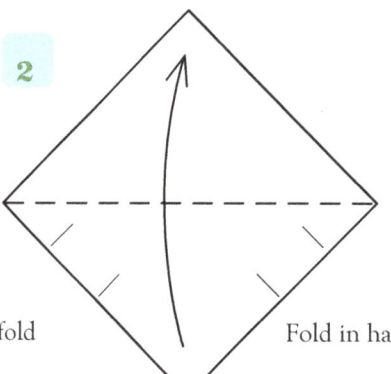

2. Fold in half.

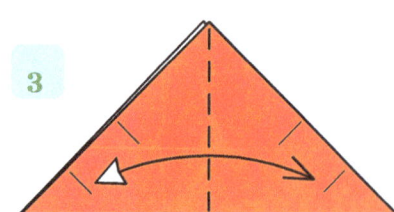

3. Fold and unfold.

40 Origami Symphony No. 1

4

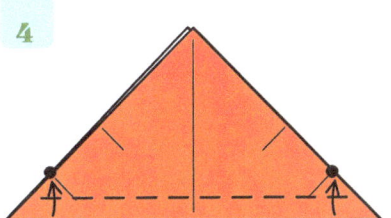

Fold a strip up so the bottom edge meets the dots.

5

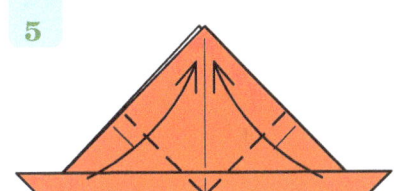

Fold to the center.

6

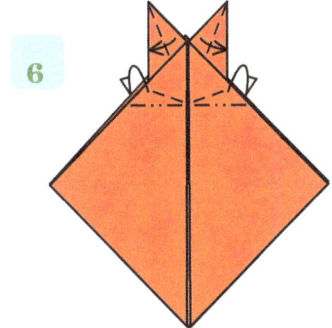

Thin the antennae.

7

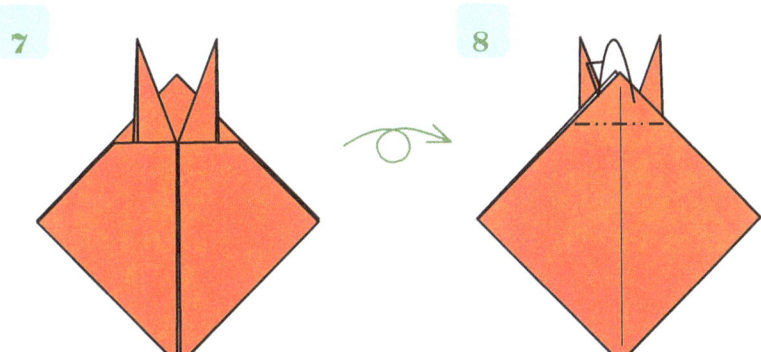

8

Fold the top layer inside.

9

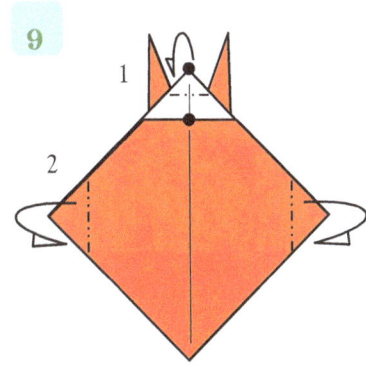

1. Fold behind so the dots meet.
2. Fold behind on the left and right.

10

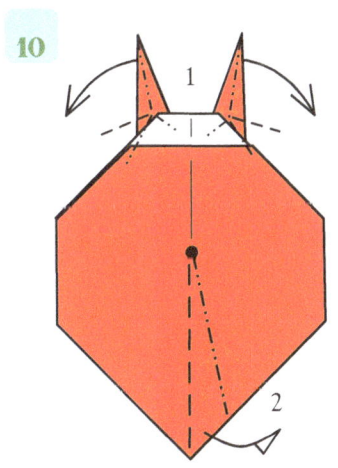

1. Make rabbit ears.
2. Puff out at the dot to make the body 3D.

11

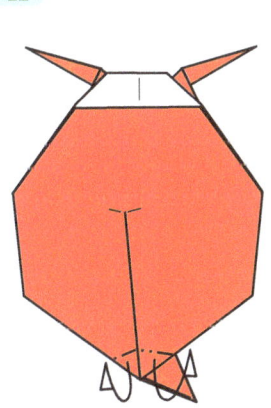

Fold behind.

12

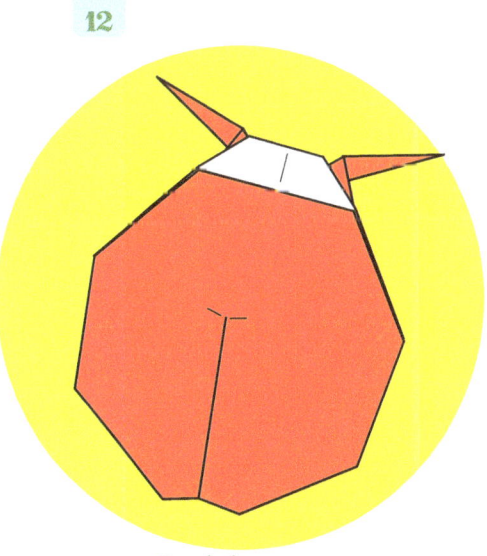

Ladybug

Ladybug **41**

Butterfly

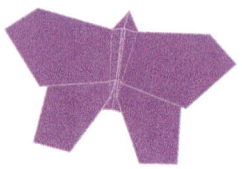

Many stories have been told throughout history of the lowly caterpillar that munches on leaves and plants, builds a cocoon for itself, rests and soon emerges from the cocoon as a beautiful and very colorful Butterfly. About 20,000 species of Butterflies can be found throughout the world except in the Antarctic.

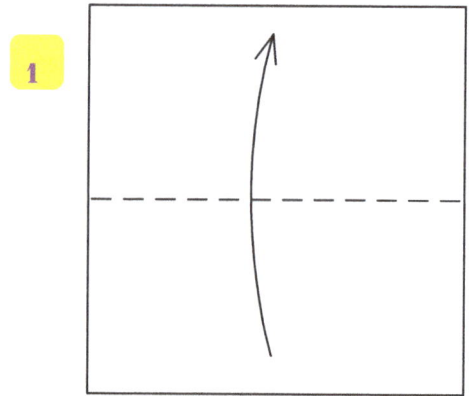

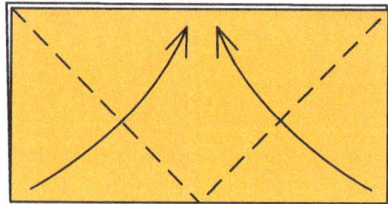

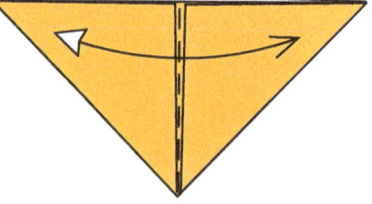

Fold and unfold.
Rotate 180°.

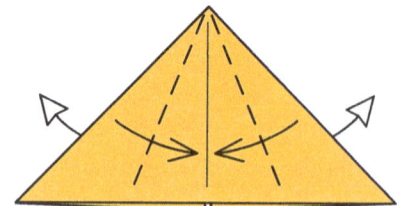

Fold to the center and swing out from behind.

42 *Origami Symphony No. 1*

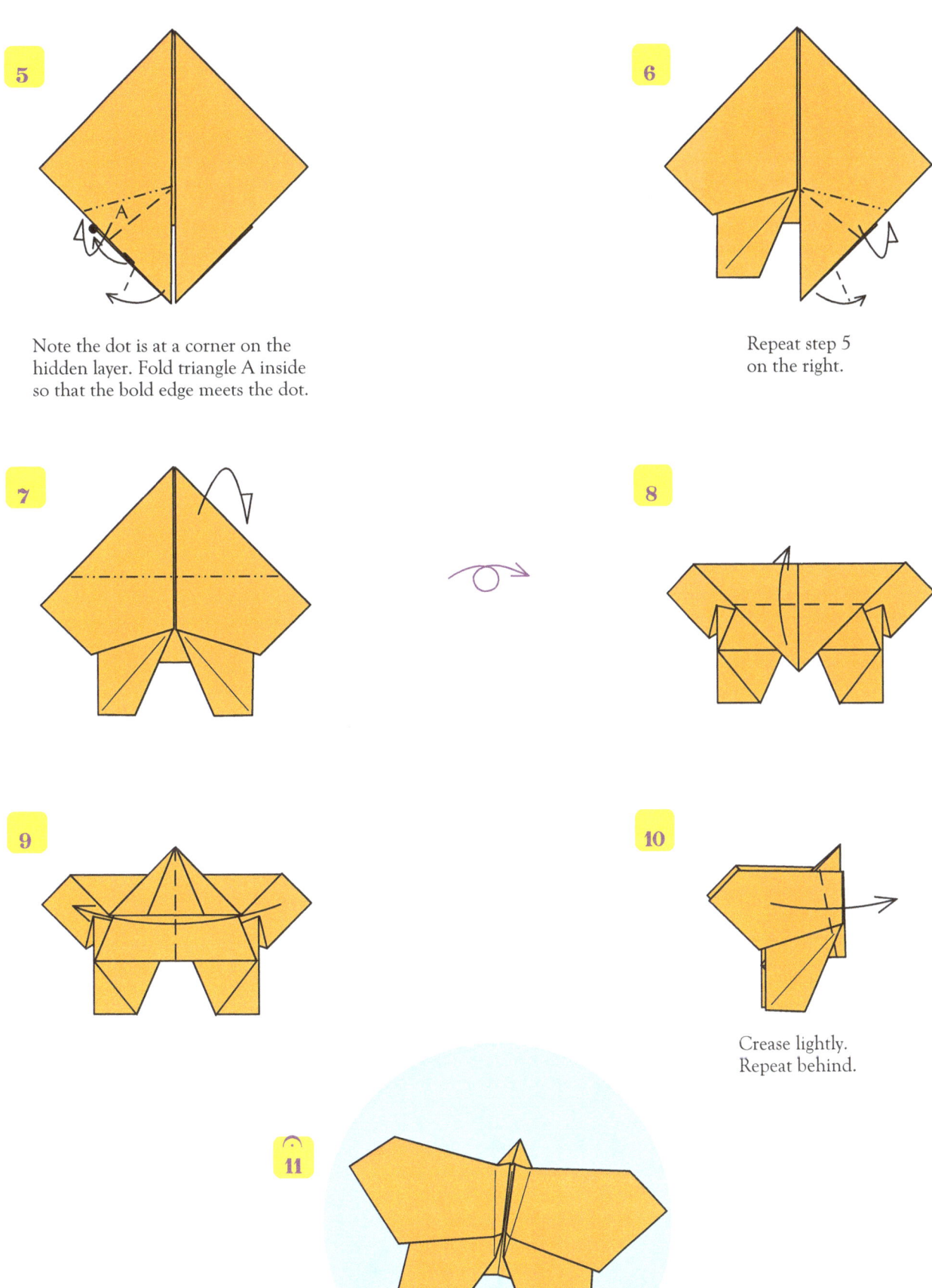

5 Note the dot is at a corner on the hidden layer. Fold triangle A inside so that the bold edge meets the dot.

6 Repeat step 5 on the right.

10 Crease lightly. Repeat behind.

Butterfly

Moth

Related to Butterflies, Moths help make the world a better place by pollinating flowers, which leads to seed production and more flowers. Over 150,000 species of Moths cover the globe. Unlike the Butterfly which has thin antennae, the Moth usually has feathery antennae.

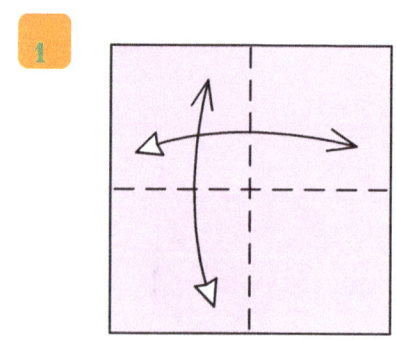

1. Fold and unfold.

 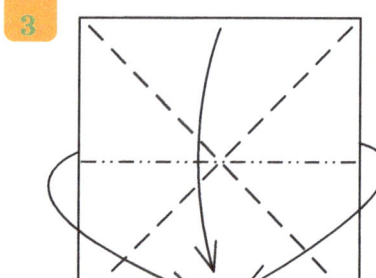

2. Fold and unfold.

3. Collapse along the creases.

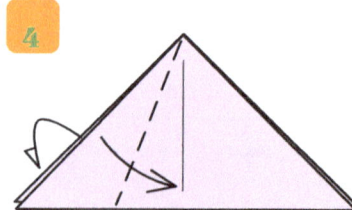

4. This is the Waterbomb Base. Fold to the center and repeat behind.

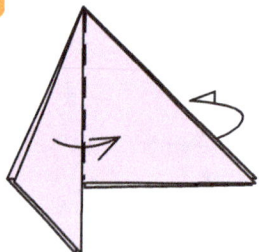

5. Fold one layer in front and one layer behind.

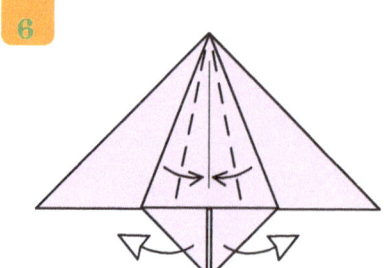

6. Fold to the center and swing out from behind.

44 Origami Symphony No. 1

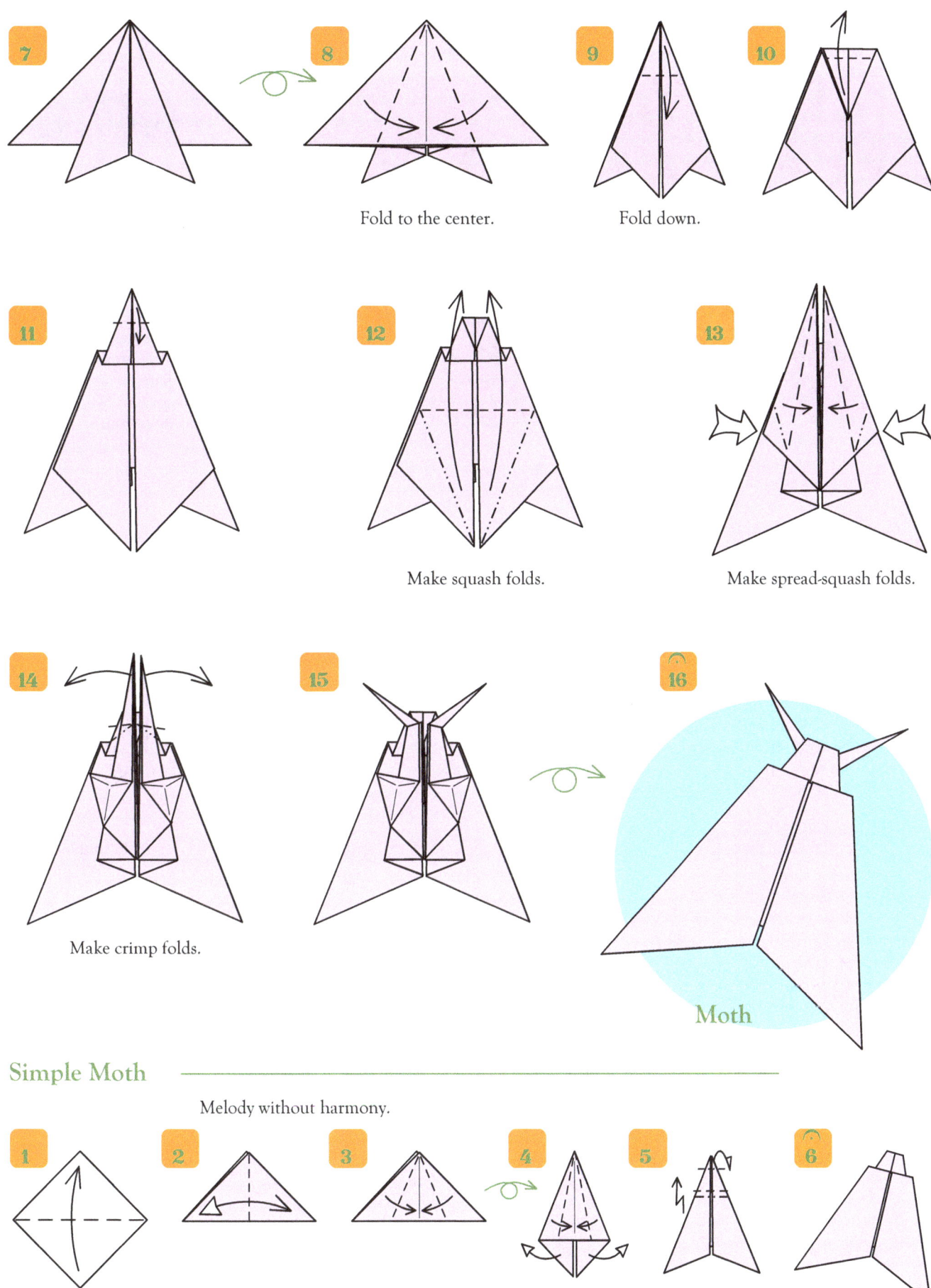

Fold to the center.

Fold down.

Make squash folds.

Make spread-squash folds.

Make crimp folds.

Moth

Simple Moth

Melody without harmony.

Moth 45

Caterpillar

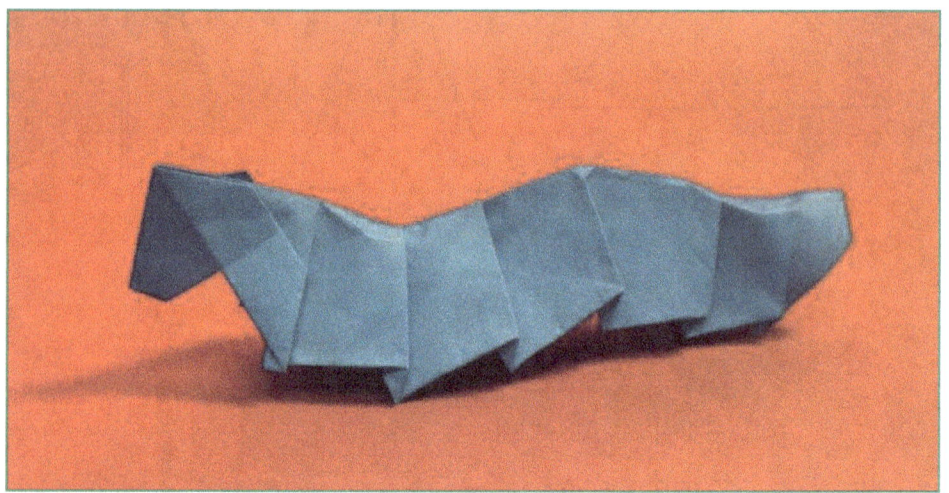
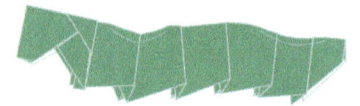

Will the Caterpillar become a Butterfly or a Moth? Depending on their coloring, size and other identifiable features, one can tell what will eventually emerge from the cocoon. For protection, some Caterpillars use camouflage to hide, or have markings to appear poisonous.

1

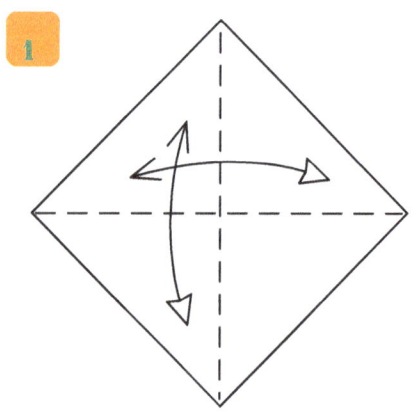

Fold and unfold.

2

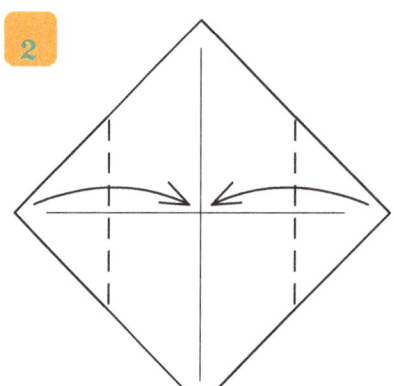

Fold to the center.

3

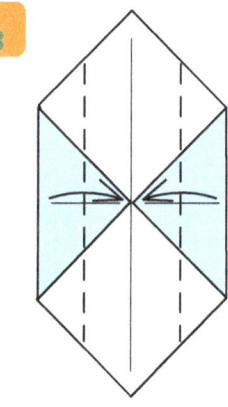

Fold to the center.

4

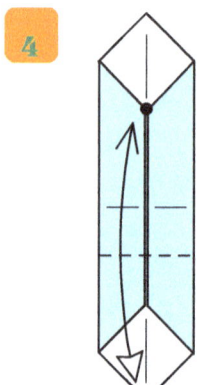

Fold and unfold.

5

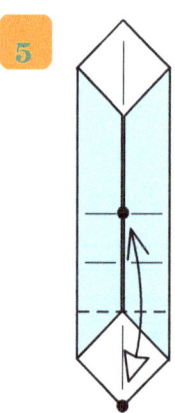

Fold and unfold. Rotate 180°.

6

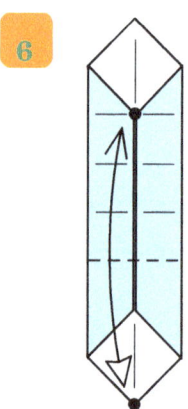

Repeat steps 4–5.

7

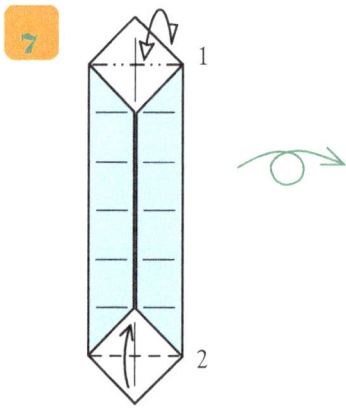

1. Fold and unfold.
2. Valley-fold.
Rotate 90°.

46 *Origami Symphony No. 1*

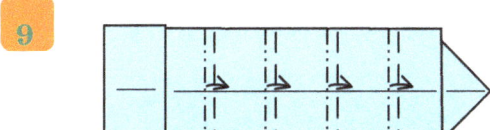

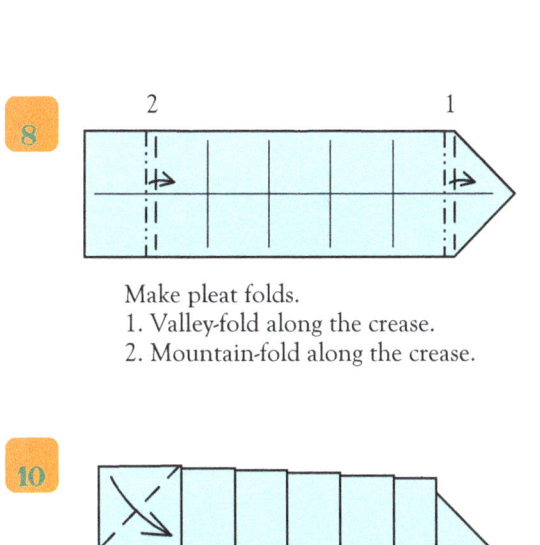

Make pleat folds.
1. Valley-fold along the crease.
2. Mountain-fold along the crease.

Make four pleat folds. Mountain-fold along the creases.

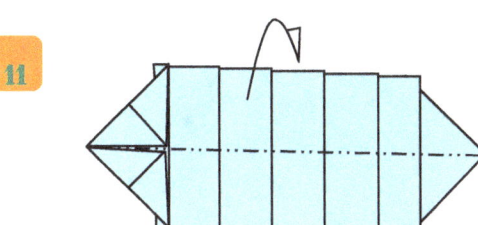

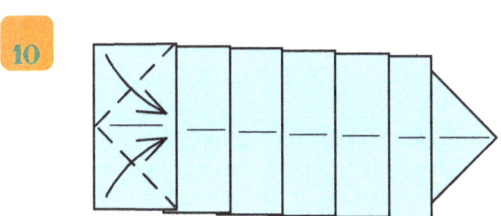

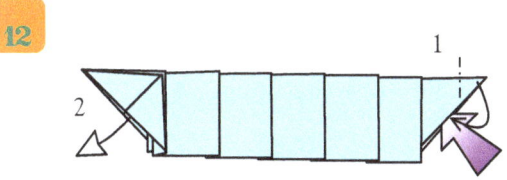

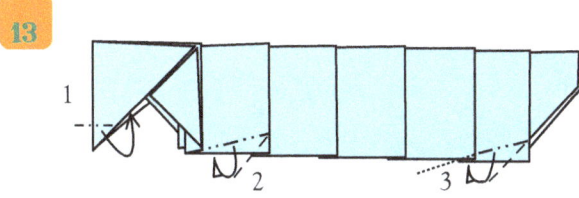

1. Reverse-fold.
2. Pull out.

1. Reverse-fold.
2. Fold inside, repeat behind.
3. Fold inside, repeat behind.

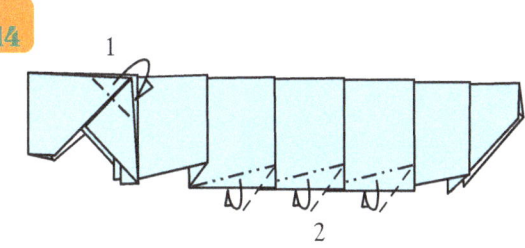

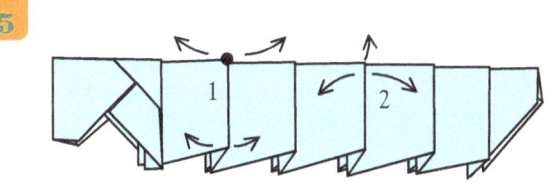

1. Fold behind.
2. Fold inside.
Repeat behind.

Spread the paper different ways for 1 and 2.

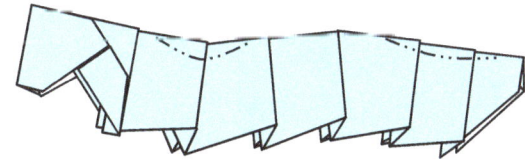

Shape the back. Steps 15–16 show ways to shape the caterpillar. You can skip or modify them.

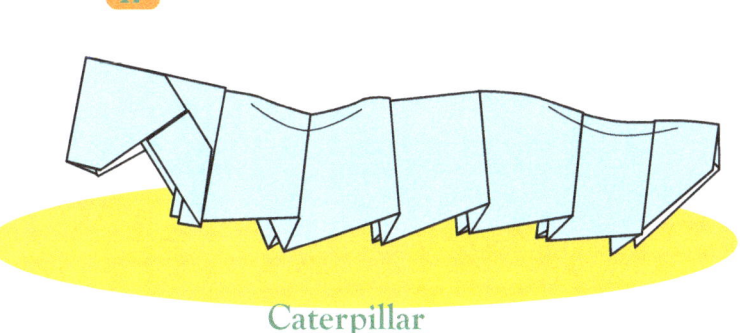

Caterpillar

Caterpillar **47**

Dragonfly

With their distinctive four wings, Dragonflies are primarily seen flying around marshes and other wetlands since they are aquatic in their nymph stage. Dragonflies eat mosquitoes, which benefits humans. Over 5,000 species can be found around the world except in Antarctica. Dragonflies have bright iridescent colors. They can fly up or down or even stay in place.

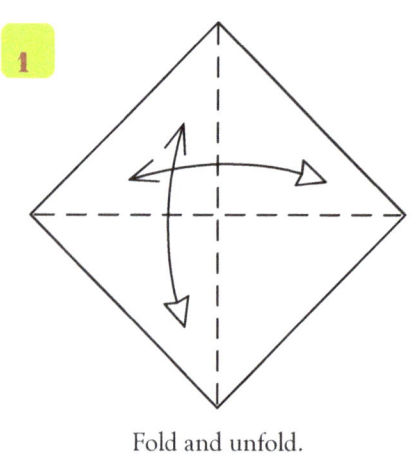

Fold and unfold.

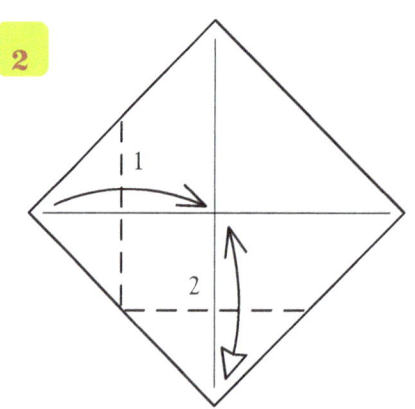

1. Fold to the center.
2. Fold and unfold.

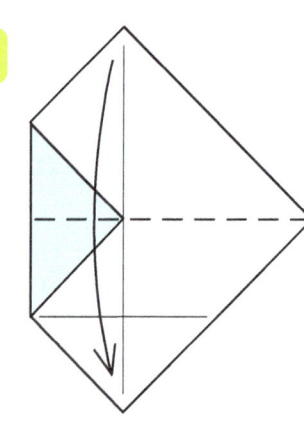

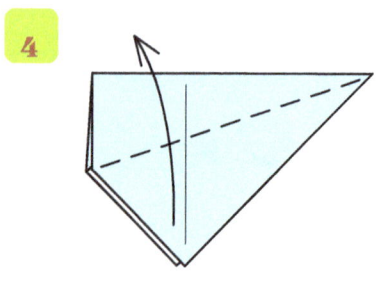

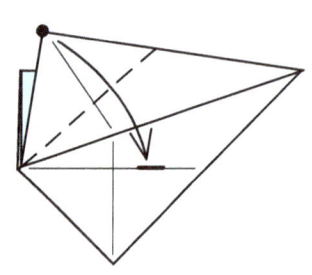

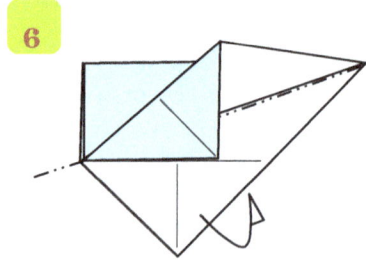

48 Origami Symphony No. 1

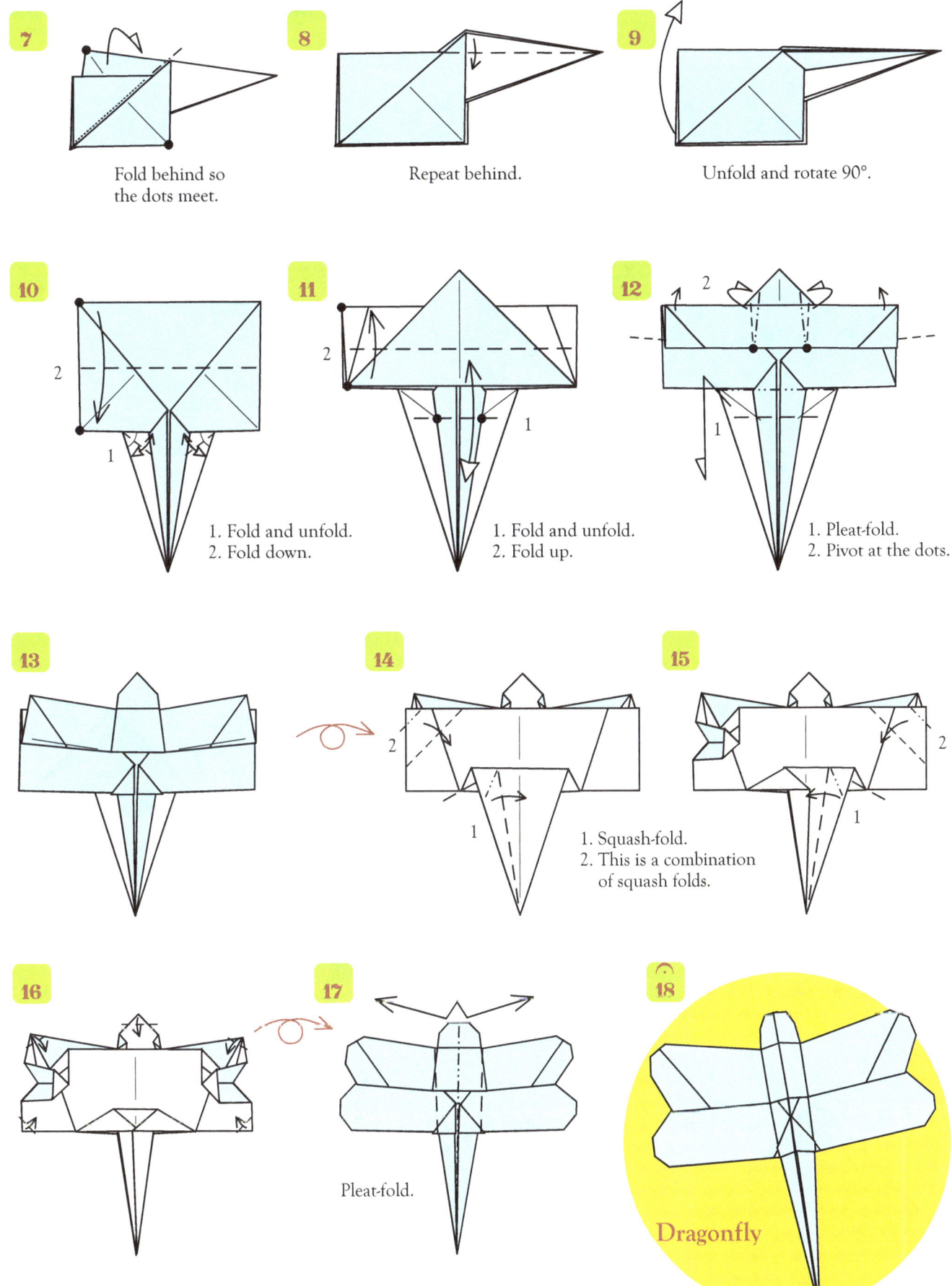

Dragonfly 49

Stink Bug

Stink Bugs are more of an invasive species of bug, and are generally pests in gardens and farms. However, they do prey on other insects that would damage plants, and in this way, they are helpful.

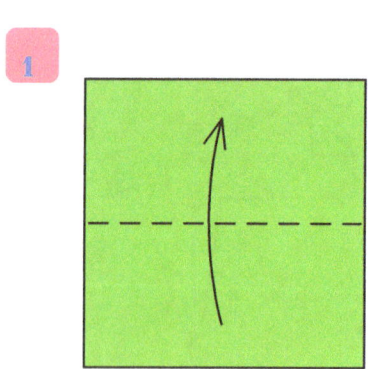

Fold in half.

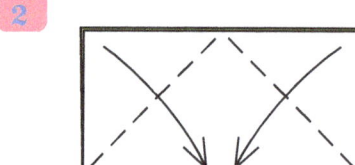

Repeat behind.

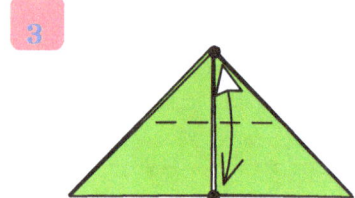

Fold and unfold the top layer.

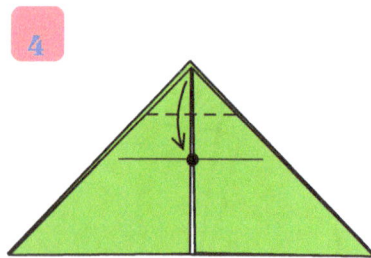

Fold the top layer to the center.

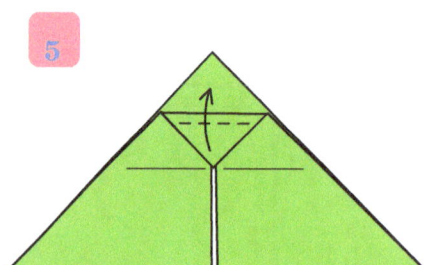

Fold down to the center.

50 *Origami Symphony No. 1*

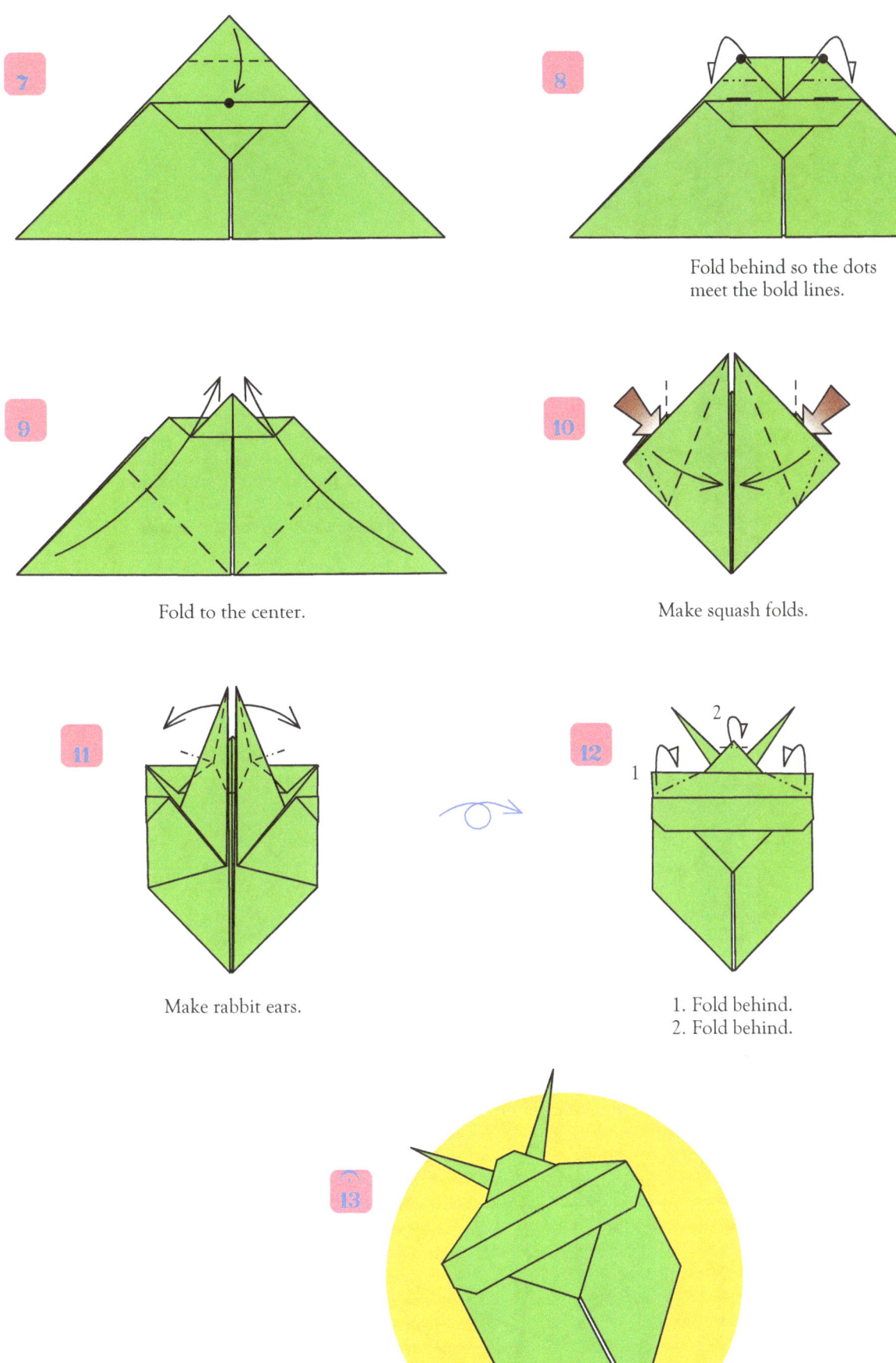

Stink Bug **51**

Stag Beetle

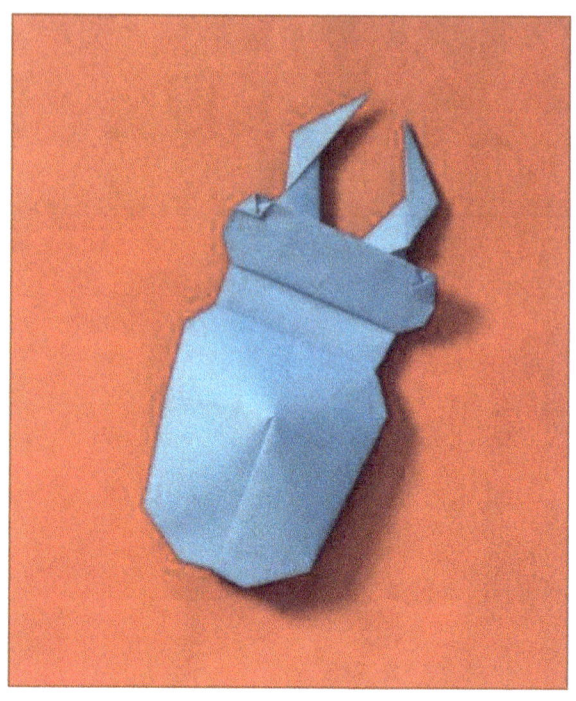

Called the Stag Beetle because the male beetle of this variety looks like it has antlers, those antlers are in fact its mighty jaws. Now endangered, the Stag Beetle is effectively extinct in some countries, and efforts are being made to rebuild the population of these spectacular beetles.

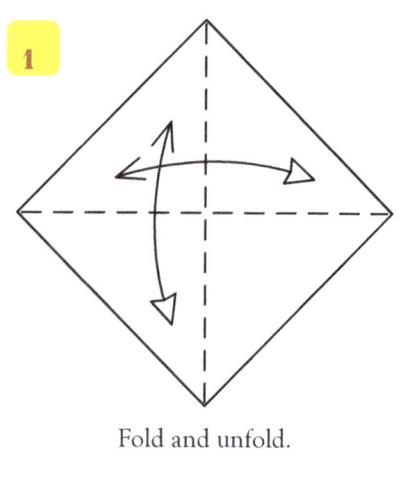

Fold and unfold.

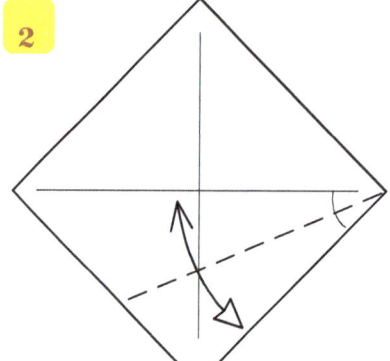

Fold and unfold.

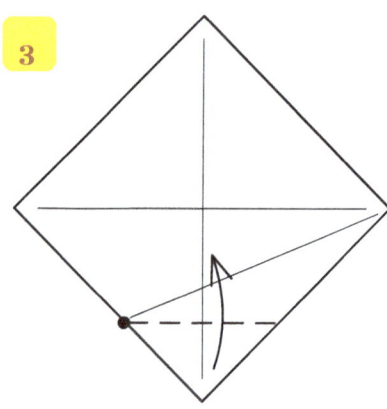

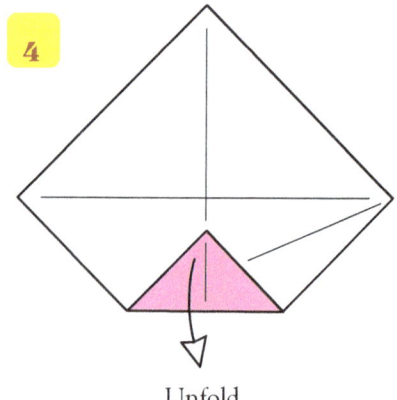

Unfold.

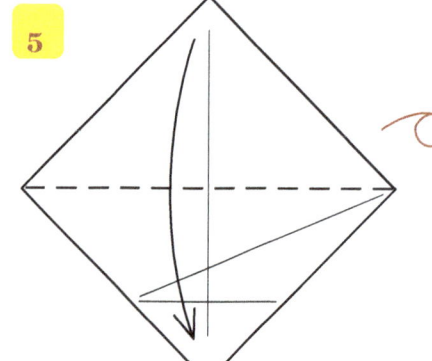

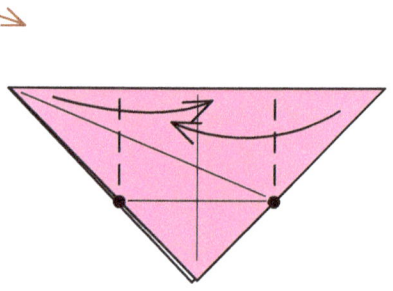

52   *Origami Symphony No. 1*

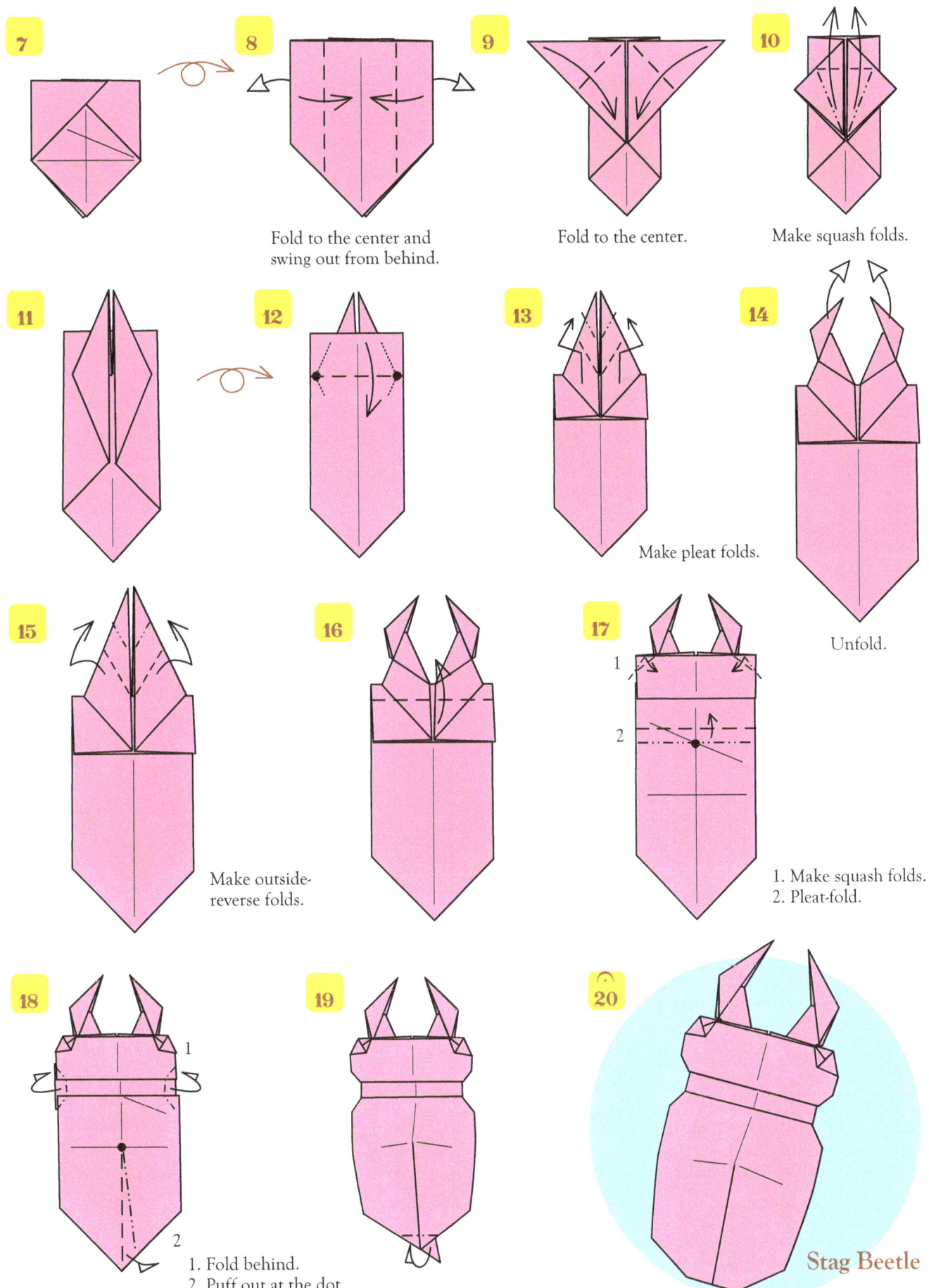

Stag Beetle

Cicada

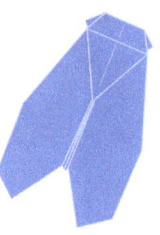

Every 17 years, people in the Eastern United States are treated to the distinct song of the Periodic Cicada. Only the males sing, and their body is similar to a violin, giving it its distinctive resonate sound. Large and red-eyed, they spend most of their lives underground, and are quite harmless.

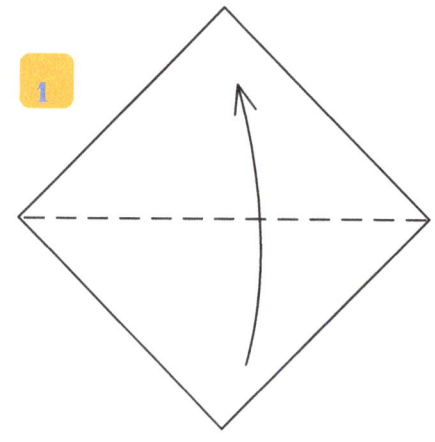

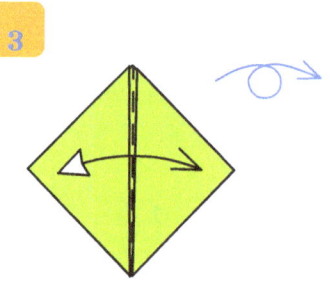

Fold and unfold.

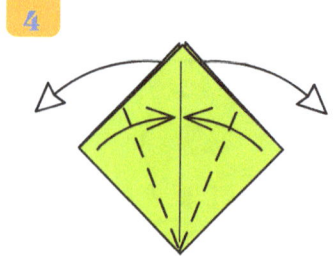

Fold to the center and swing out from behind.

Unfold.

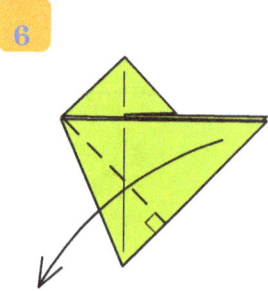

Note the right angle.

54   Origami Symphony No. 1

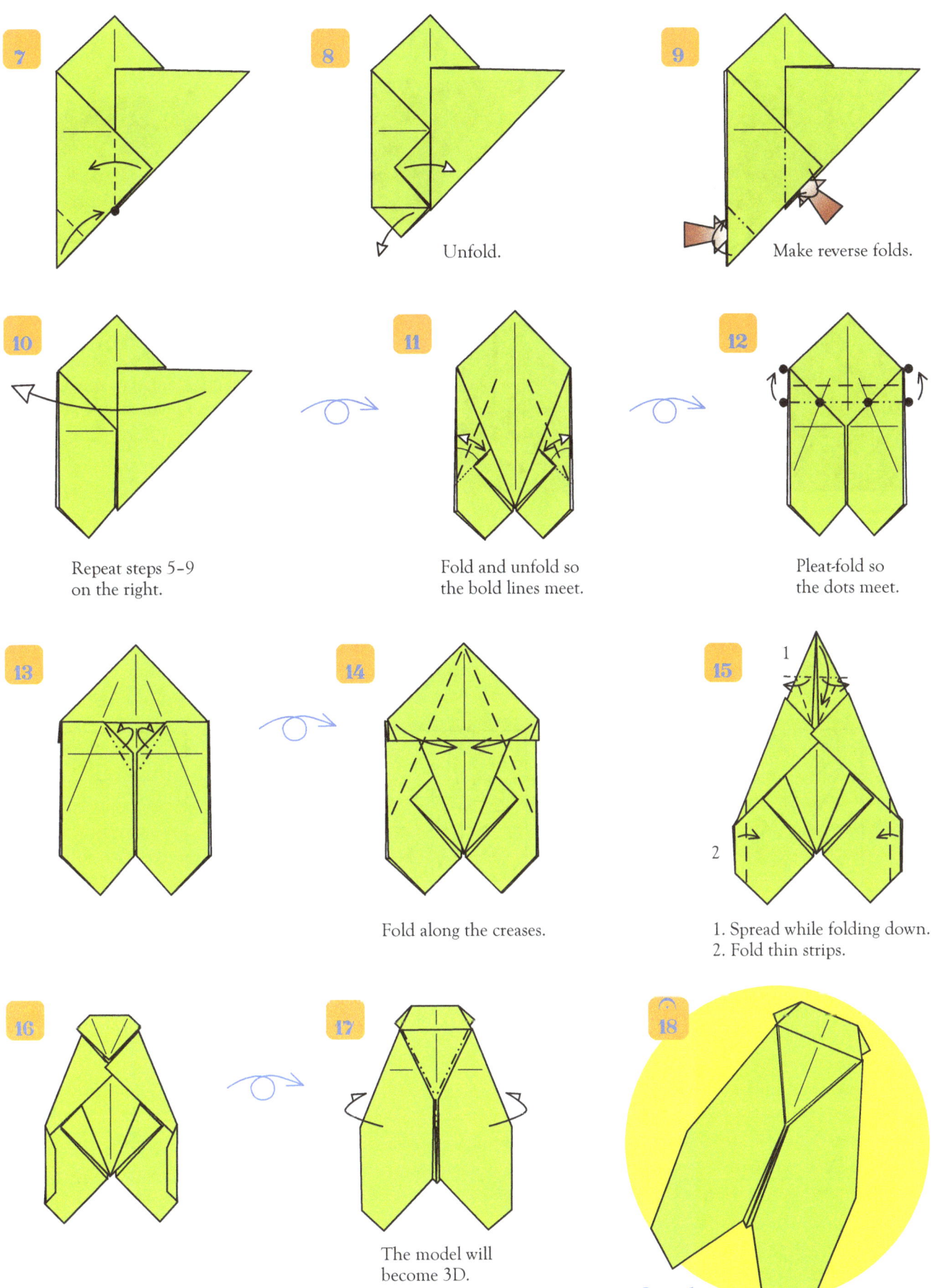

Cicada 55

Ant

Sometimes busy minding their own business at work and sometimes on the attack, the many varieties of Ants have fascinated humans for millennia. Known for their amazing strength, there are over 12,000 species of Ants. Ants form complex colonies with specialized groups of ants, all working together, to support and protect the colony.

1

Fold and unfold.

2

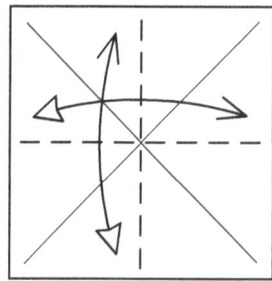

Fold and unfold.

3

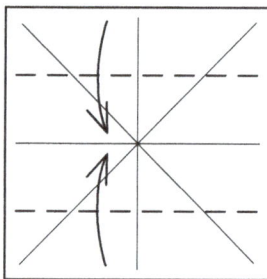

Fold to the center.

4

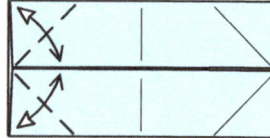

Fold and unfold along the creases.

5

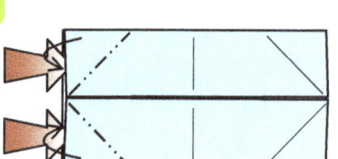

Make reverse folds.

6

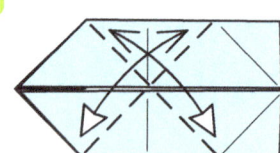

Fold and unfold along hidden creases. Rotate 90°.

56 *Origami Symphony No. 1*

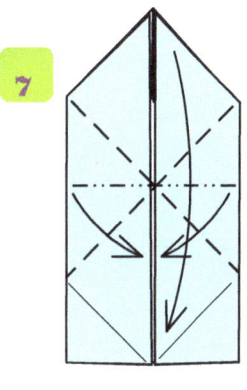

Fold along the creases.

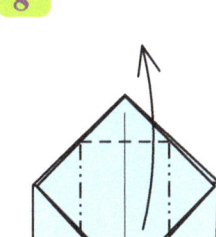

Petal-fold.

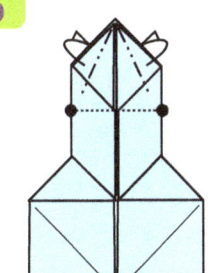

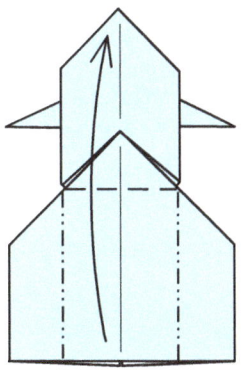

Petal-fold.

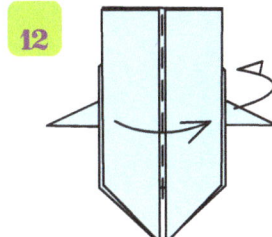

Fold a layer on top and repeat behind.

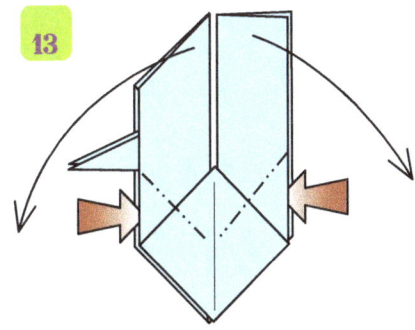

Make reverse folds.

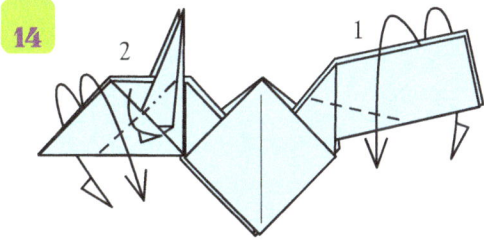

1. Outside-reverse-fold.
2. This is a combination of reverse folds.

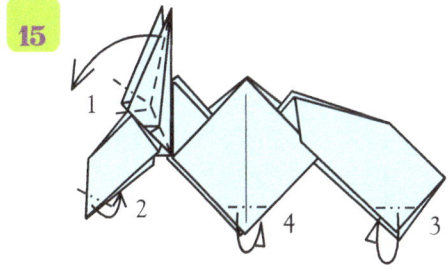

1. Rabbit-ear.
2. Reverse-fold.
3. Fold inside.
4. Fold inside.
Repeat behind.

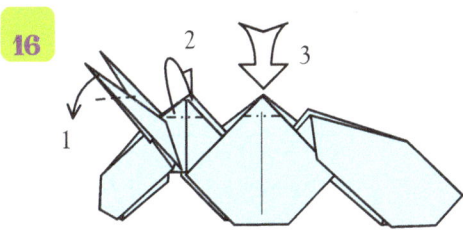

1. Reverse-fold.
2. Fold inside.
3. Push in.
Repeat behind.

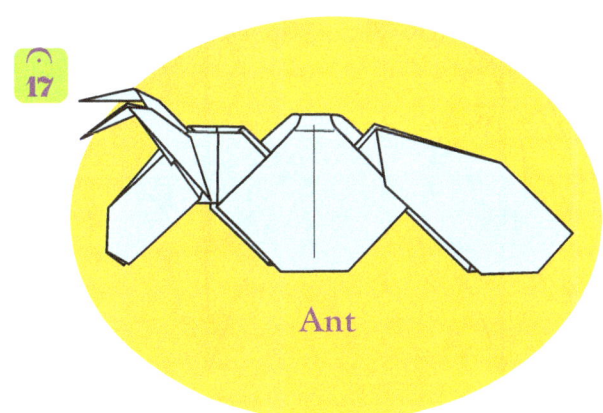

Ant

Ant 57

Wasp

Wasp resembles both the Bee and the Ant in shape and coloring, though it is neither. Some species are very social and some are solitary, and it is the female Wasp that stings, while the male does not have the stinger. Wasps build nests made of wood fibers which they convert into paper-like pulp.

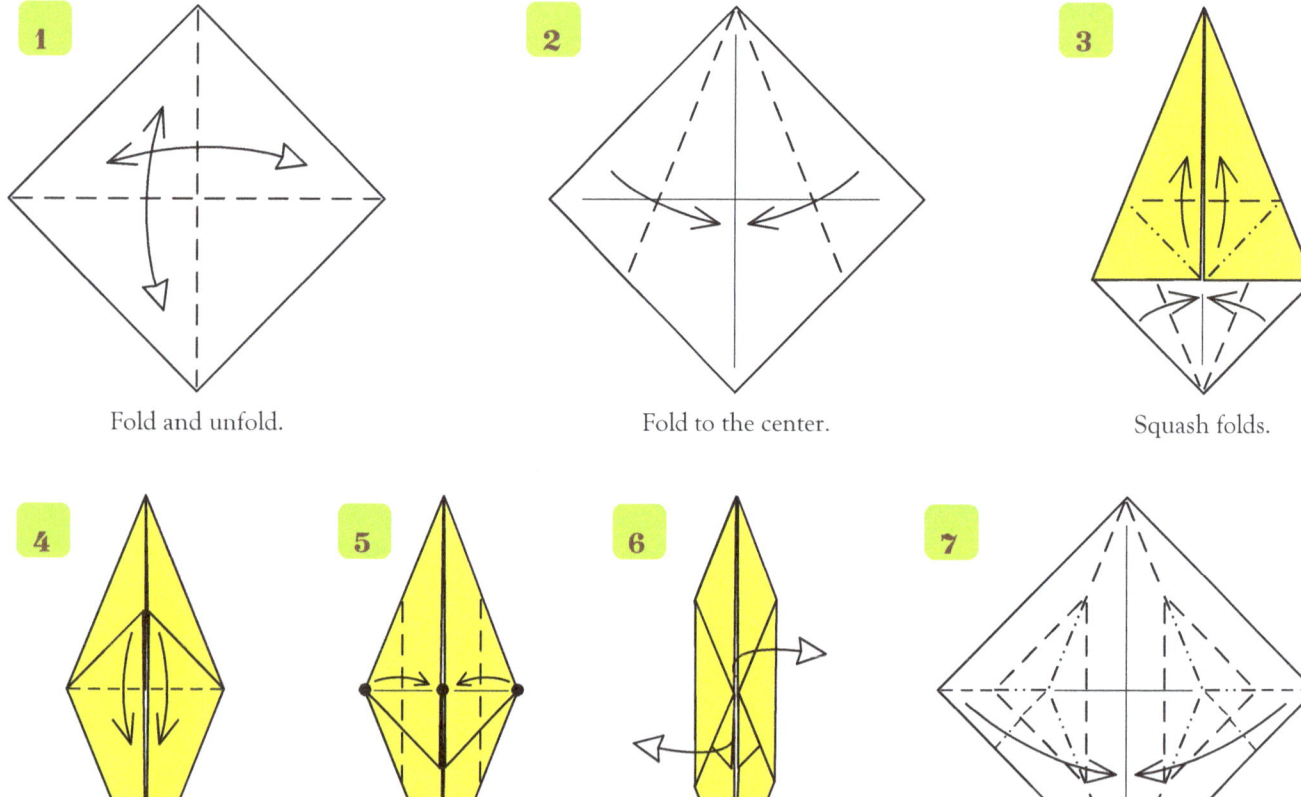

1. Fold and unfold.
2. Fold to the center.
3. Squash folds.
4.
5.
6. Unfold everything.
7. Fold along the creases.

58 *Origami Symphony No. 1*

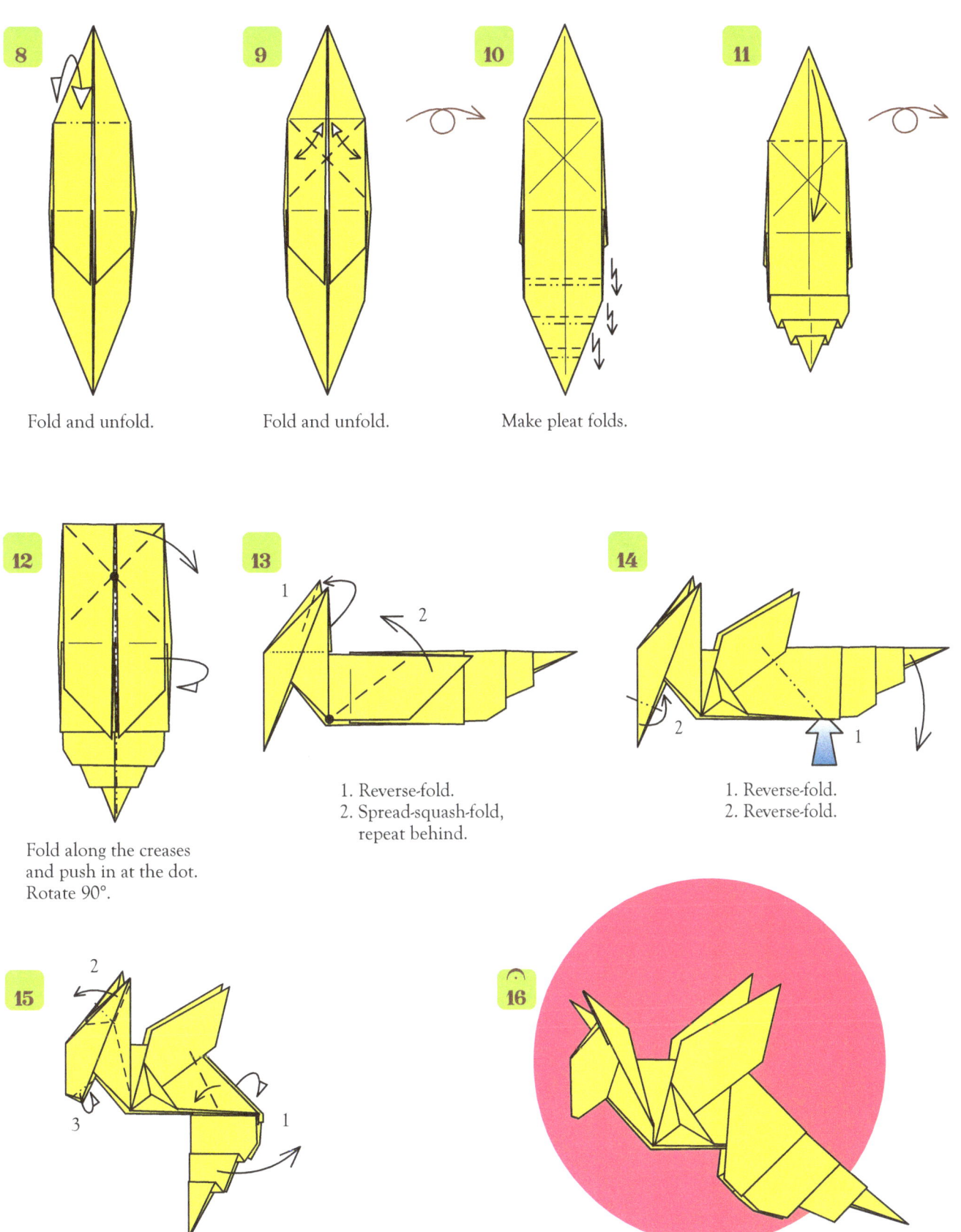

Wasp

Grasshopper

The Grasshopper has been around in some form since the Triassic Period and has a familiar chirping song that is often heard on warm Summer nights. They can jump three feet. Grasshoppers will eat anything from plants to other insects or spiders.

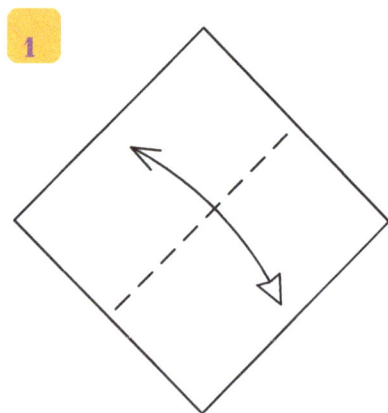

1. Fold and unfold.

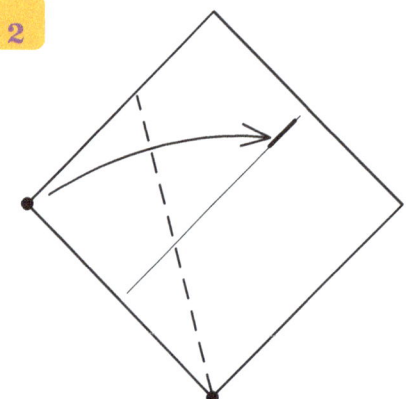

2. Bring the corner to the line.

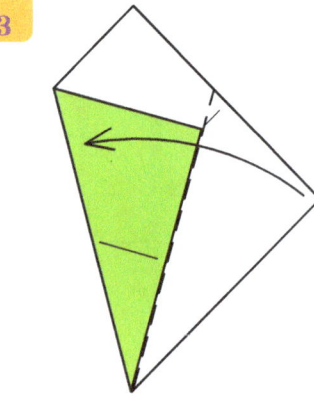

3.

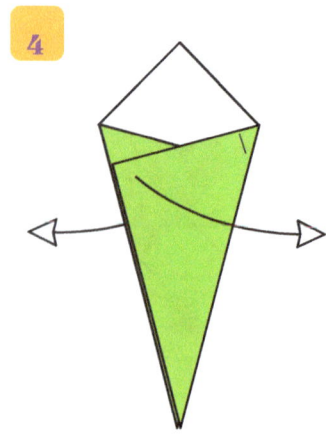

4. Unfold.

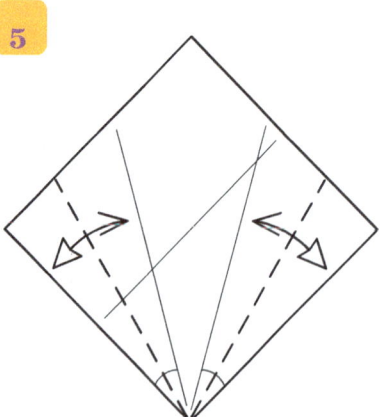

5. Fold and unfold. Rotate 180°.

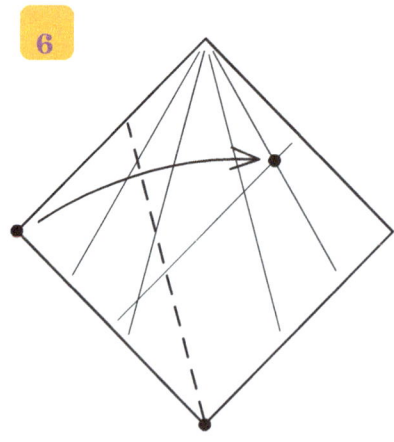

6. Repeat steps 2–5.

60   Origami Symphony No. 1

7
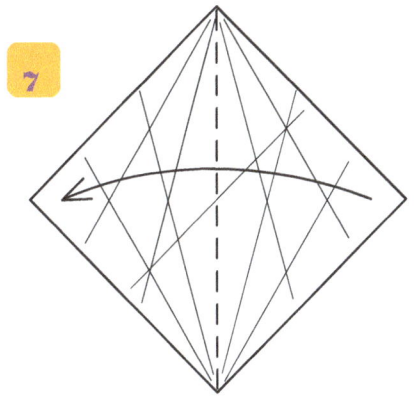

8
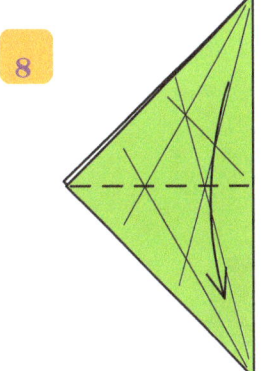

9
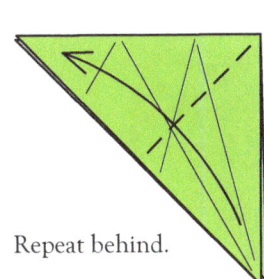

Repeat behind.

10
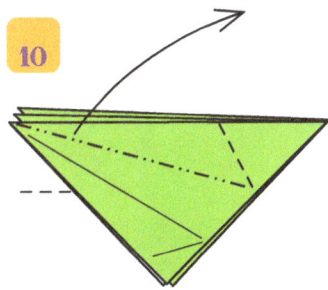

Mountain-fold along the crease for this squash fold. Repeat behind.

11
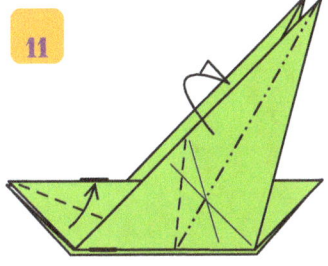

Note the bold lines are parallel. Mountain-fold along the crease and repeat behind.

12
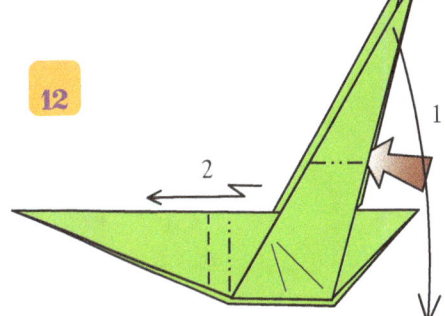

1. Reverse-fold, repeat behind.
2. Crimp-fold.

13
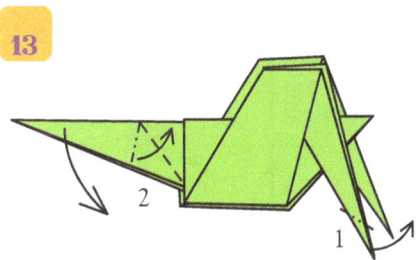

1. Reverse-fold, repeat behind.
2. Crimp-fold.

14
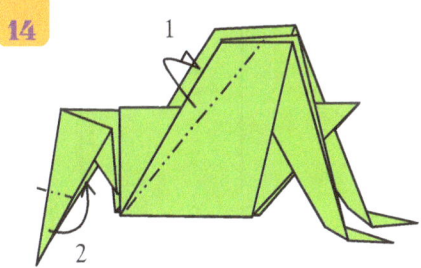

1. Fold behind, repeat behind.
2. Reverse-fold.

15
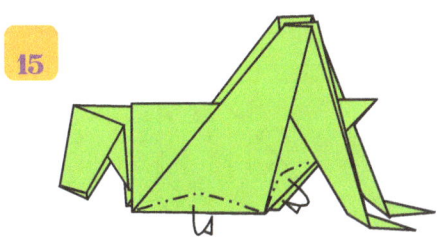

Curve and shape the legs. Repeat behind.

16
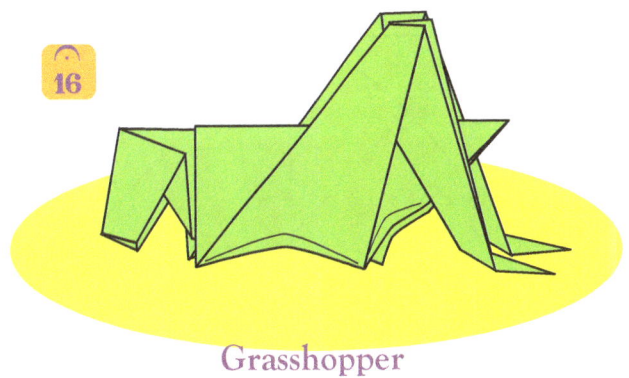

Grasshopper

Fly

Though there are over 120,000 species of Flies, the ones humans are most familiar with are houseflies. Attracted to decaying meat and other organic material, the Common House Fly has paid a visit to most everyone's home.

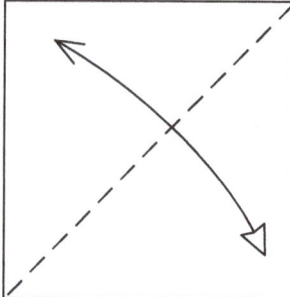

1. Fold and unfold.

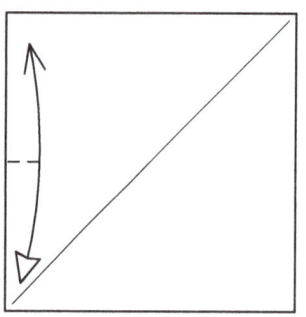

2. Fold and unfold on the left.

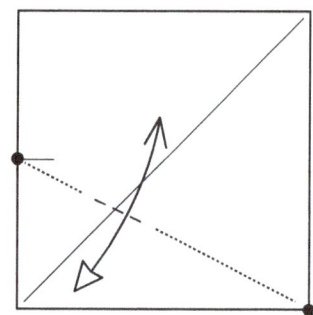

3. Fold and unfold on the diagonal.

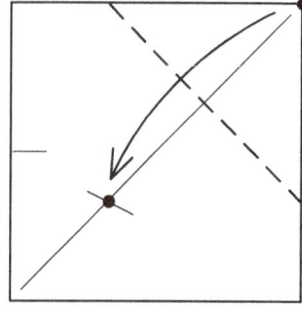

4. Rotate.

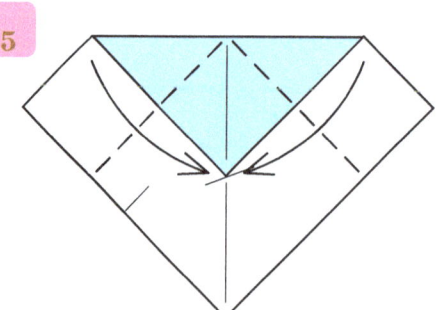

5.

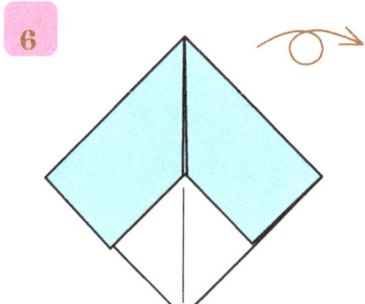

6.

62 Origami Symphony No. 1

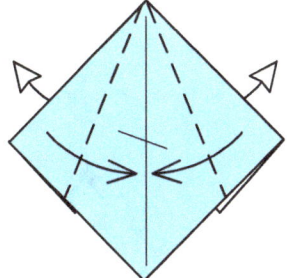

Fold to the center and swing out from behind.

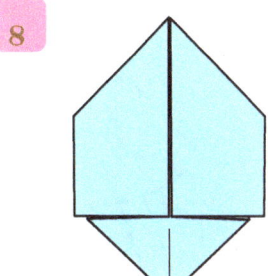

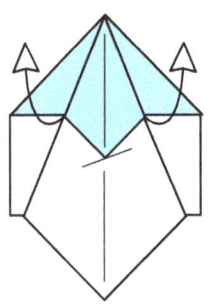

Pull out.

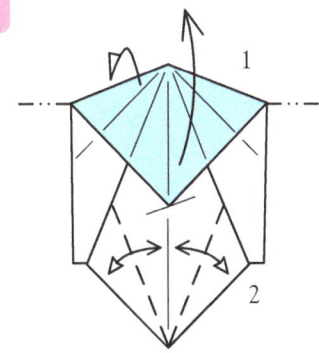

1. Pivot around the mountain-fold line.
2. Fold and unfold.

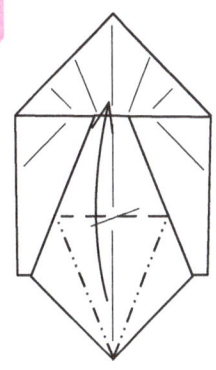

Petal-fold.

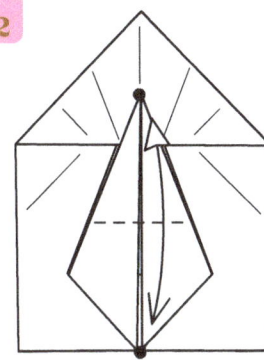

Fold and unfold.

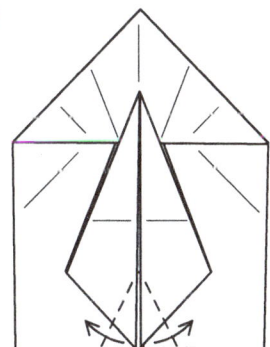

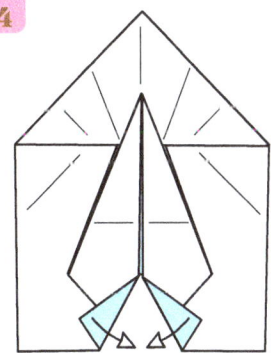

Unfold.

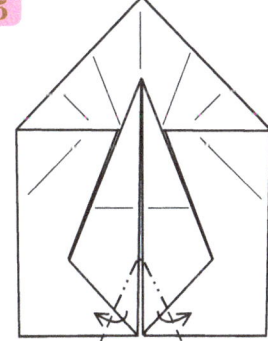

Make reverse folds.

Fly

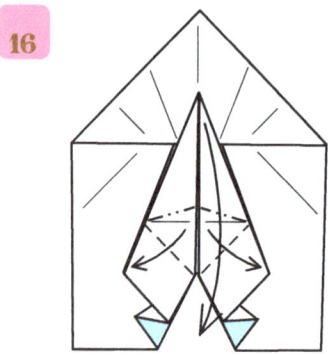

Spread while folding down.

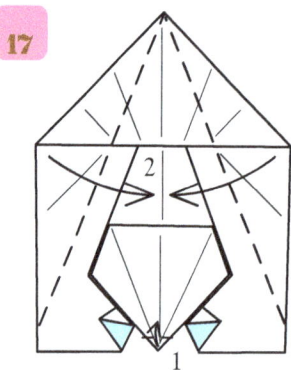

1. Fold up.
2. Fold to the center.

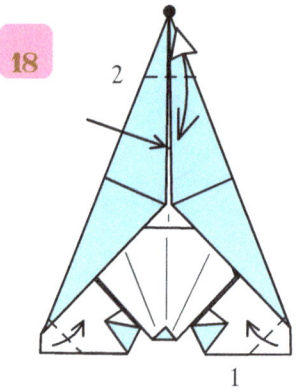

1. Fold up on the left and right.
2. Fold and unfold. Bring the dot down to the line which is mostly hidden.

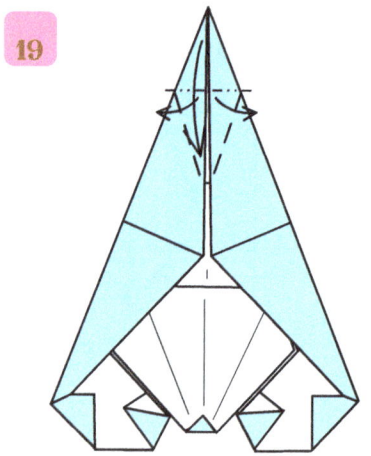

Spread while folding down.

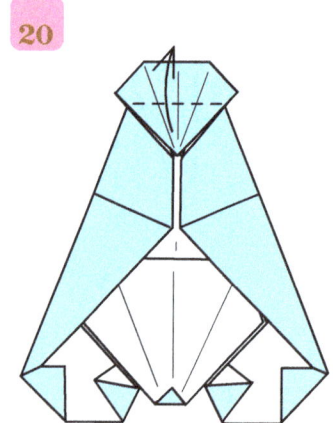

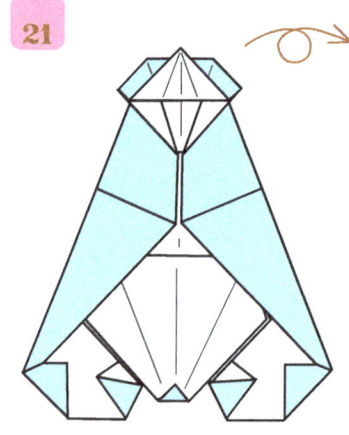

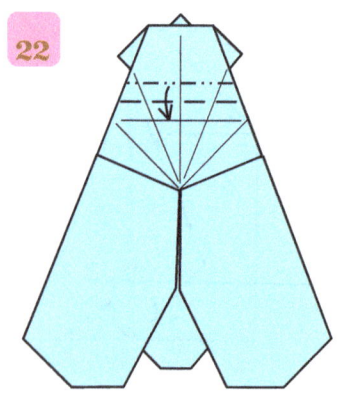

Pleat-fold.

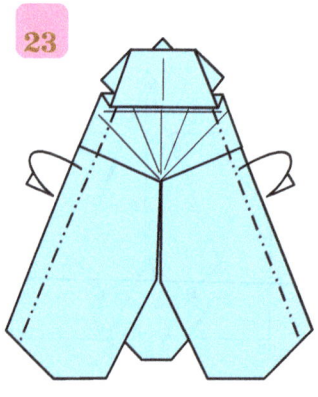

Fold behind.

Fly

64 Origami Symphony No. 1

Snail

Snails are gastropods with shells. Slow and slimy, some Snails live on land, such as Garden Snails, and some live in the water, such as Periwinkles. Some large Land Snails are eaten as Escargot.

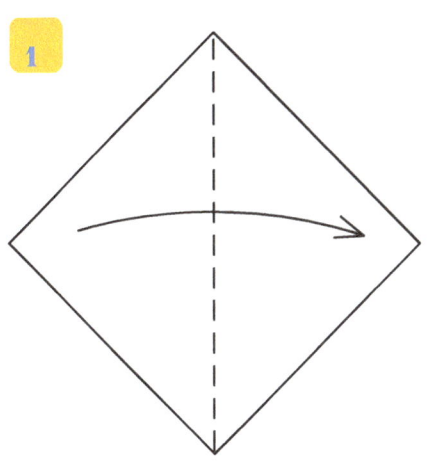

1

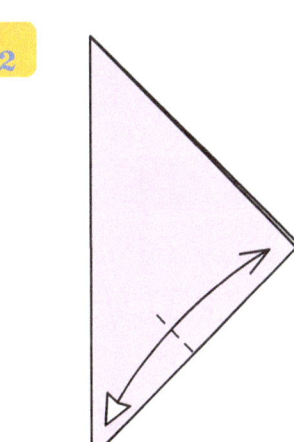

2

Fold and unfold.

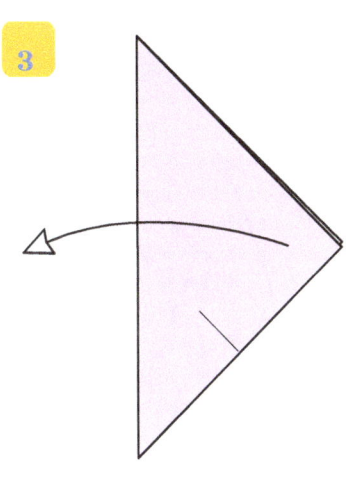

3

Unfold.

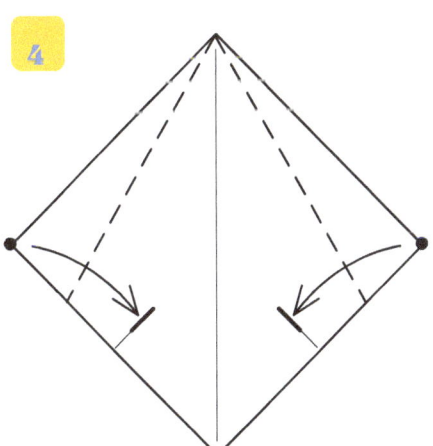

4

Bring the corners to the lines.

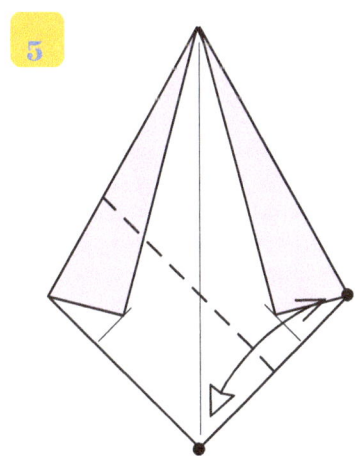

5

Fold and unfold.

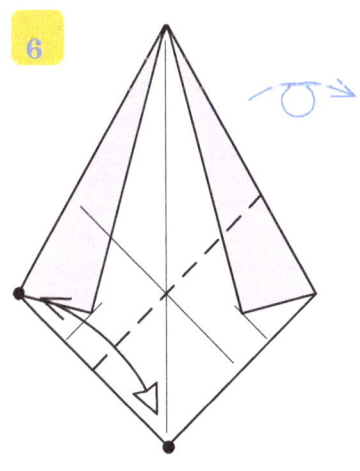

6

Fold and unfold.

Snail **65**

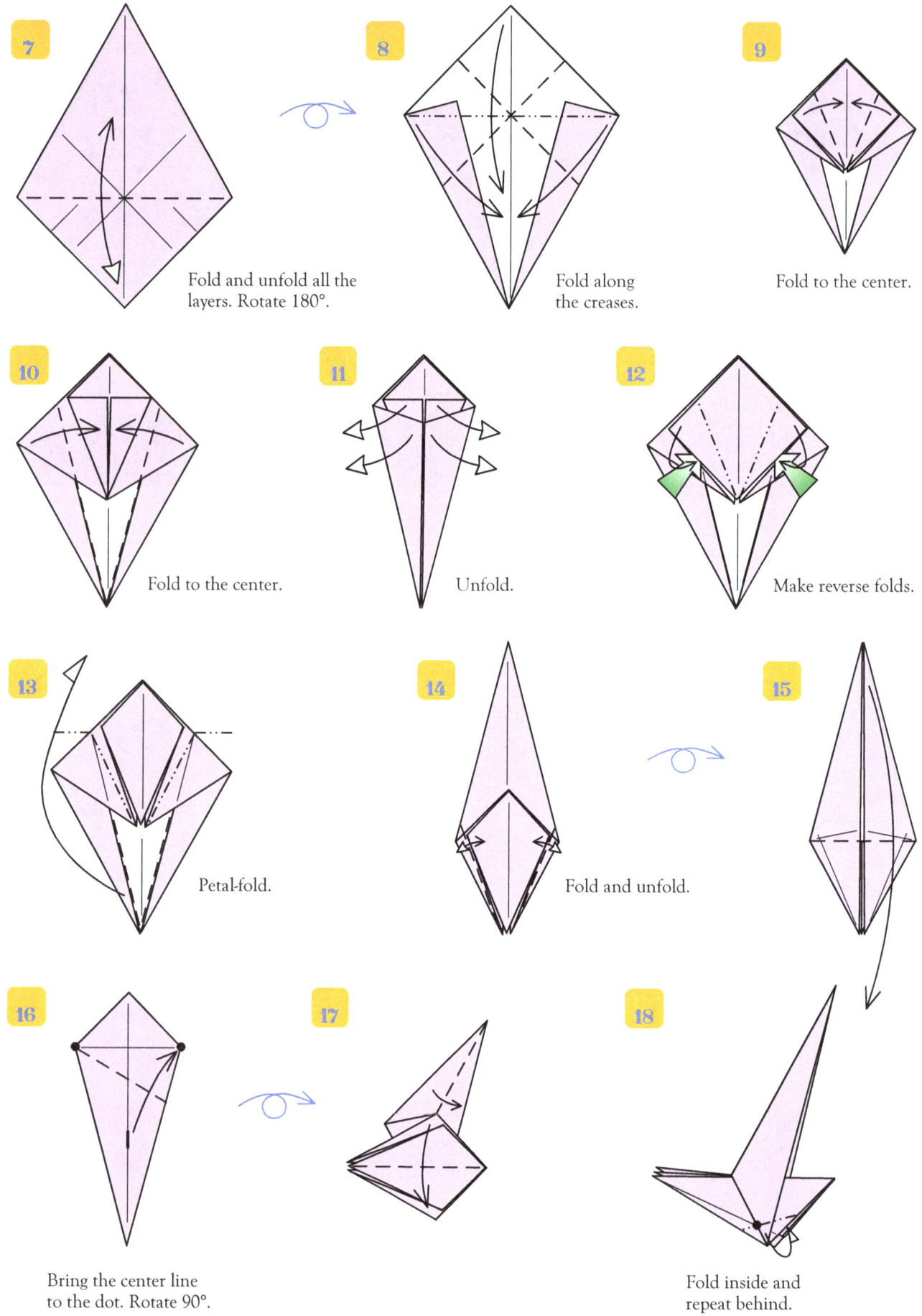

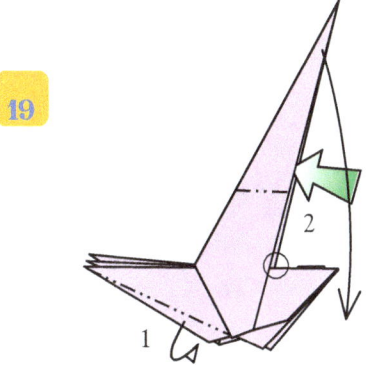

1. Fold inside, repeat behind.
2. Reverse-fold on a line parallel to the bold line. Leave a small space by the circle.

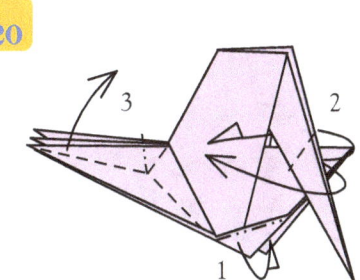

1. Fold inside, repeat behind.
2. Outside-reverse-fold.
3. Rabbit-ear, repeat behind.

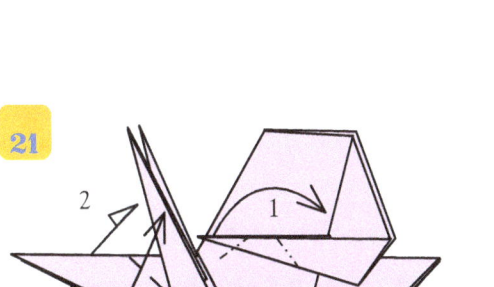

1. Continue with reverse folds.
2. Outside-reverse-fold.
Rotate.

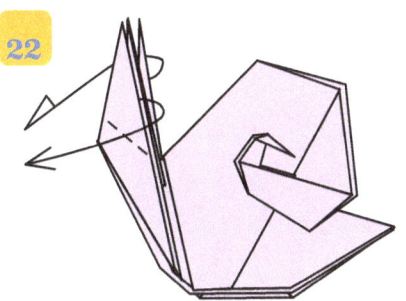

Outside-reverse-fold.

1. Reverse-fold.
2. Spread the tip to round it.
3. Bend the antenna.
Repeat behind.

Snail

Frog

Popular as pets, these hopping amphibians have a variety of songs, from high chirps to deep croaks. Throughout history, Frogs have been popular as the subjects of folk tales, often in the form of princes who have been turned into a Frog by a magic spell.

1

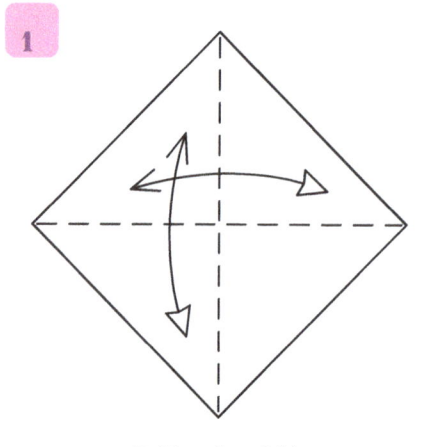

Fold and unfold.

2

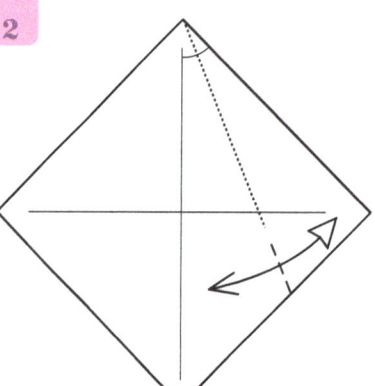

Fold and unfold on the edge.

3

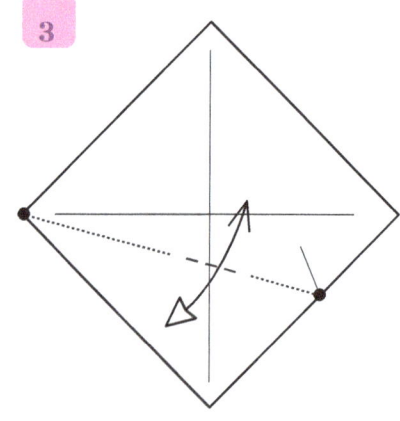

Fold and unfold on the diagonal.

4

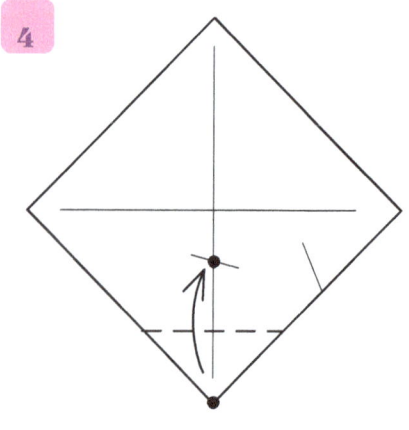

5

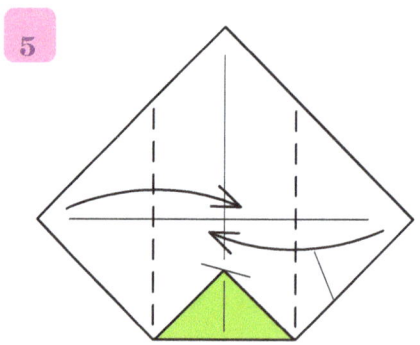

6

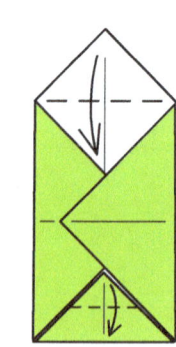

68 *Origami Symphony No. 1*

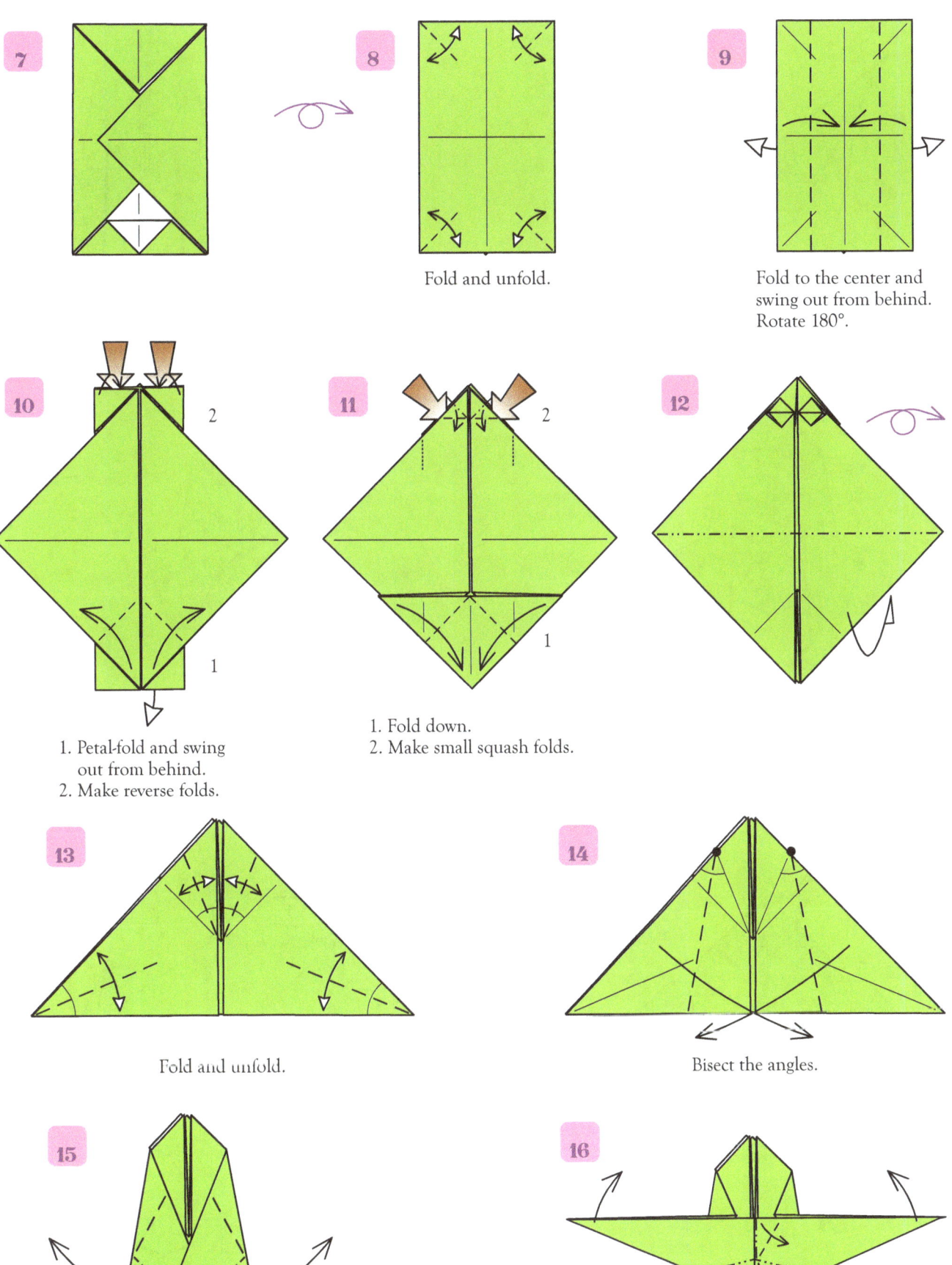

Fold and unfold.

Fold to the center and swing out from behind. Rotate 180°.

1. Petal-fold and swing out from behind.
2. Make reverse folds.

1. Fold down.
2. Make small squash folds.

Fold and unfold.

Bisect the angles.

Fold the legs in half.

Pivot on the dots as you slide the legs.

Frog **69**

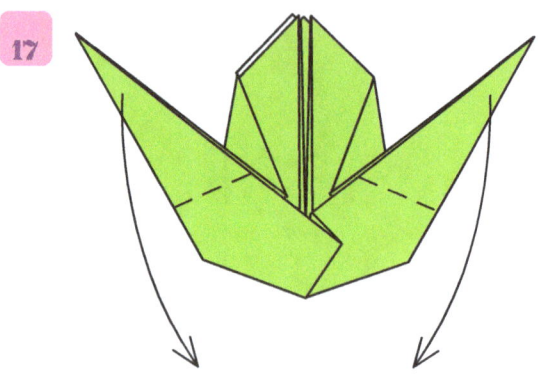

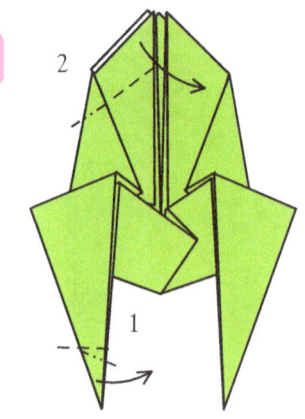

1. Squash fold.
2. Reverse-fold.

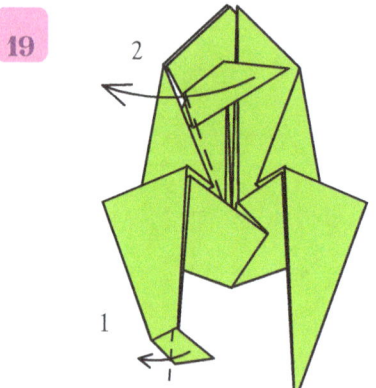

1. Fold the foot with a possible small squash fold.
2. Valley-fold.

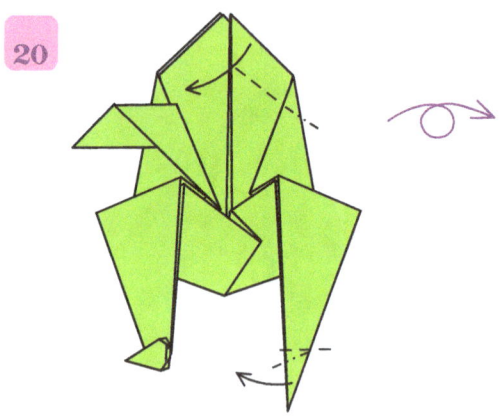

Repeat steps 18–19 on the right.

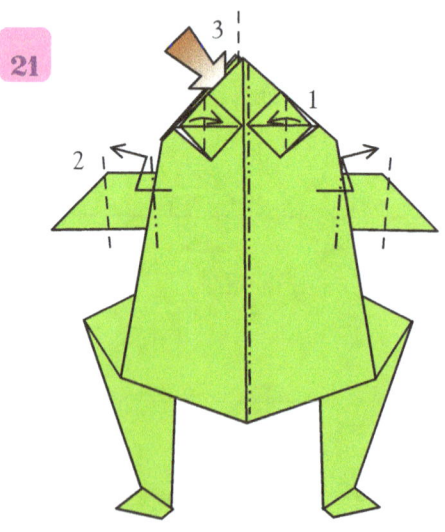

1. Fold the eyes.
2. Bend the legs.
3. Open the mouth and fold the back slightly in half.

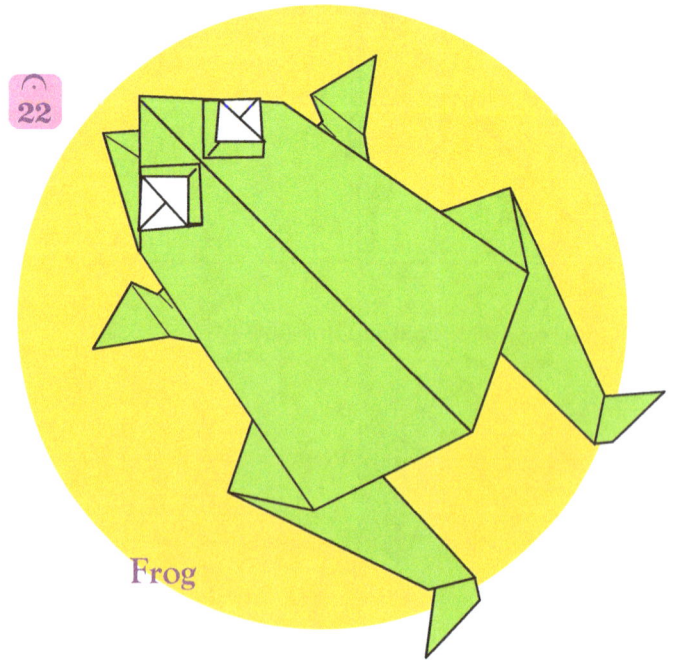

Frog

70 Origami Symphony No. 1

Third Movement

Minuet of Platonic Solids with a Trio of Sunken Solids

 The minuet of geometric shapes highlights the five Platonic Solids. To Plato, the Greek philosopher, they represent the classic Elements of Fire, Earth, Air, Water, and the Universe. Folding these three-dimensional shapes, each from one square sheet, shows varied techniques. The trio shows three models built on Sunken Triangles, Squares, and Pentagons. Models range from simple to very complex in skill level. Light up the room with these geometric wonders.

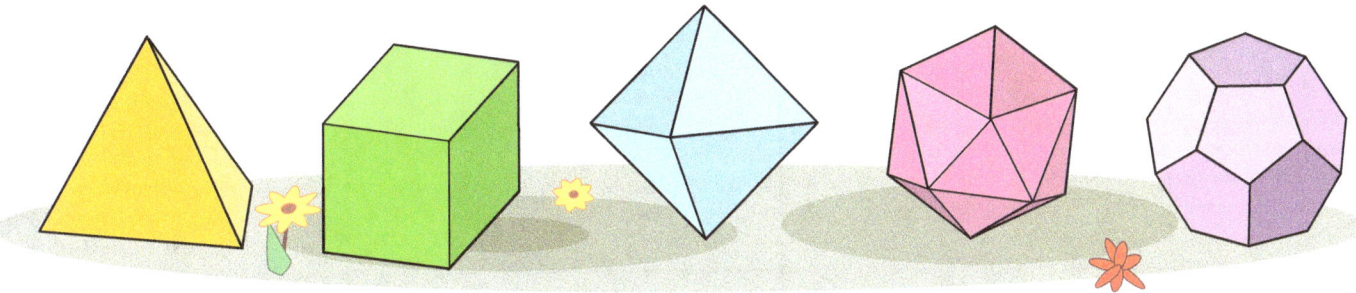

Tetrahedron

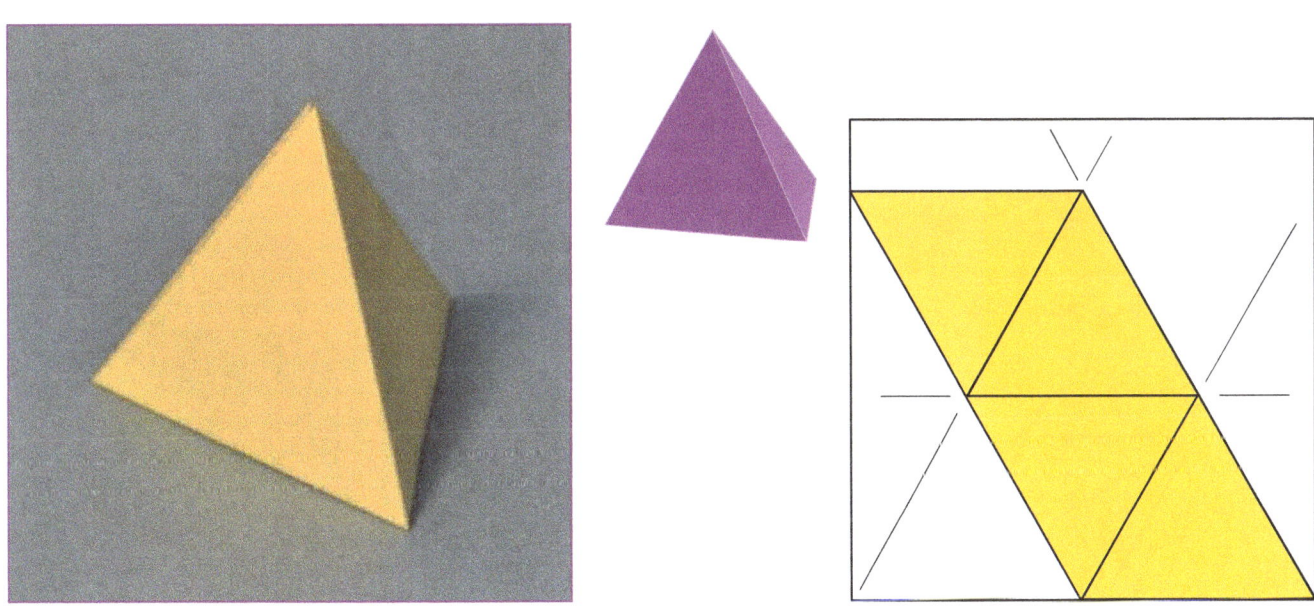

Composed of four equilateral triangles, this is the simplest of the five Platonic Solids. To Plato, the Tetrahedron represents fire because of its sharpness and simplicity.

The image on the right shows the crease pattern. The four sides of the model are the colored triangles, showing their placement on the square sheet of paper. The crease pattern shows a band of four triangles. The extra paper on top is used as the tab to lock the model.

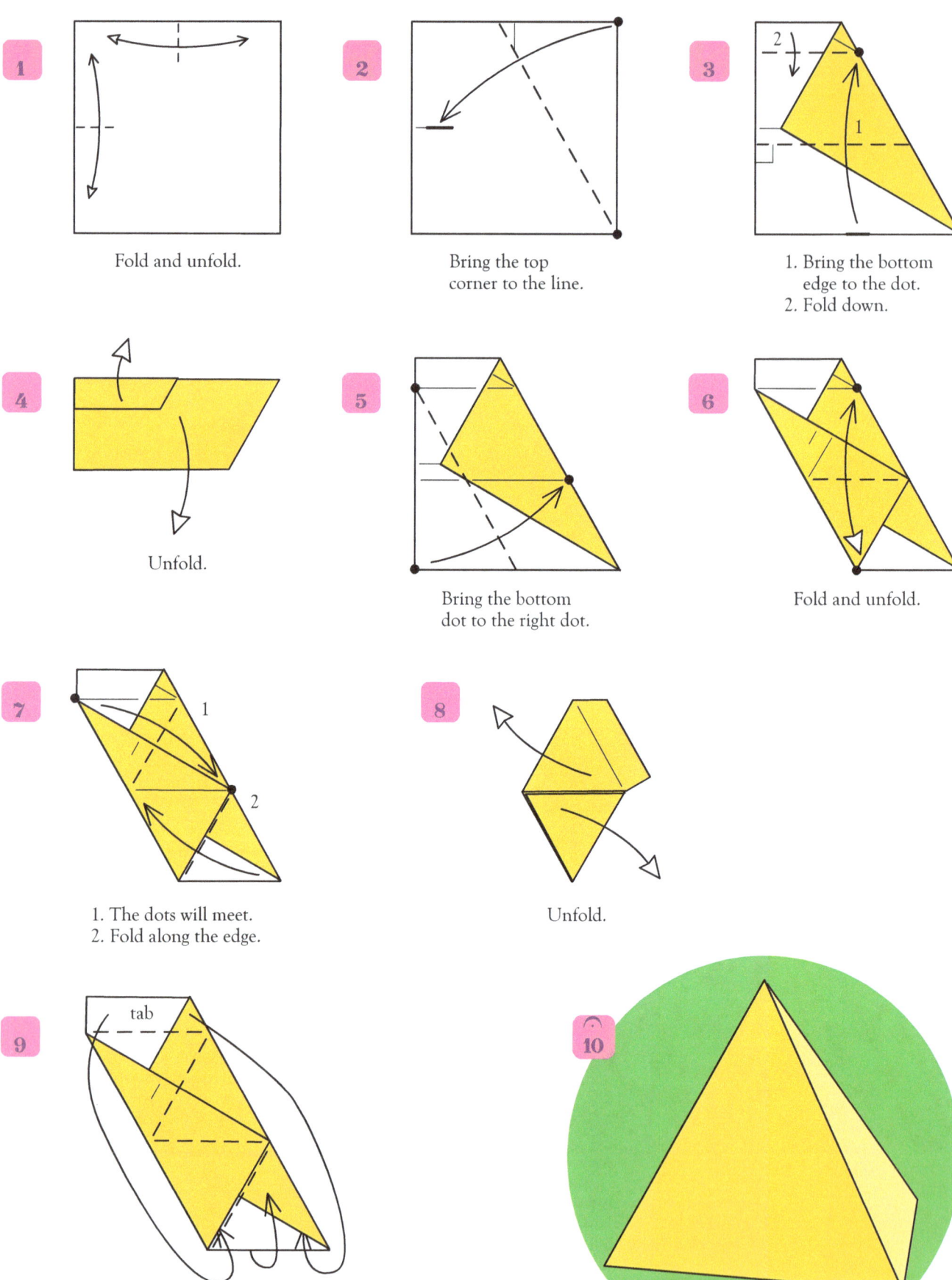

Cube

Plato believed the Cube, with six square faces, symbolized Earth because of its stability.

Six squares forming a cross become the six sides of the cube. Even symmetry is used.

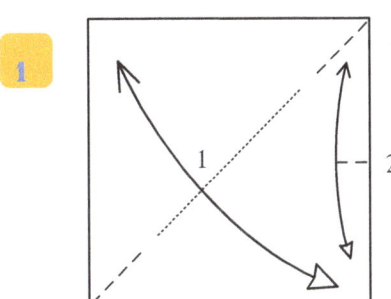

1. Fold and unfold on the corners.
2. Fold and unfold on the right.

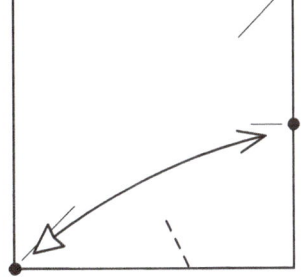

Fold and unfold on the bottom.

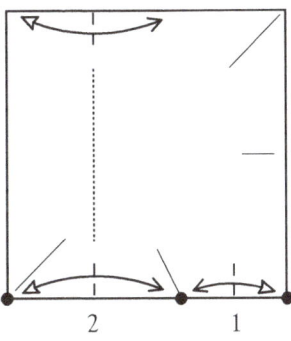

1. Fold and unfold on the bottom.
2. Fold and unfold on the top and bottom.

Rotate 45°.

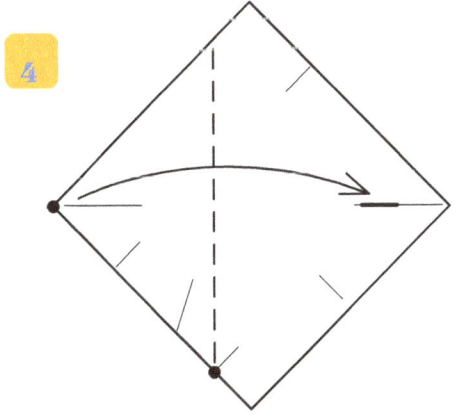

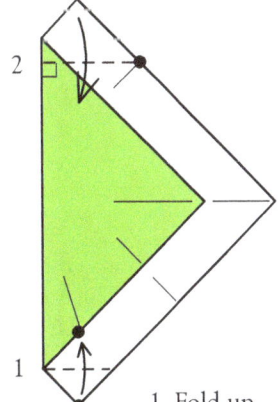

1. Fold up.
2. Fold down.

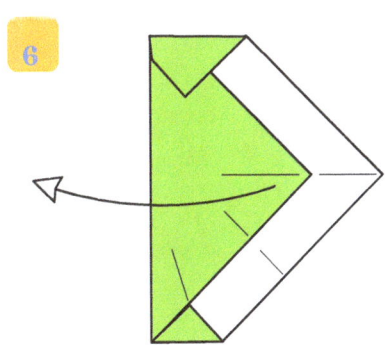

Pull out.

Cube **73**

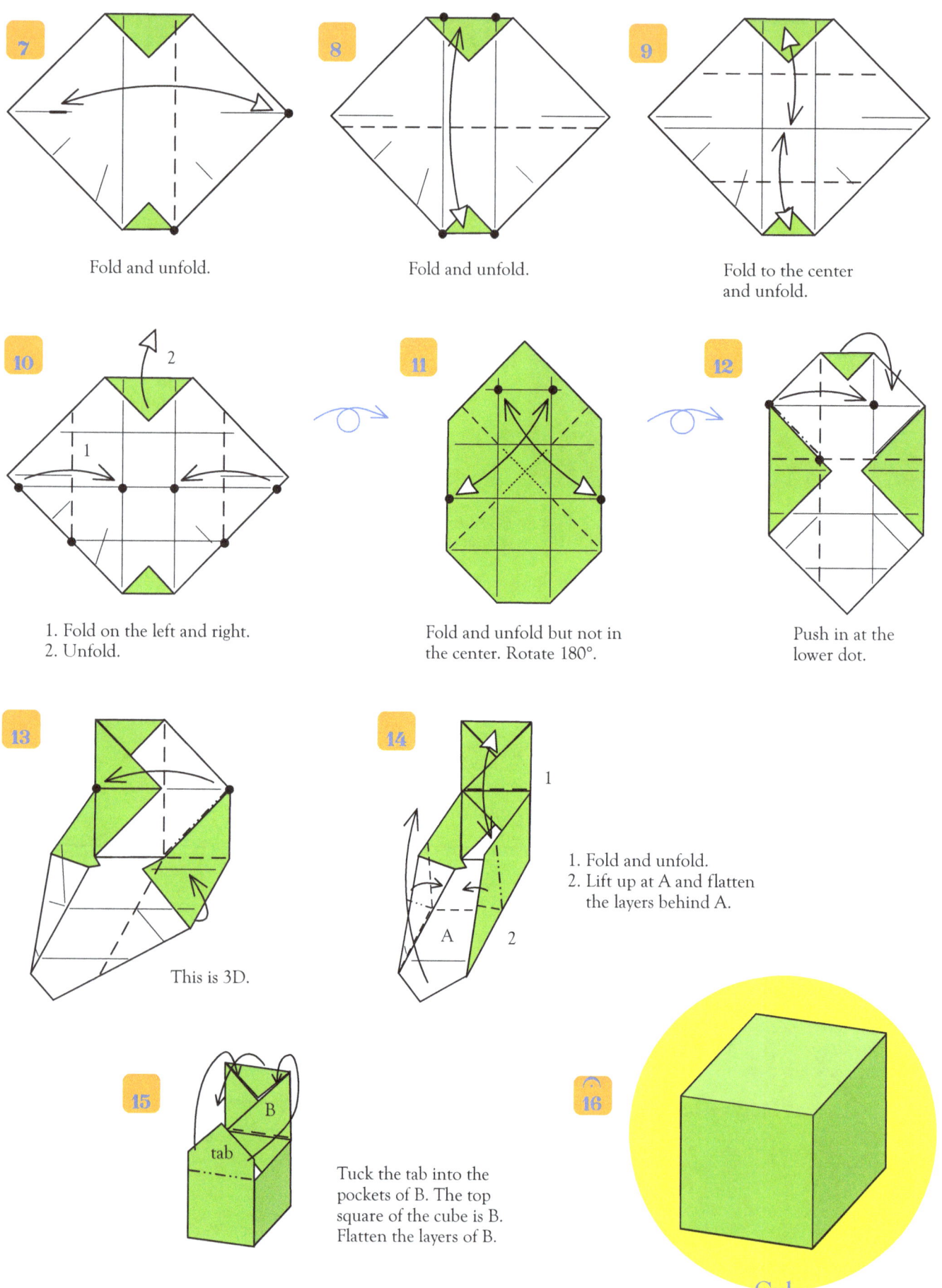

Octahedron

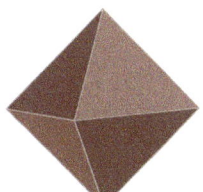
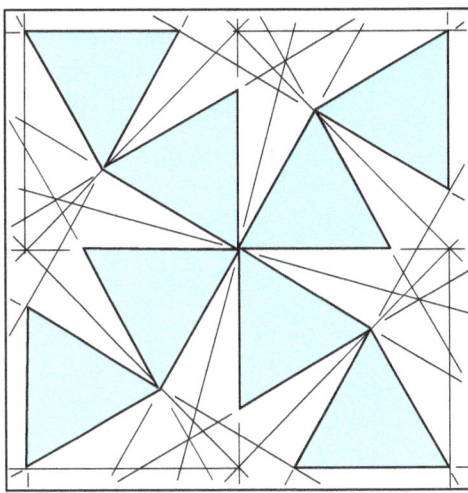

The Octahedron is composed of eight equilateral triangles. According to Plato, the Octahedron represents air because it appears to be suspended.

The crease pattern shows the arrangement of the eight triangular faces. If it is rotated 90°, the pattern would be the same, so this model uses square symmetry. At the end of the folding, the model closes with a four-way twist lock. Using an unusual method of folding, none of the triangular faces are adjacent.

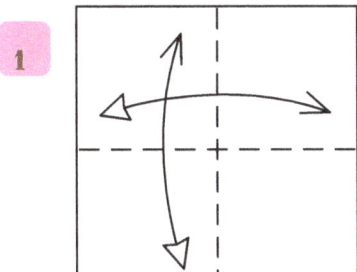

1. Fold and unfold.

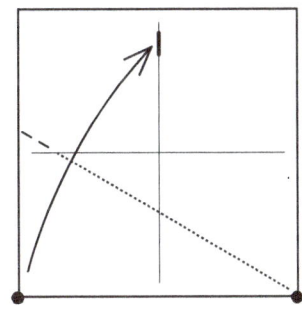

2. Bring the left dot to the line. Crease on the left.

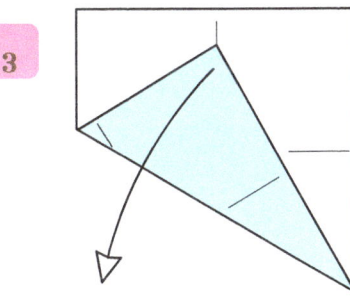

3. Unfold and rotate 180°.

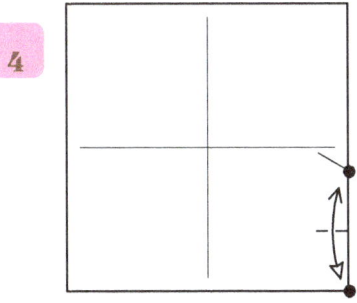

4. Fold and unfold.

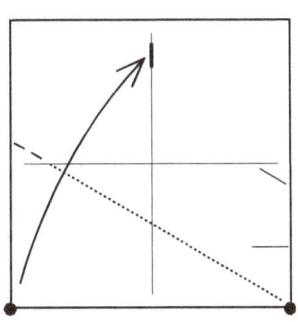

5. Repeat steps 2–4.

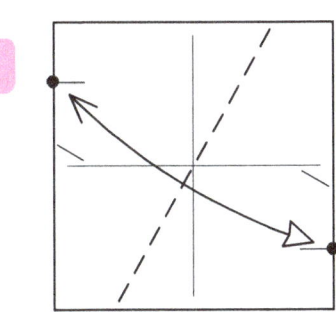

6. Fold and unfold.

Octahedron 75

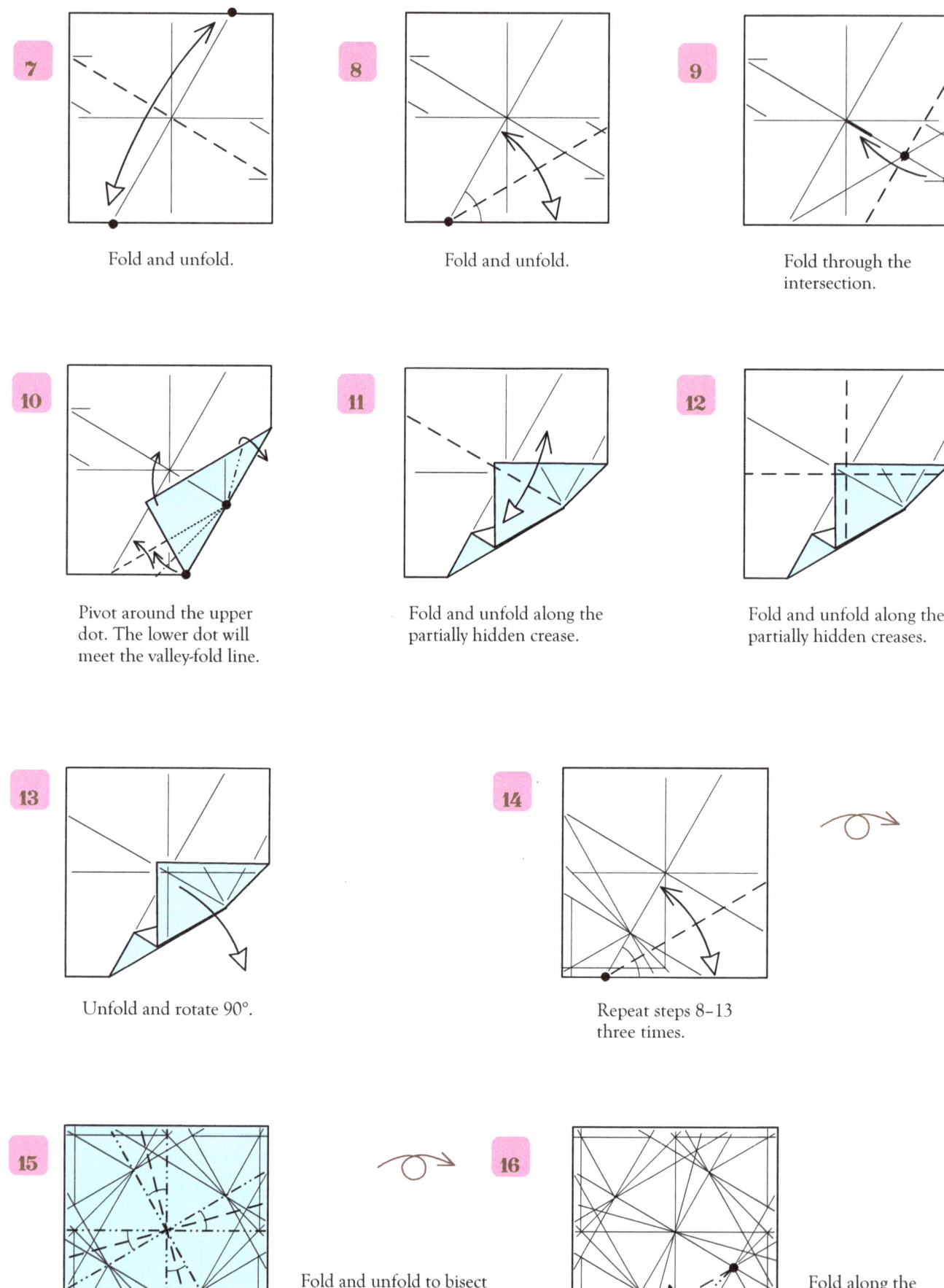

76   Origami Symphony No. 1

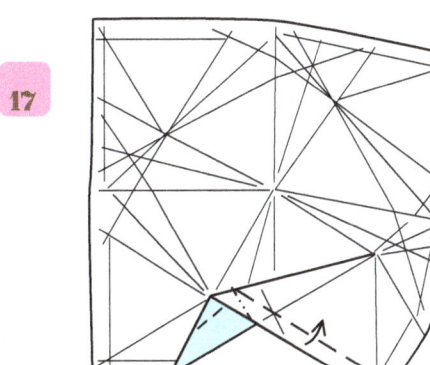

Squash-fold along the crease.

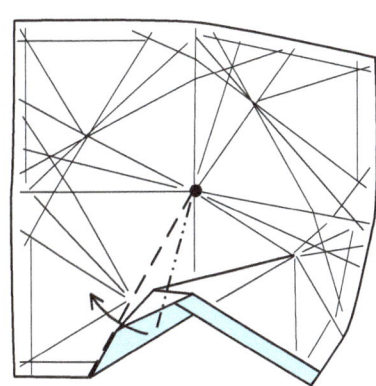

Fold along the creases and push in at the dot.

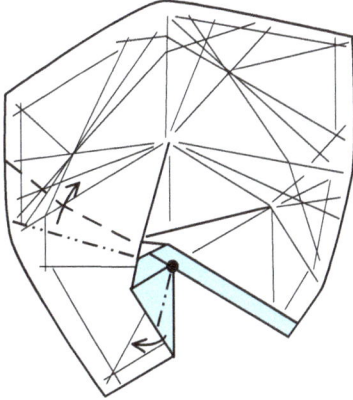

Repeat steps 16–18 three times. Rotate to view the outside.

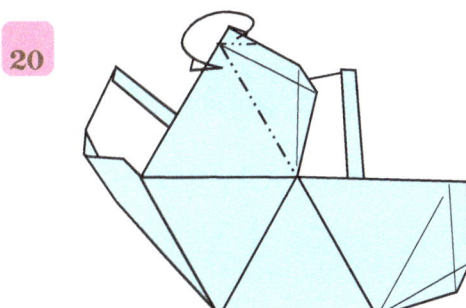

Wrap around.

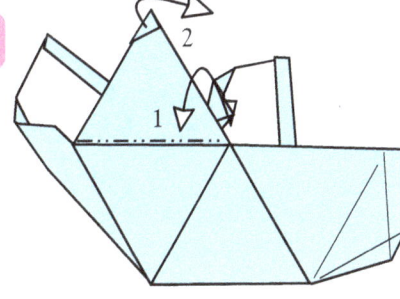

1. Fold and unfold.
2. Unfold.
Repeat steps 20–21 three times.

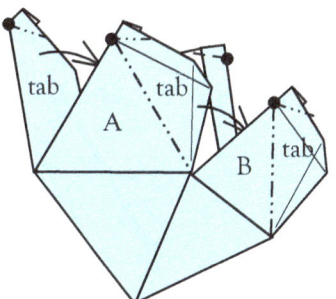

Tuck the tabs under A and B and continue all around. The dots will meet at the top. The model closes with a four-way twist lock.

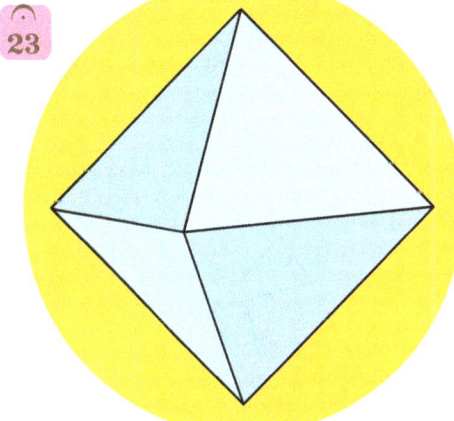

Octahedron

Icosahedron

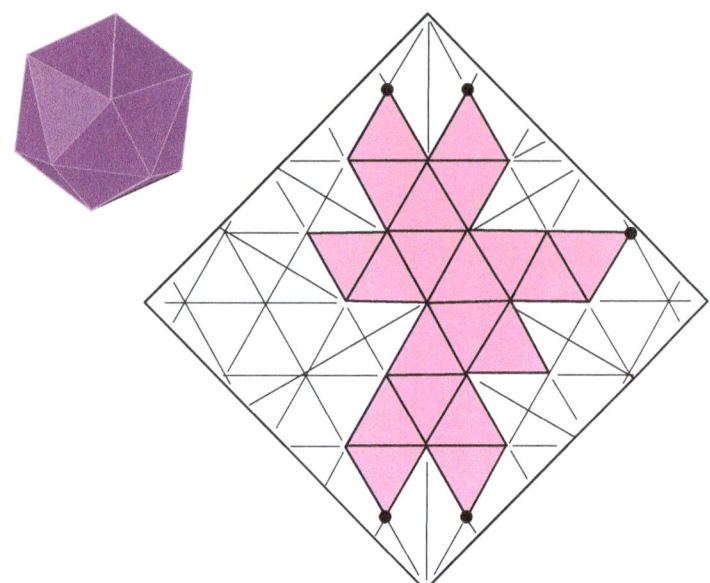

The Icosahedron is composed of 20 equilateral triangles. Plato attributed this model to water because of its ability to roll.

The model was designed to close with a five-way lock. The five dots in the layout all meet at a vertex, to close the model.

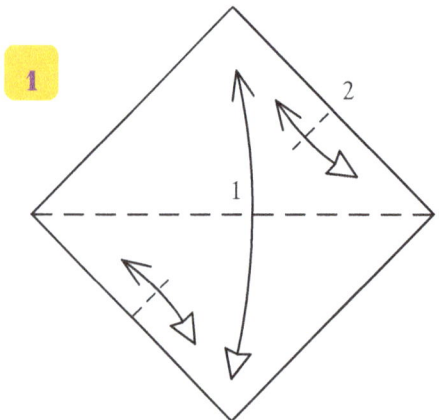

1. Fold and unfold.
2. Fold and unfold on the edges.

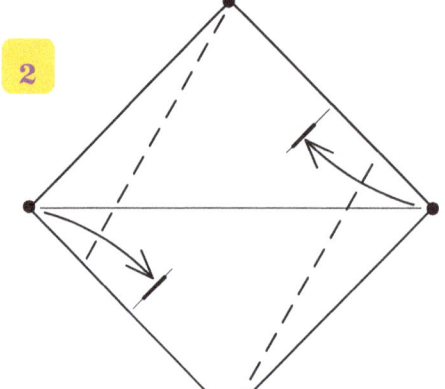

Bring the corners to the lines.

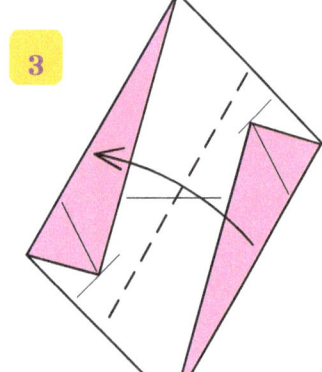

Fold in half.

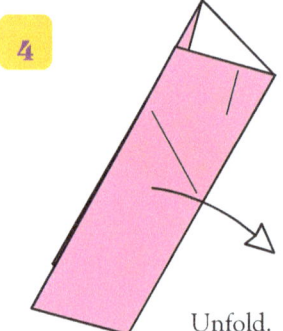

Unfold.

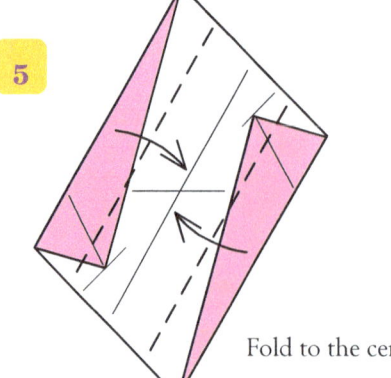

Fold to the center.

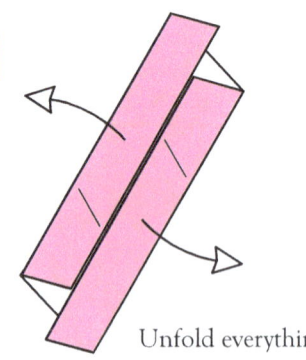

Unfold everything.

78   Origami Symphony No. 1

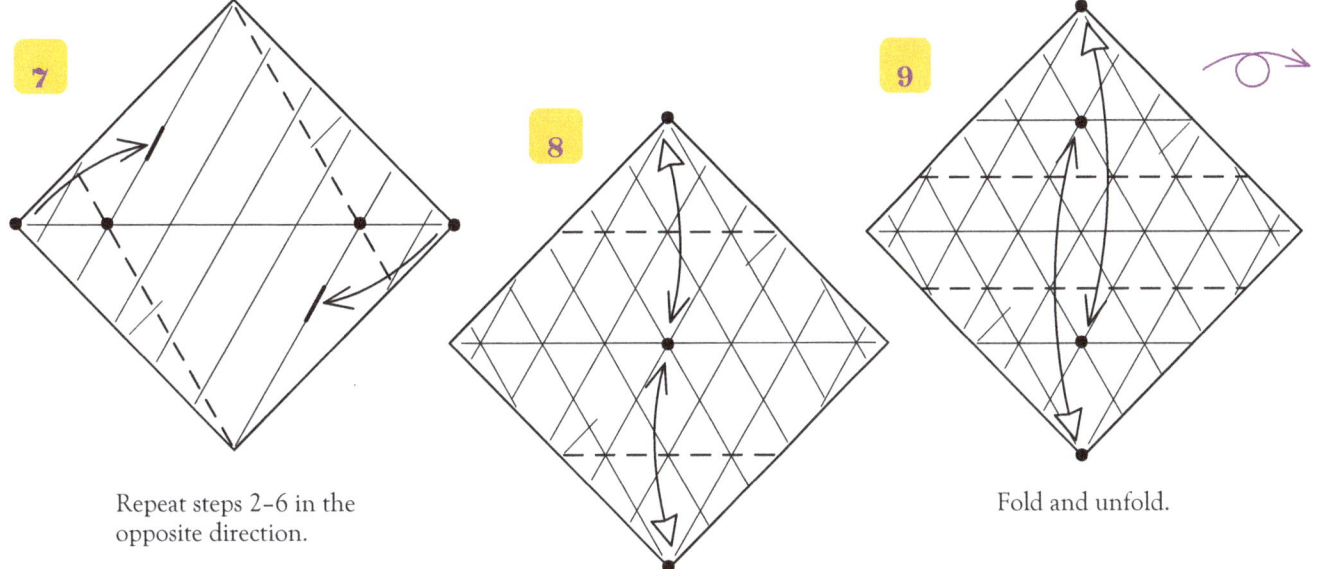

7. Repeat steps 2–6 in the opposite direction.

8. Fold to the center and unfold.

9. Fold and unfold.

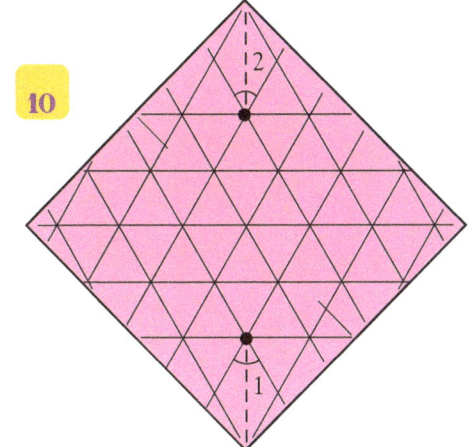

10. Fold and unfold at 1 and 2.

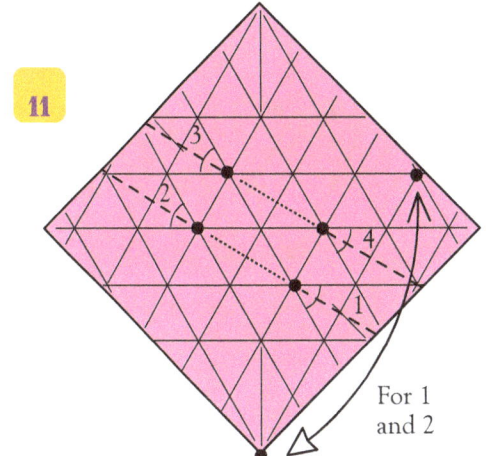

11. Fold and unfold at 1 and 2. Rotate 180° for 3 and 4 (same as 1 and 2).

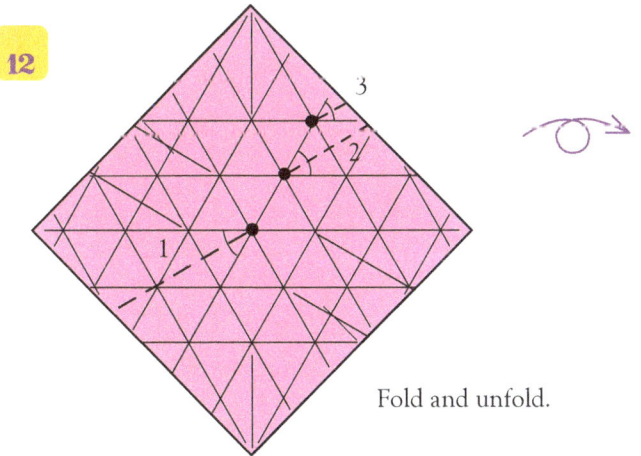

12. Fold and unfold.

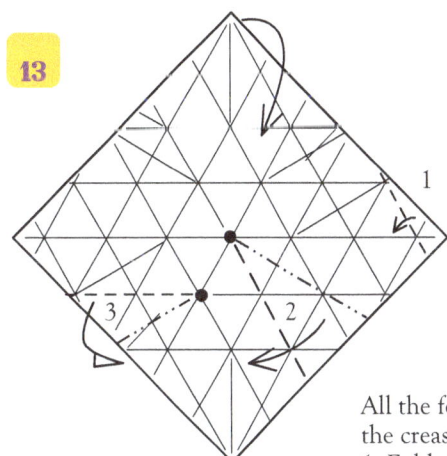

13. All the folds are along the creases.
1. Fold along the crease.
2. Push in at the dot.
3. Push in at the dot.

Icosahedron **79**

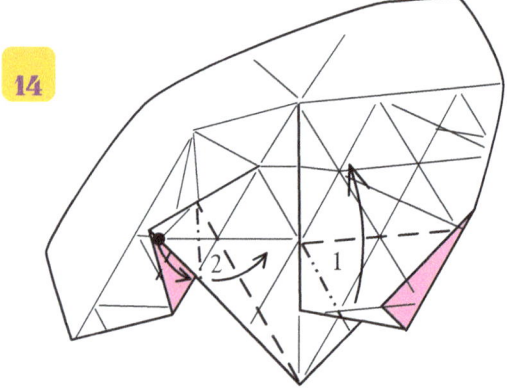

1. Squash-fold along the creases.
2. Squash-fold. Valley-fold along the crease. The dot will meet the edge.

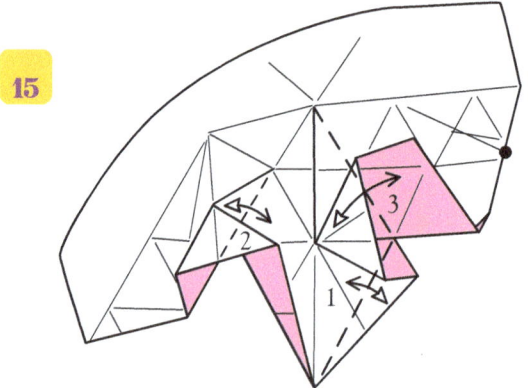

Fold and unfold three times. Rotate to view the outside so the dot is center and top.

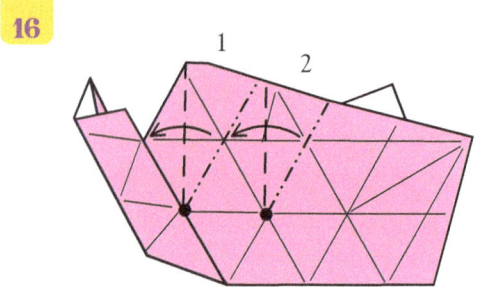

Fold along the creases, in order. Puff out at the dots.

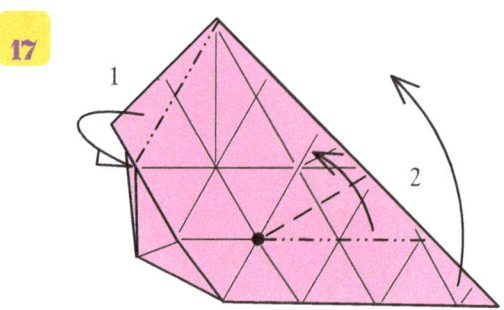

1. Wrap around.
2. Puff out at the dot.

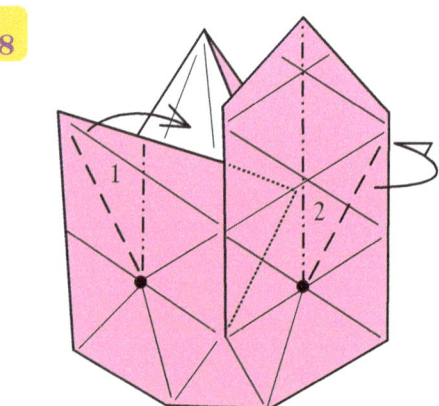

1. Puff out at the dot.
2. Puff out at the dot and wrap around the paper shown with the dotted lines.

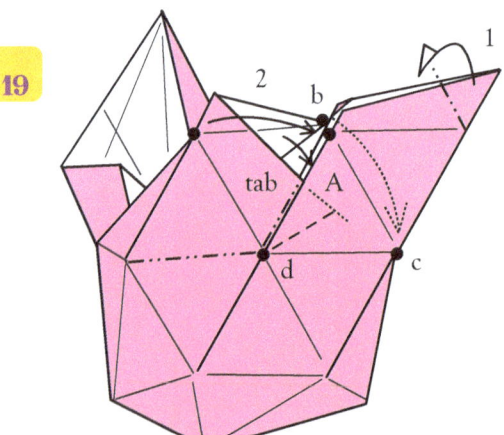

1. Fold behind along the crease.
2. Fold along the creases to tuck the tab between the layers, with A on top. The upper dots will meet and dot b will meet c inside. Puff out at dot d.

80 Origami Symphony No. 1

20

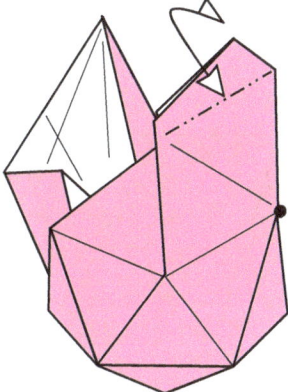

Fold and unfold along the crease. Rotate the dot to the center.

21

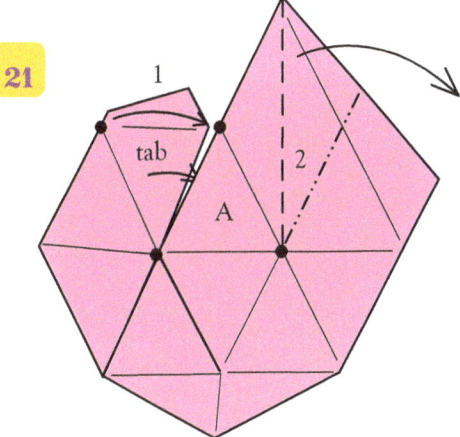

1. A will cover the tab as the upper dots meet. Puff out at the lower left dot.
2. Puff out at the dot below 2.

22

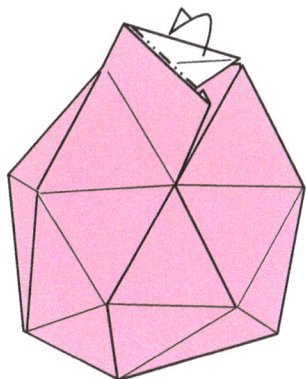

Fold behind.

23

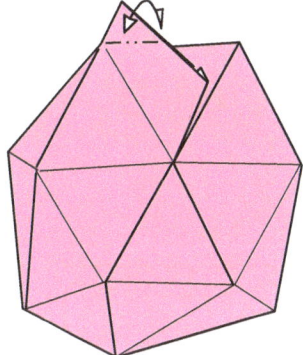

Fold and unfold.

24

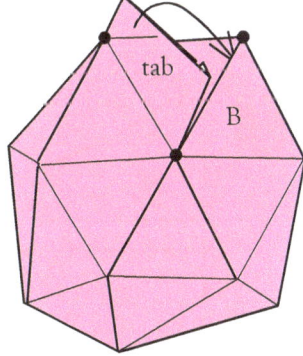

The tab will go under B so the two upper dots meet. Puff out at the lower dot. Slide the top, at the upper left dot, so it catches with the inside flaps to lock it.

25

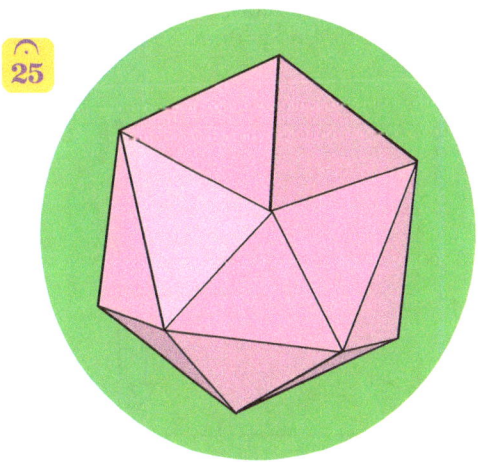

Icosahedron

Icosahedron **81**

Dodecahedron

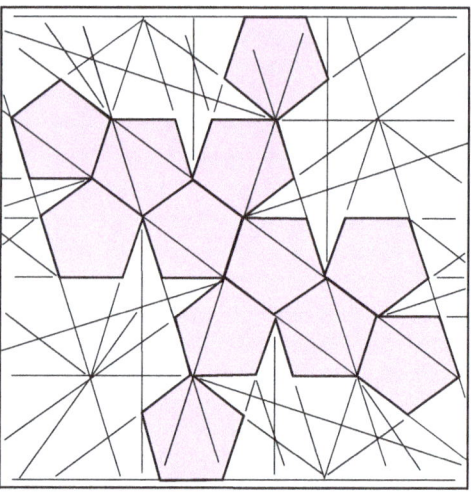

The Dodecahedron has twelve pentagonal faces. To Plato, the Dodecahedron, the quintessence (the "fifth being"), represented the whole universe.

This was very difficult to design, especially to be foldable from standard origami paper and hold together. The crease pattern shows odd symmetry, that is, the pattern is the same when rotated 180°.

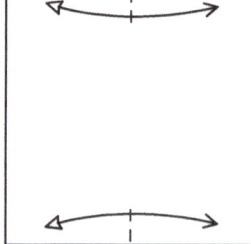

1

Fold and unfold at the top and bottom.

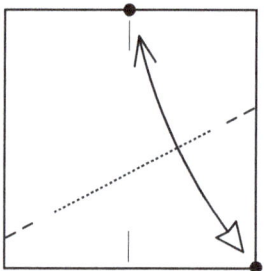

2

Fold and unfold on the left and right. Rotate 180°.

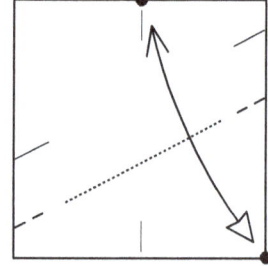

3

Repeat step 2.

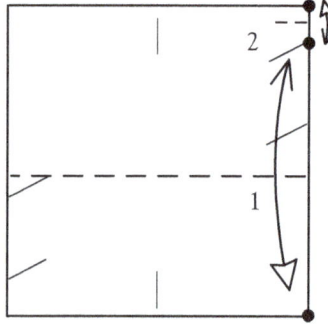

4

1. Fold and unfold.
2. Fold and unfold part way. Rotate 180°.

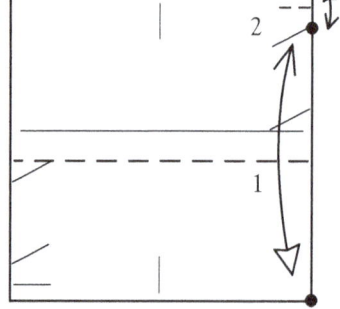

5

Repeat step 4.

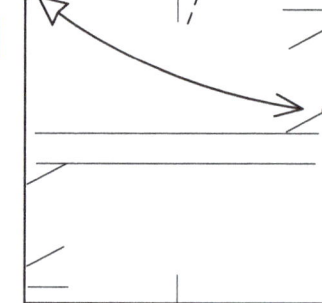

6

Fold and unfold at the top.

82   *Origami Symphony No. 1*

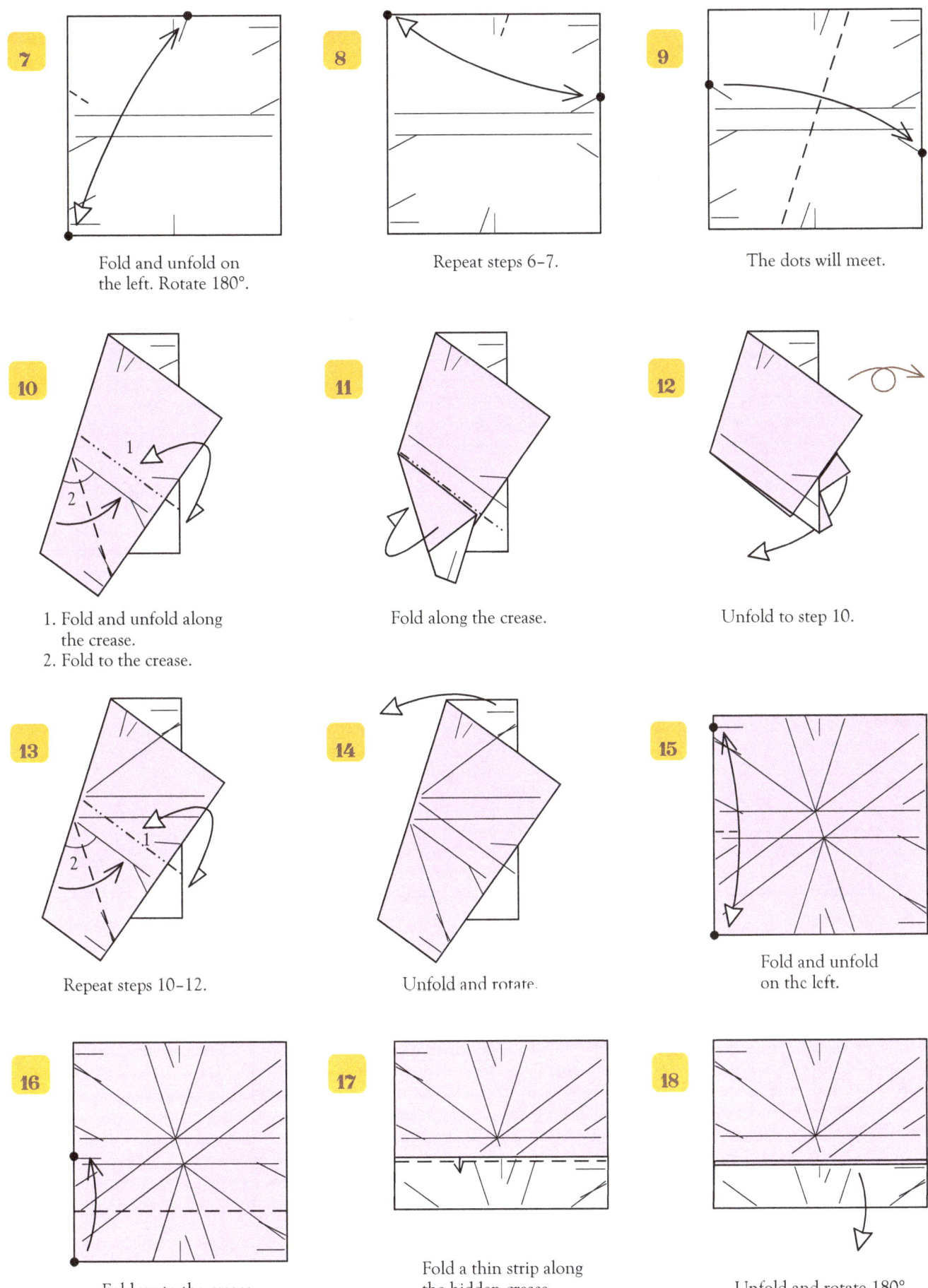

Dodecahedron

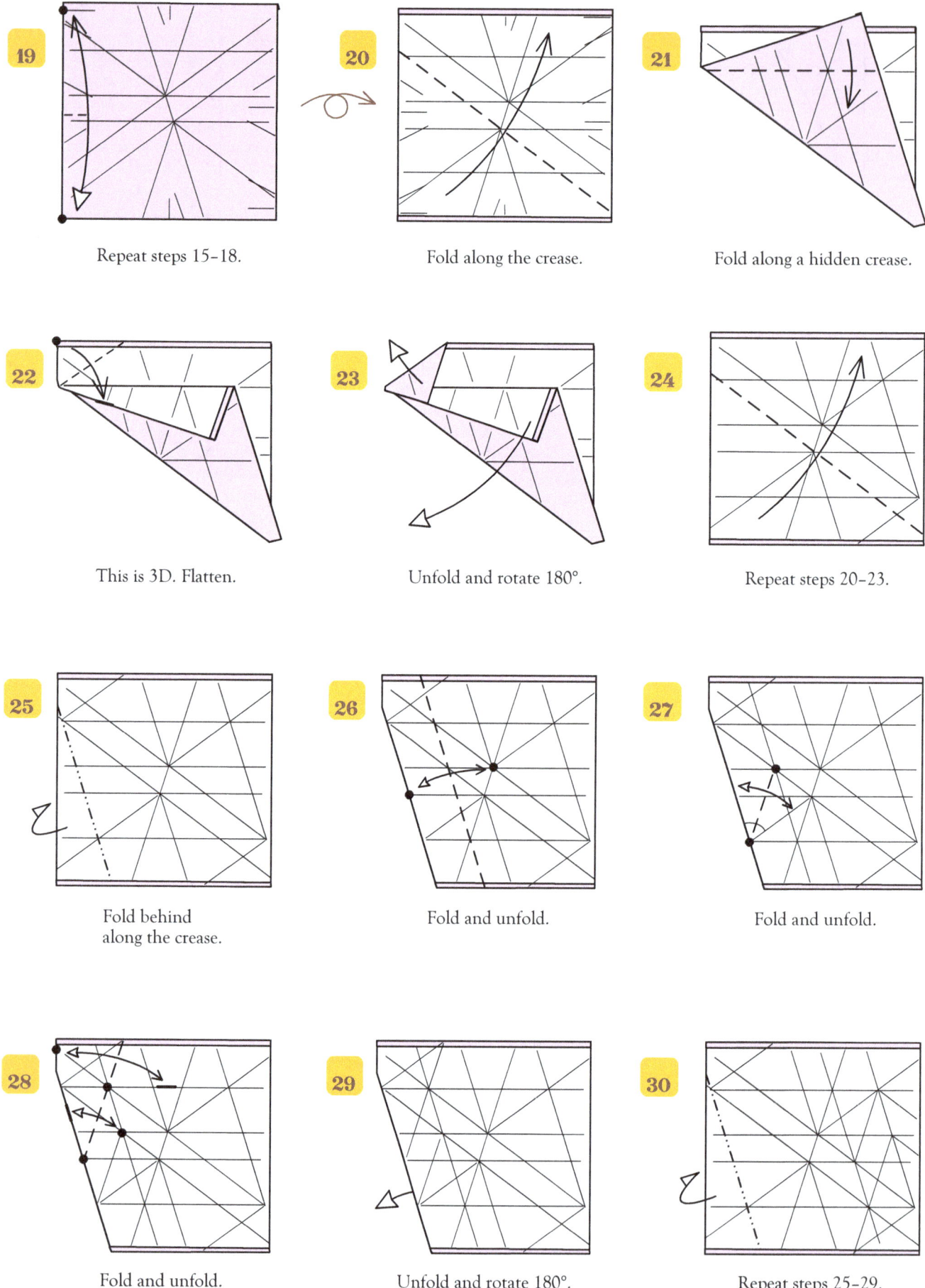

84 Origami Symphony No. 1

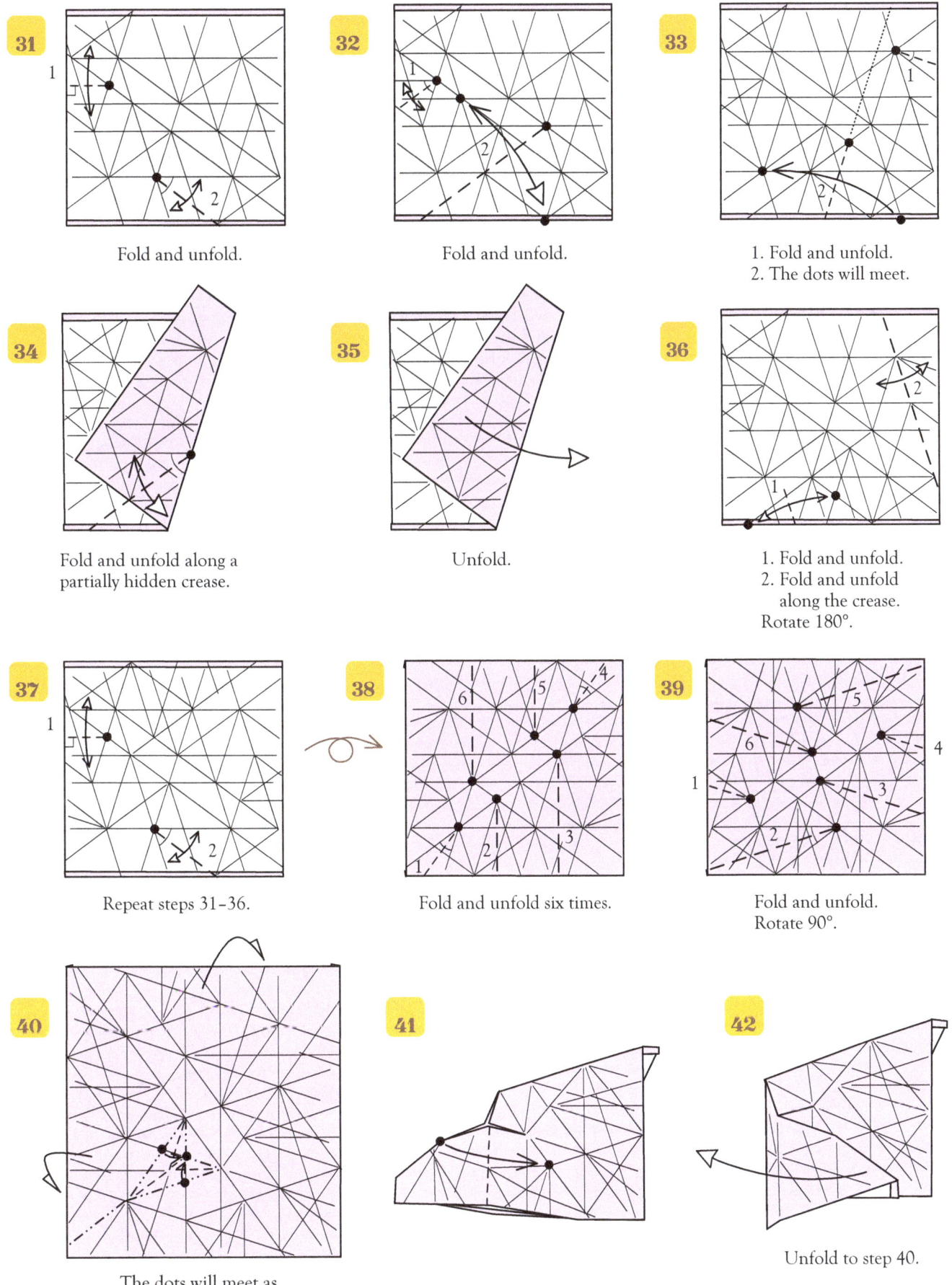

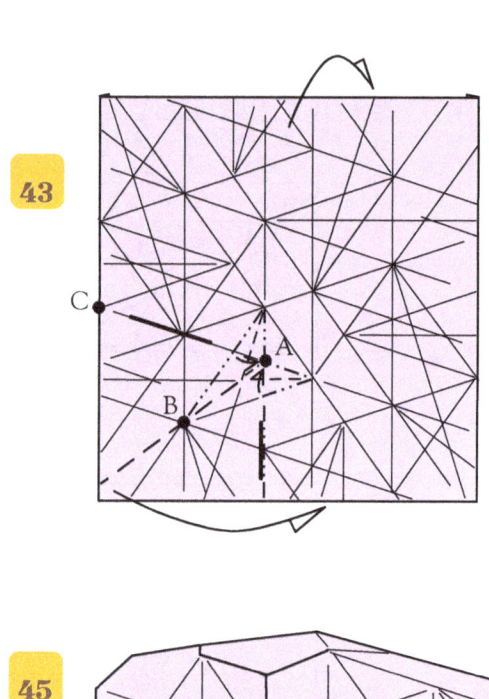

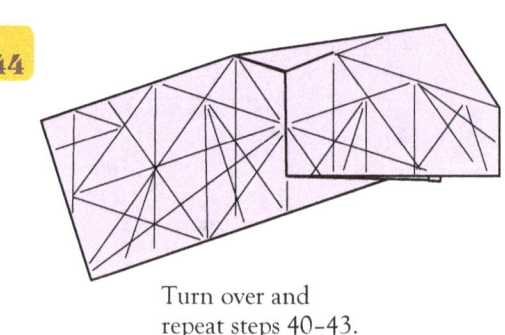

Refold along the creases. Push in at dot B, puff out at dot A. The bold lines will meet and the model will become 3D. Rotate dot C to the bottom and center.

Turn over and repeat steps 40–43.

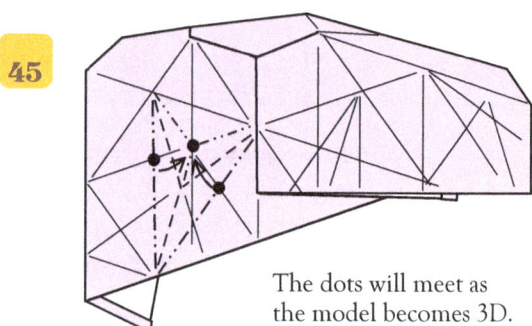

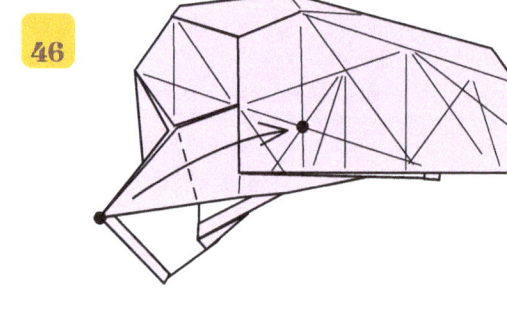

The dots will meet as the model becomes 3D.

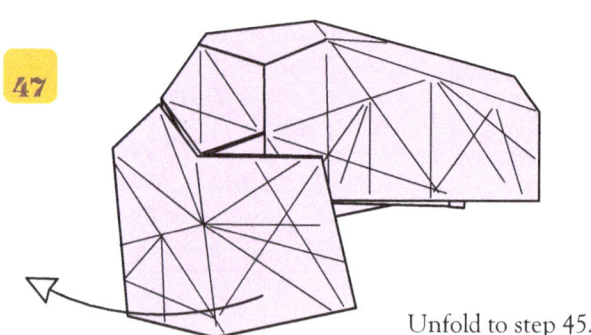

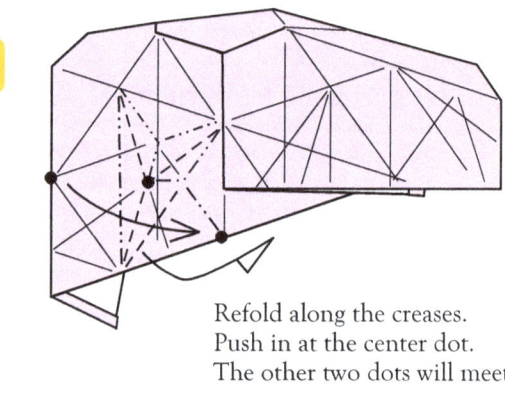

Unfold to step 45.

Refold along the creases. Push in at the center dot. The other two dots will meet.

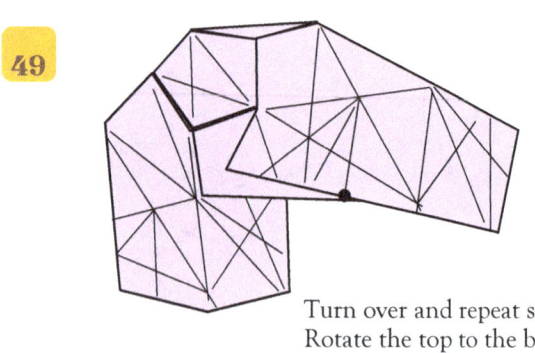

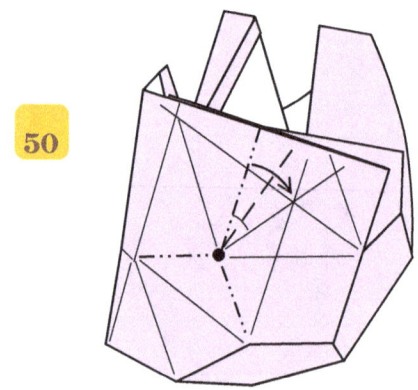

Turn over and repeat steps 45–48. Rotate the top to the bottom so the dot will be at the top and center.

Fold two layers together. Puff out at the dot.

86 *Origami Symphony No. 1*

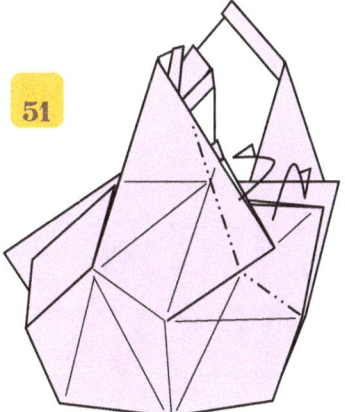

Fold along the creases. Fold behind and flatten.

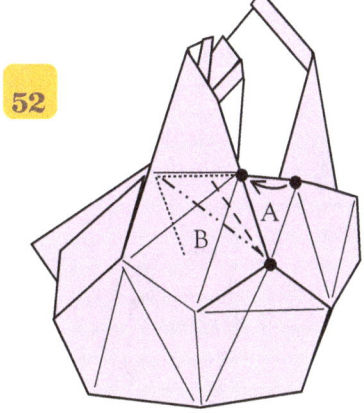

Puff out at the lower dot. The upper dots will meet. The folds are done on panel A, which is covered by region B. Mountain-fold along the crease.

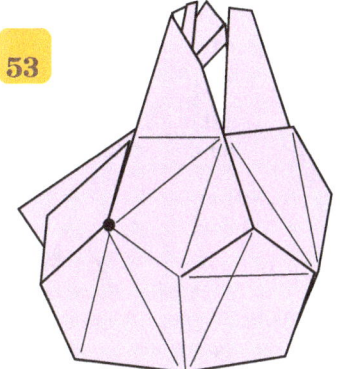

Turn over and repeat steps 50–52. Rotate the dot to the center.

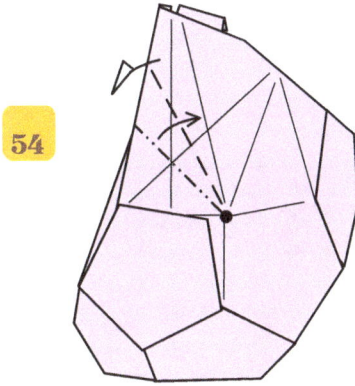

Fold along the creases and puff out at the dot. Turn over and repeat.

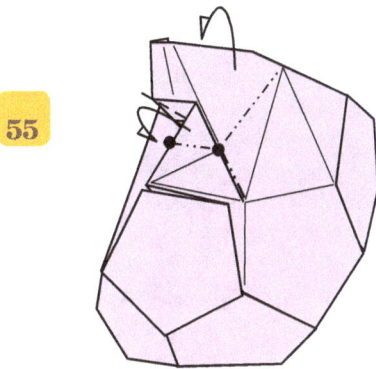

Fold inside but do not completely flatten. There is no crease for the mountain-fold between the dots. Turn over and repeat.

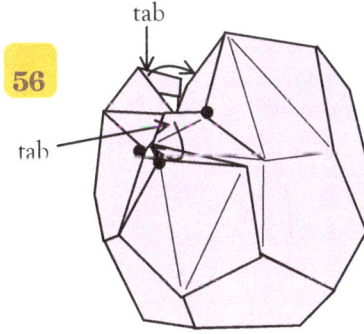

Tuck the two tabs into the pockets. The three dots will meet. You can also inflate into it to round it out.

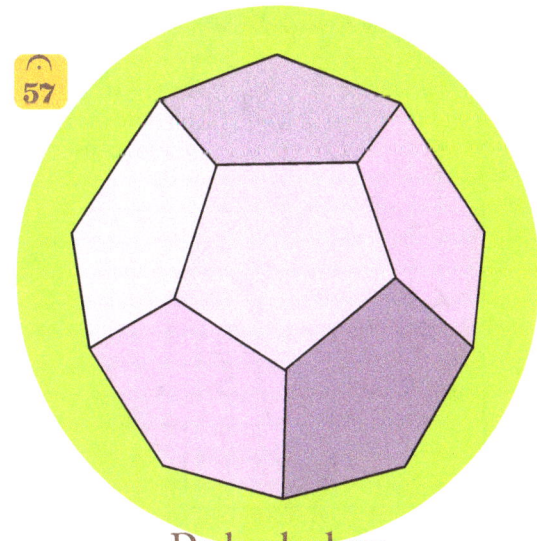

Dodecahedron

Trio of Sunken Solids

In the minuet is a trio of three sunken polyhedra, with sunken triangles, squares, and pentagons. Dive deep to master these mind-boggling shapes.

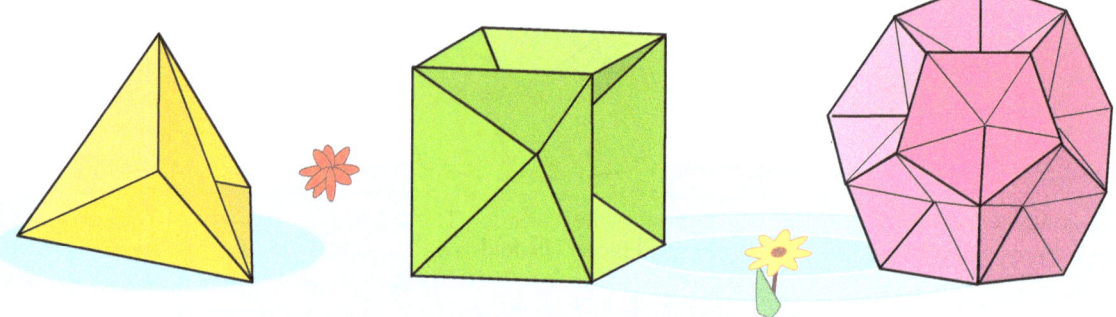

Sunken Tetrahedron

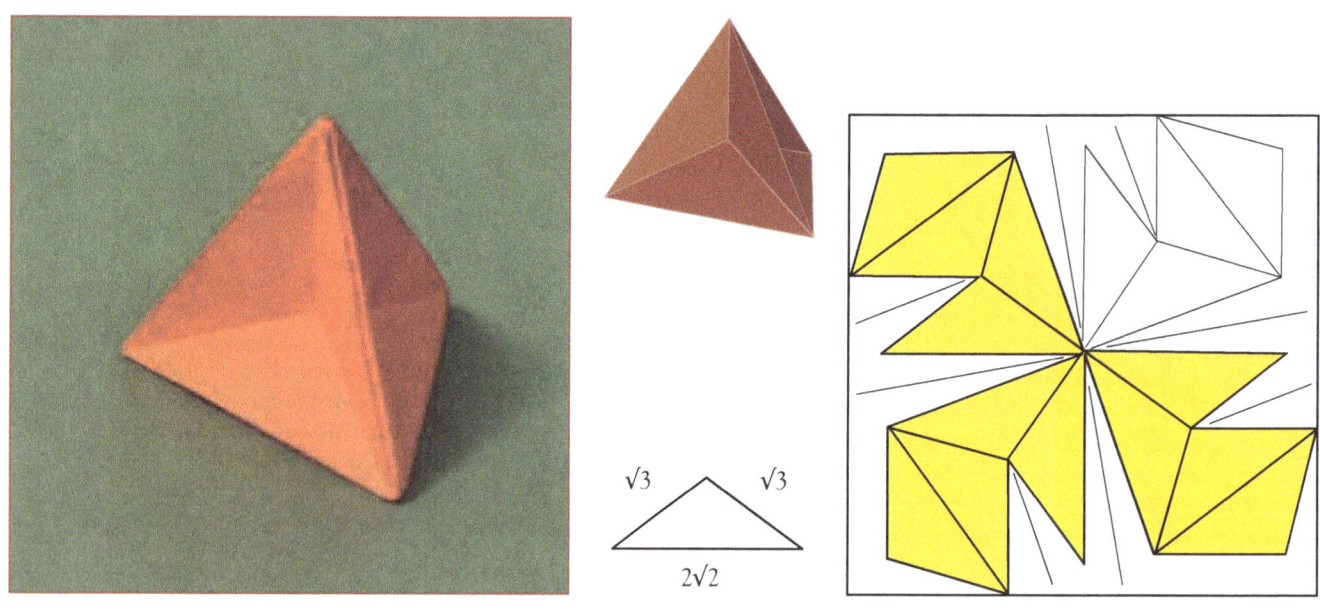

The twelve faces of the Sunken Tetrahedron are isosceles triangles. The sides of each triangular face are proportional to $2\sqrt{2}$, $\sqrt{3}$, and $\sqrt{3}$. The crease pattern shows 3/4 square symmetry.

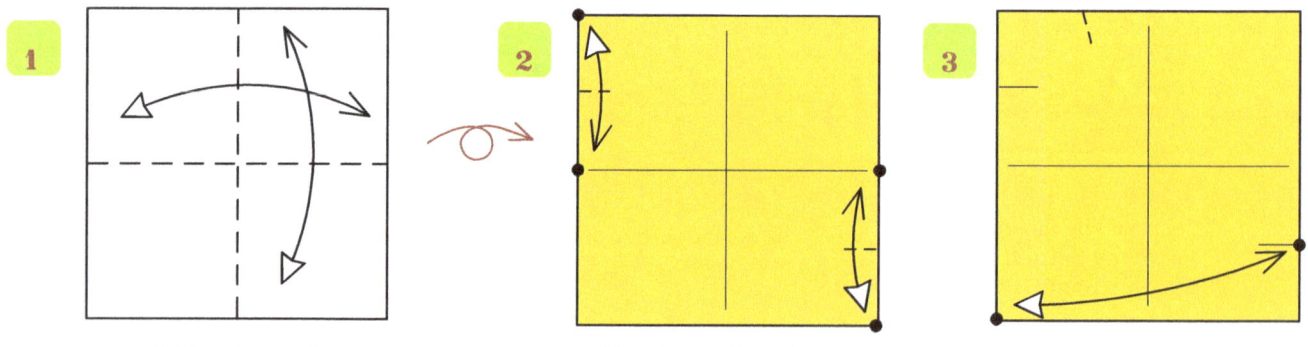

1. Fold and unfold.
2. Fold and unfold on the edges.
3. Fold and unfold on the top.

88   *Origami Symphony No. 1*

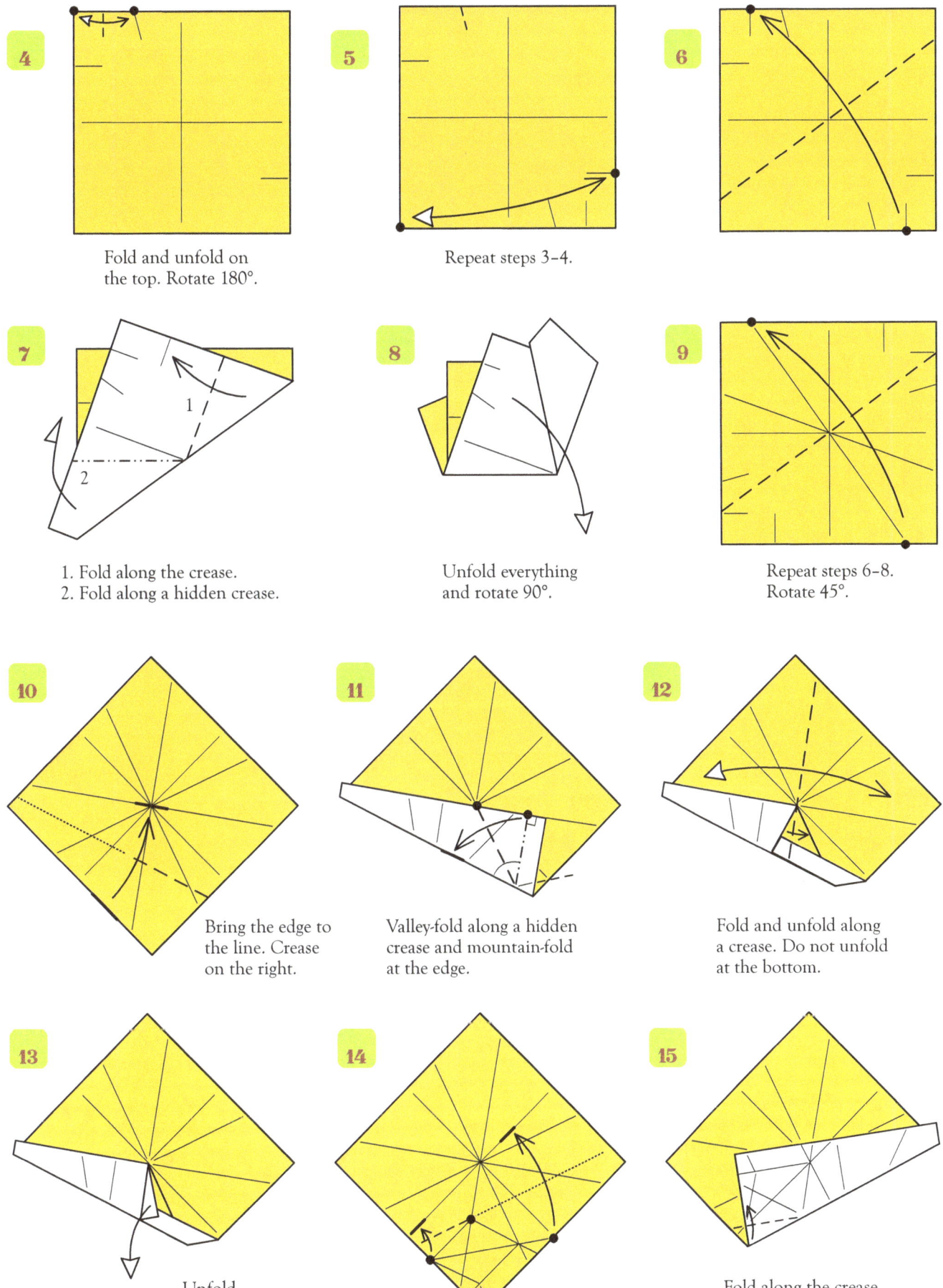

Sunken Tetrahedron **89**

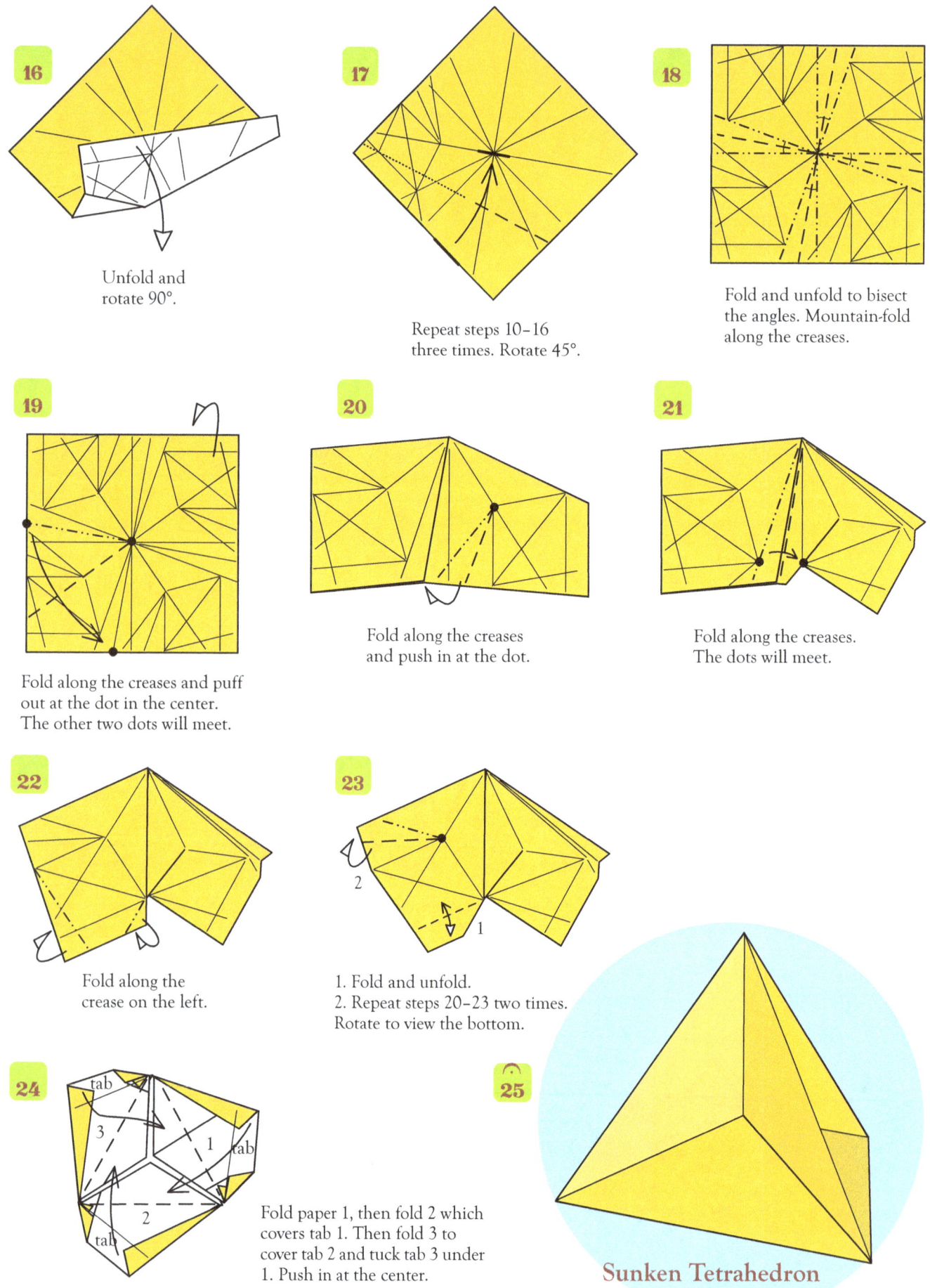

90 Origami Symphony No. 1

Sunken Cube

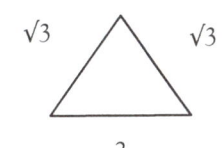
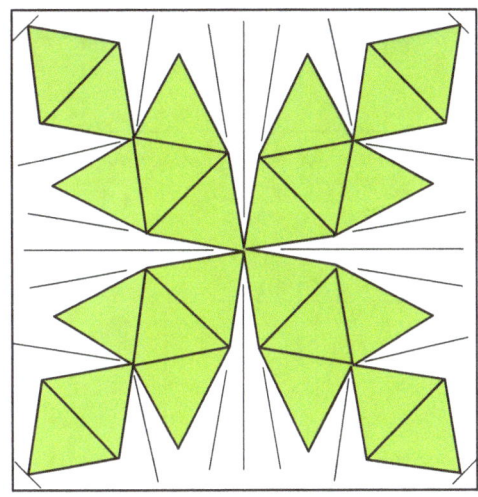

The Sunken Cube is composed of 24 isosceles triangles all meeting at the center. Each face has sides proportional to 2, $\sqrt{3}$, and $\sqrt{3}$. The crease pattern shows square symmetry.

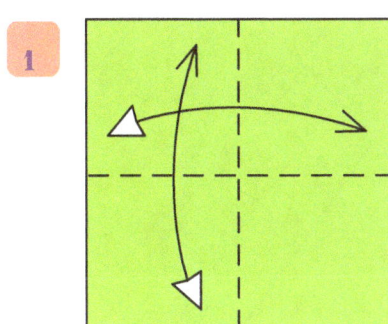

1. Fold and unfold.

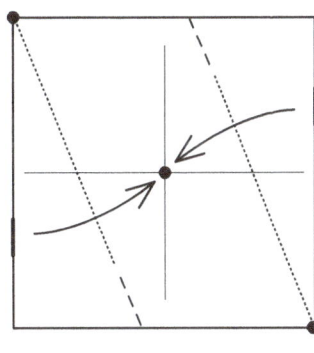

2. Bring the edges to the center creasing on the edges.

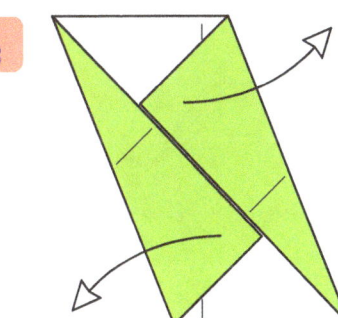

3. Unfold.

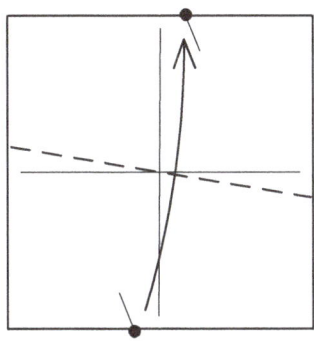

4.

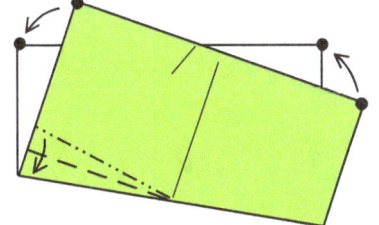

5. Valley-fold along the crease. Turn over and repeat.

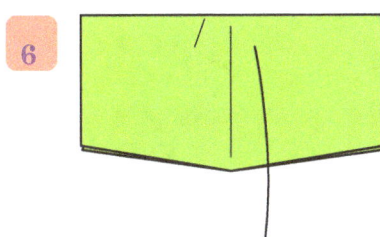

6. Unfold and rotate 90°.

Sunken Cube **91**

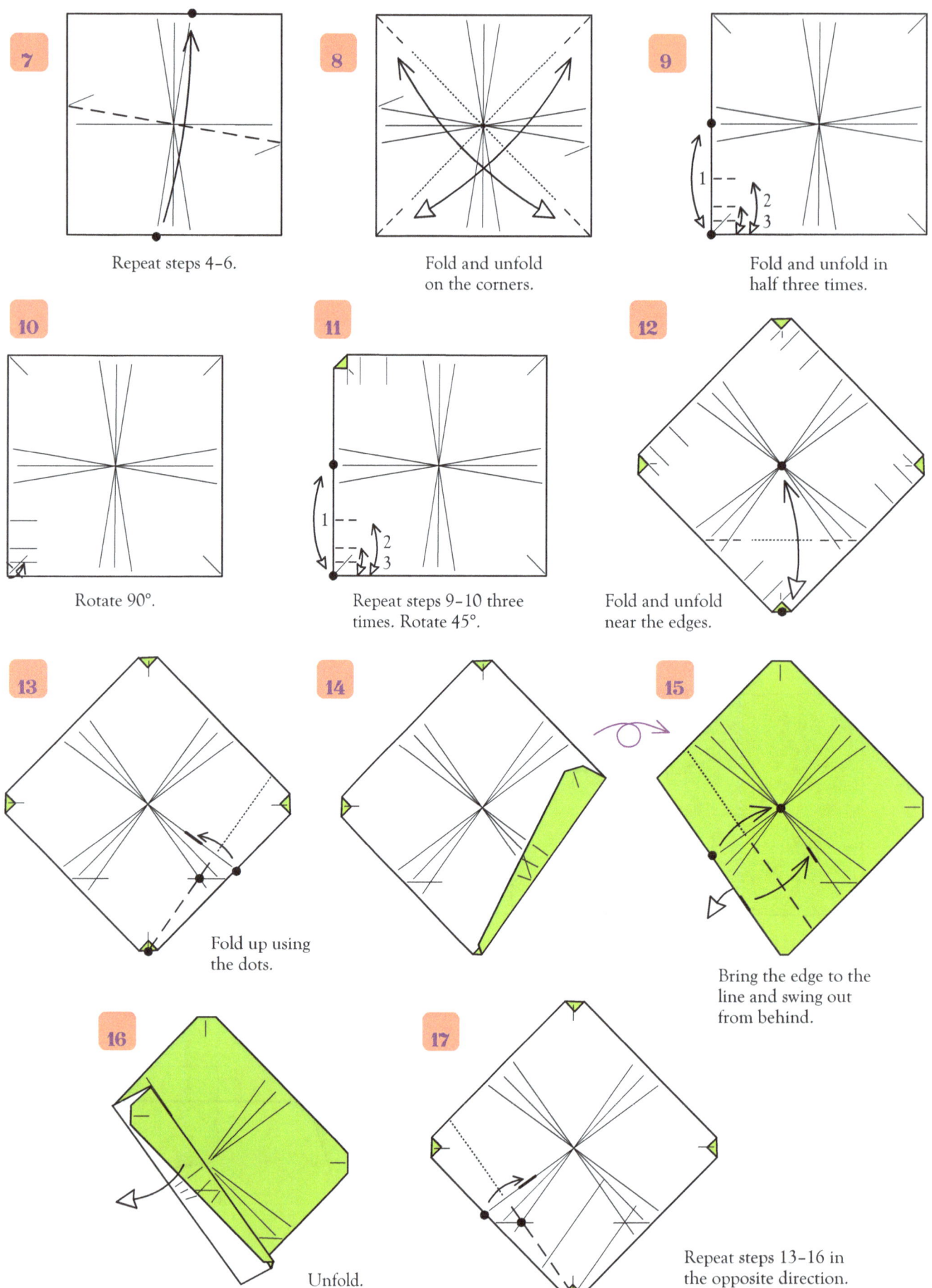

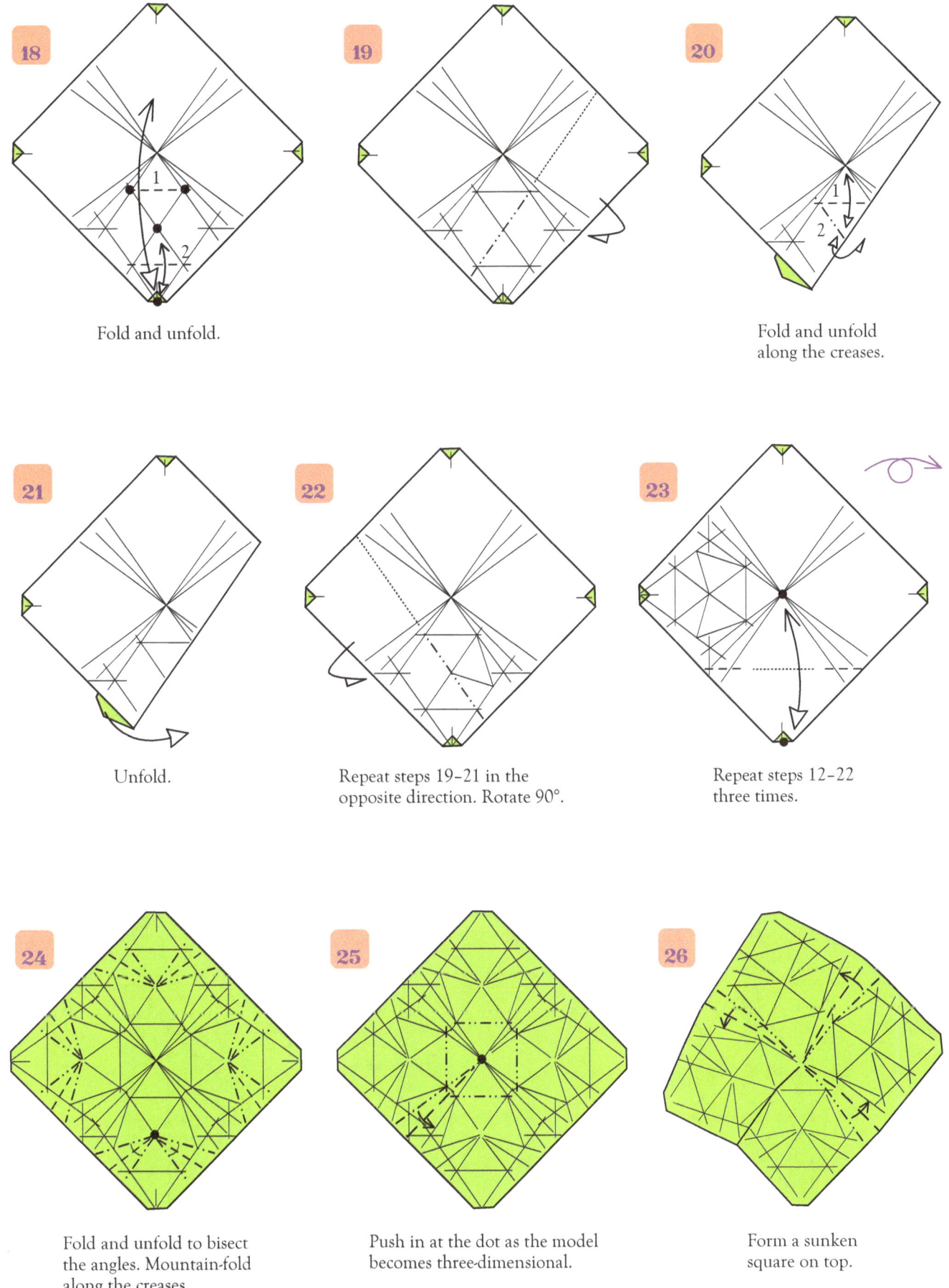

Sunken Cube 93

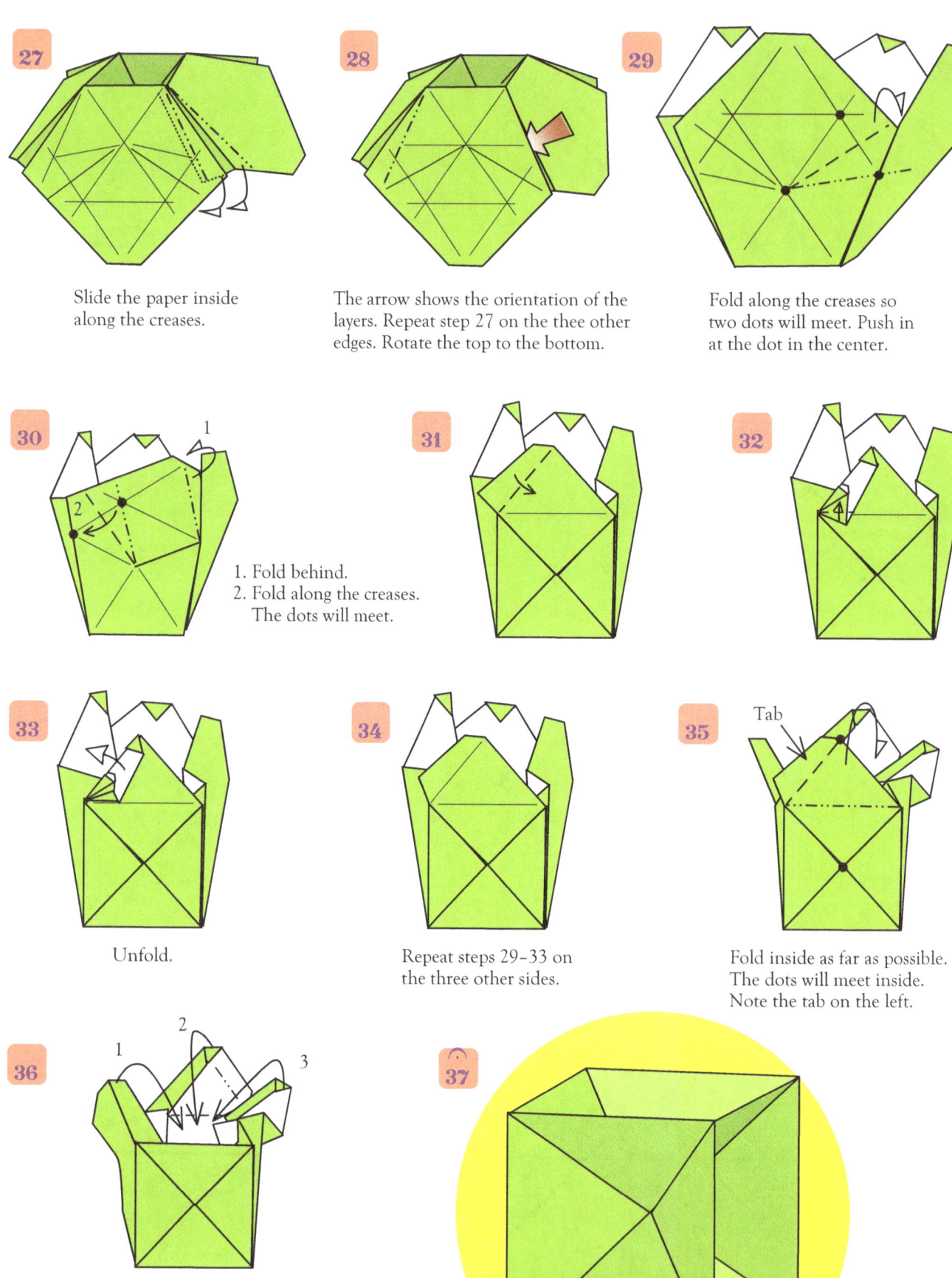

27. Slide the paper inside along the creases.

28. The arrow shows the orientation of the layers. Repeat step 27 on the thee other edges. Rotate the top to the bottom.

29. Fold along the creases so two dots will meet. Push in at the dot in the center.

30.
   1. Fold behind.
   2. Fold along the creases. The dots will meet.

33. Unfold.

34. Repeat steps 29–33 on the three other sides.

35. Fold inside as far as possible. The dots will meet inside. Note the tab on the left.

36. Continue folding inside in the order shown. For each of the three folds, cover the tabs. For the third fold, also tuck the tab inside.

37. Sunken Cube

94 *Origami Symphony No. 1*

Sunken Dodecahedron

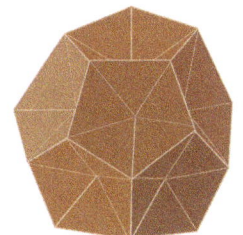
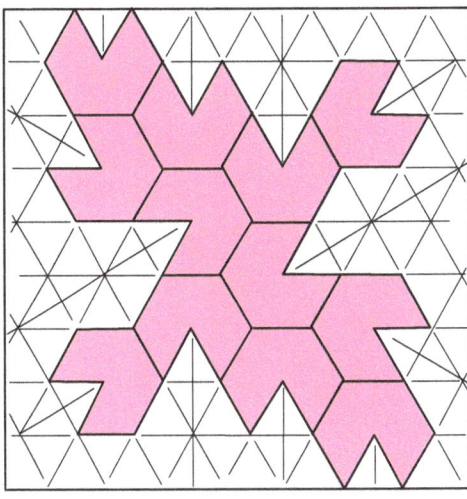

This Sunken Dodecahedron, one of several stellated icosahedrons, is composed of 60 equilateral triangles. This version has the same surface as an icosahedron. The crease pattern shows odd symmetry. The beauty of this model is that the shape is very complex yet the folding structure is so efficient that it only takes 35 steps, and the resulting model is large in proportion to the square sheet of paper.

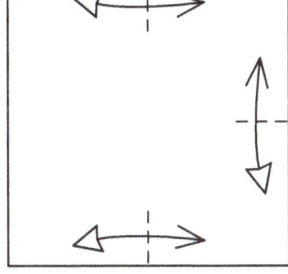

1. Fold and unfold on three edges.

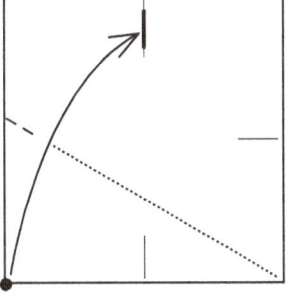

2. Bring the left dot to the line. Crease on the left.

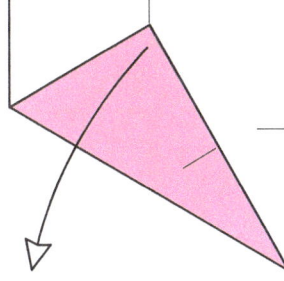

3. Unfold and rotate 180°.

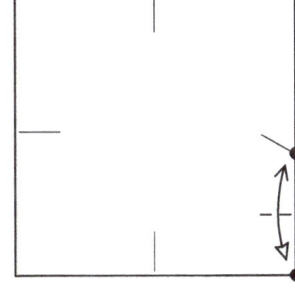

4. Fold and unfold on the right.

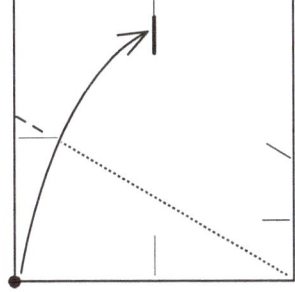

5. Repeat steps 2–4.

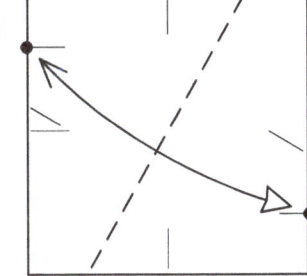

6. Fold and unfold.

Sunken Dodecahedron   **95**

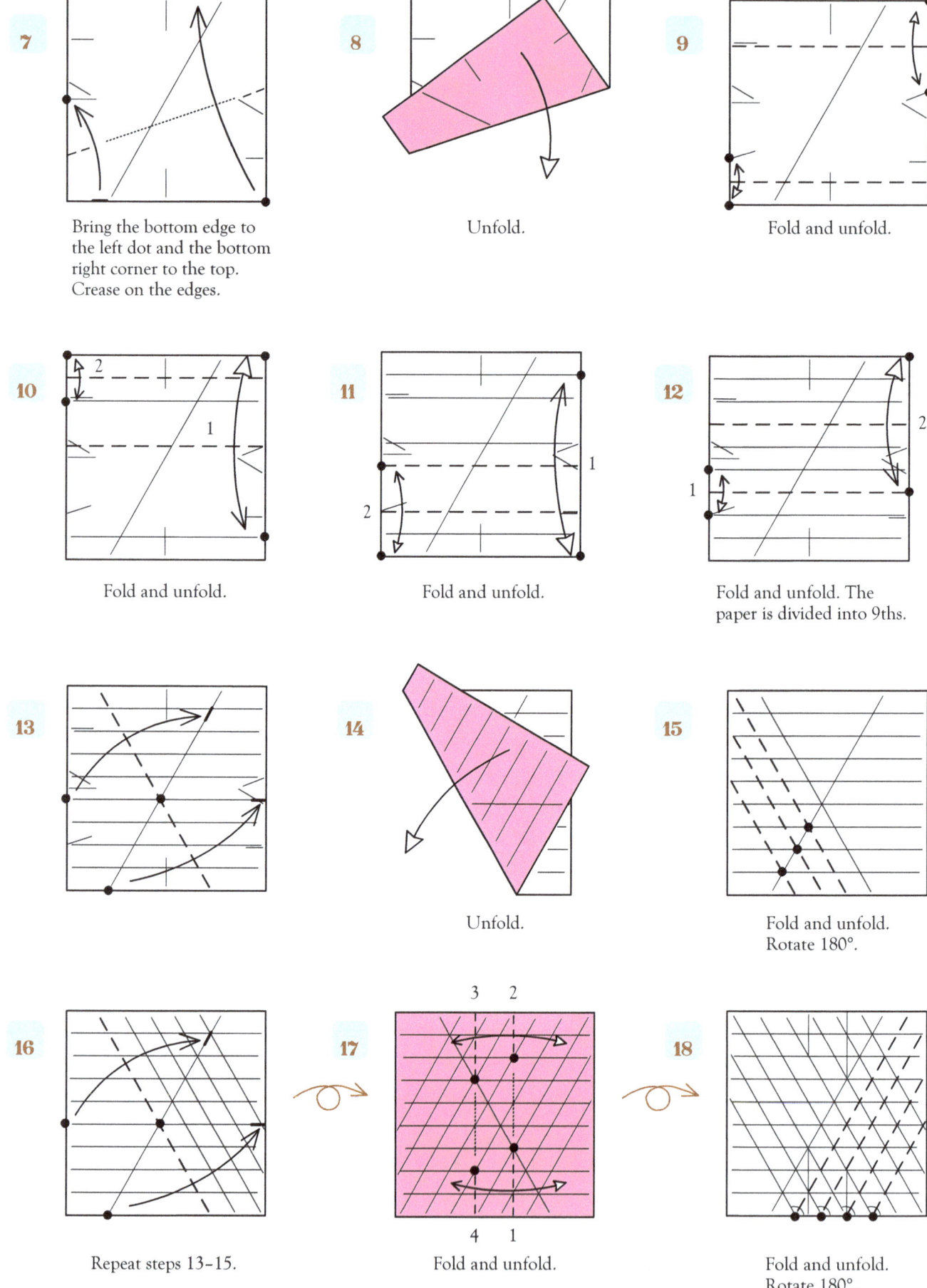

96 Origami Symphony No. 1

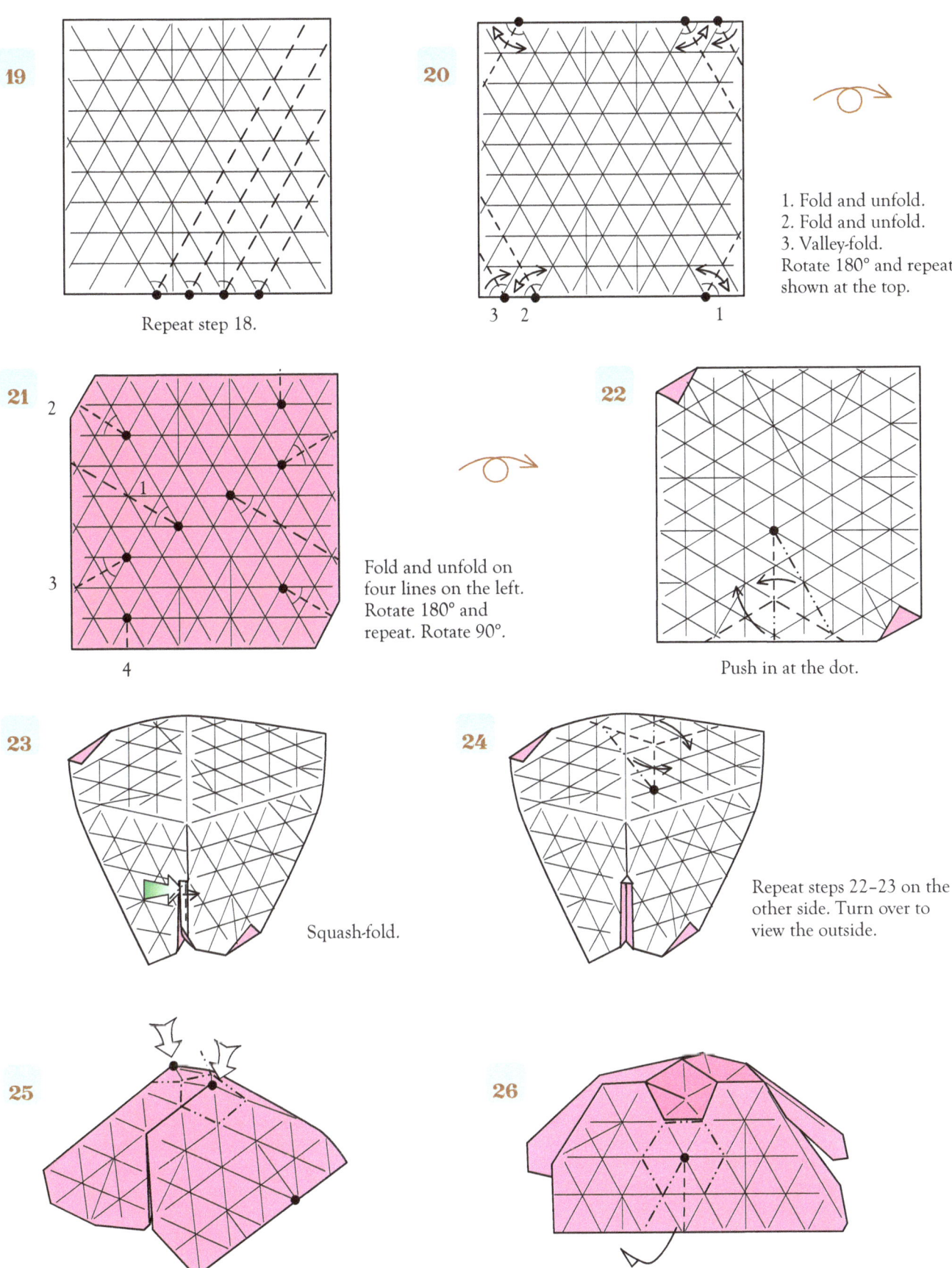

Sunken Dodecahedron **97**

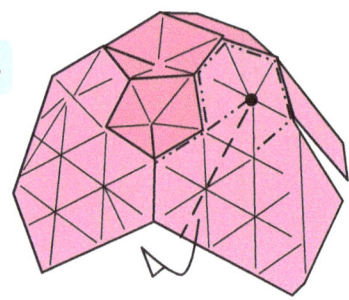

27. Push in at the dot and tuck under the left side to form a sunken pentagon. Turn over and repeat.

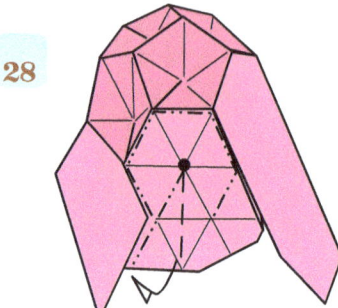

28. Push in at the dot to form a sunken pentagon. Turn over and repeat.

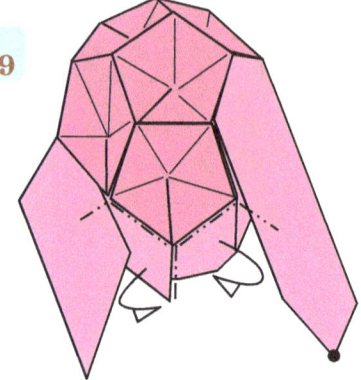

29. Turn over and repeat. Rotate to view the dot at the top, center.

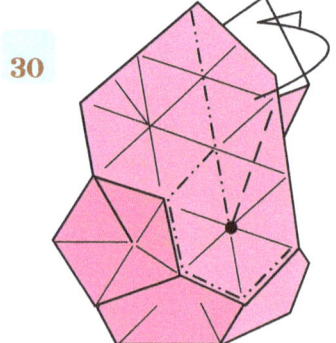

30. Push in at the dot to form a sunken pentagon. Turn over and repeat.

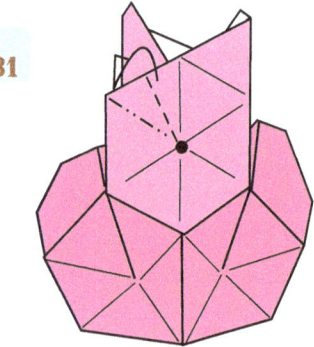

31. Push in at the dot and tuck into a hidden pocket. Turn over and repeat.

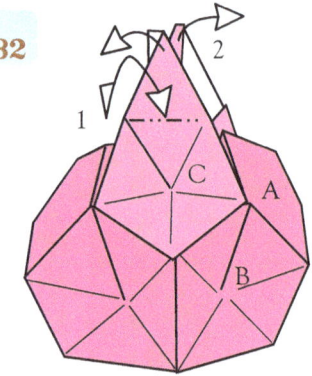

32.
1. Fold and unfold. Turn over and repeat.
2. Spread at the top to view the inside. Follow pentagons A, B, and C into the next step.

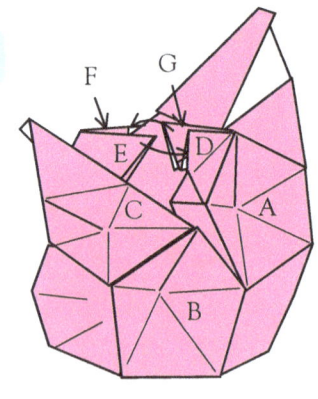

33. There are four flaps at the top, flaps D, E, F, and G. Flaps E and G larger than D and F. Tuck E into D, and G into F. This will create a pocket at the top.

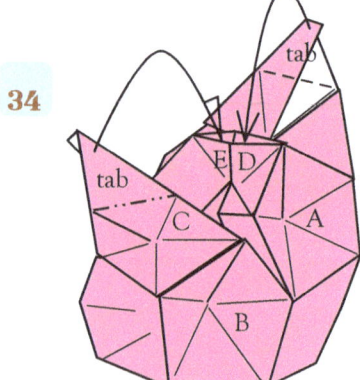

34. Tuck the tabs into the pocket.

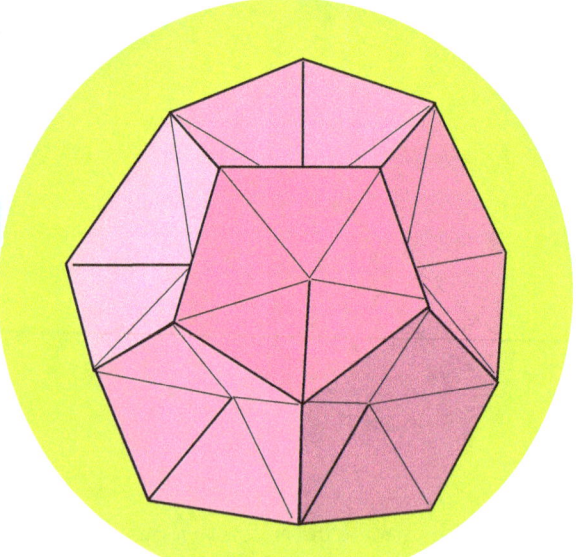

35.

Sunken Dodecahedron

98 *Origami Symphony No. 1*

Fourth Movement

March of the Large African Animals

𝄢 The symphony comes to a roaring conclusion with a March of these large and detailed animals. You can hear the Lion's roar and the Elephant's trumpet call. Models are complex in skill level. Come ride on the Elephant's back for a majestic view.

Rhinoceros

Rhinos are known for their horns, which are in fact made out of keratin, the same protein that forms our hair and fingernails. Some species of rhinos have two horns and some have only one. Rhinos spend much of the time grazing.

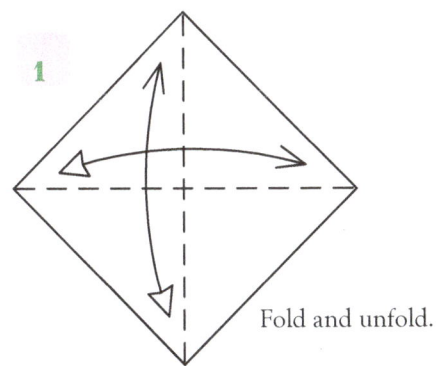

1. Fold and unfold.

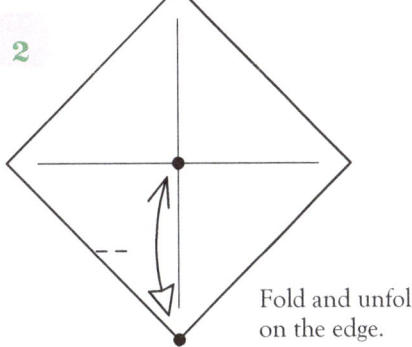

2. Fold and unfold on the edge.

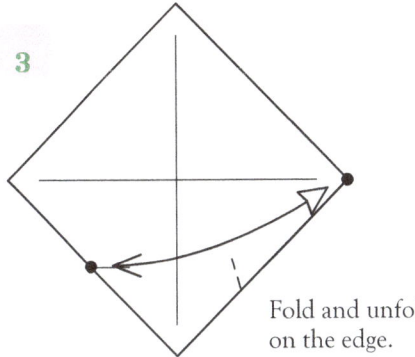

3. Fold and unfold on the edge.

Rhinoceros 99

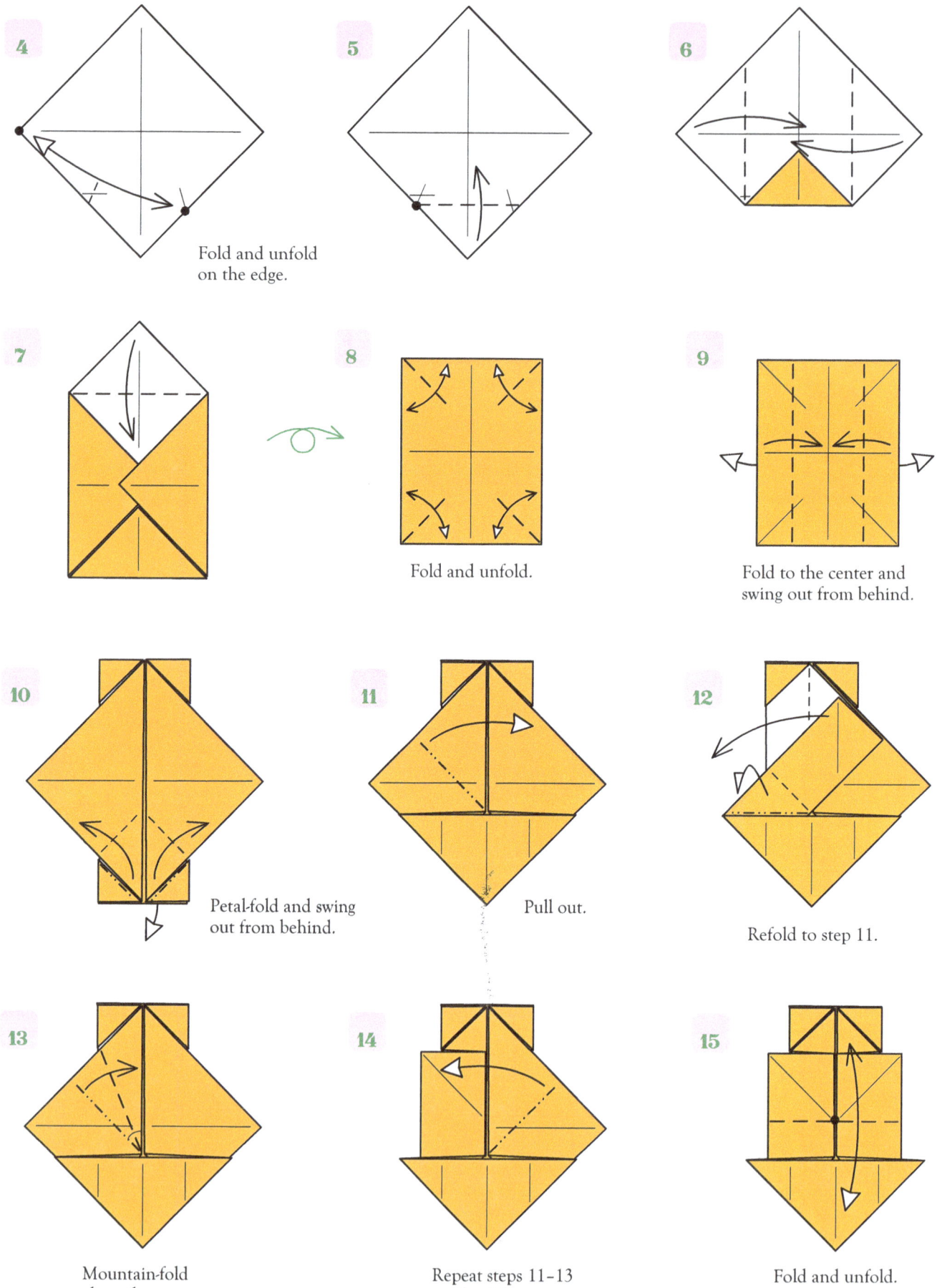

100 Origami Symphony No. 1

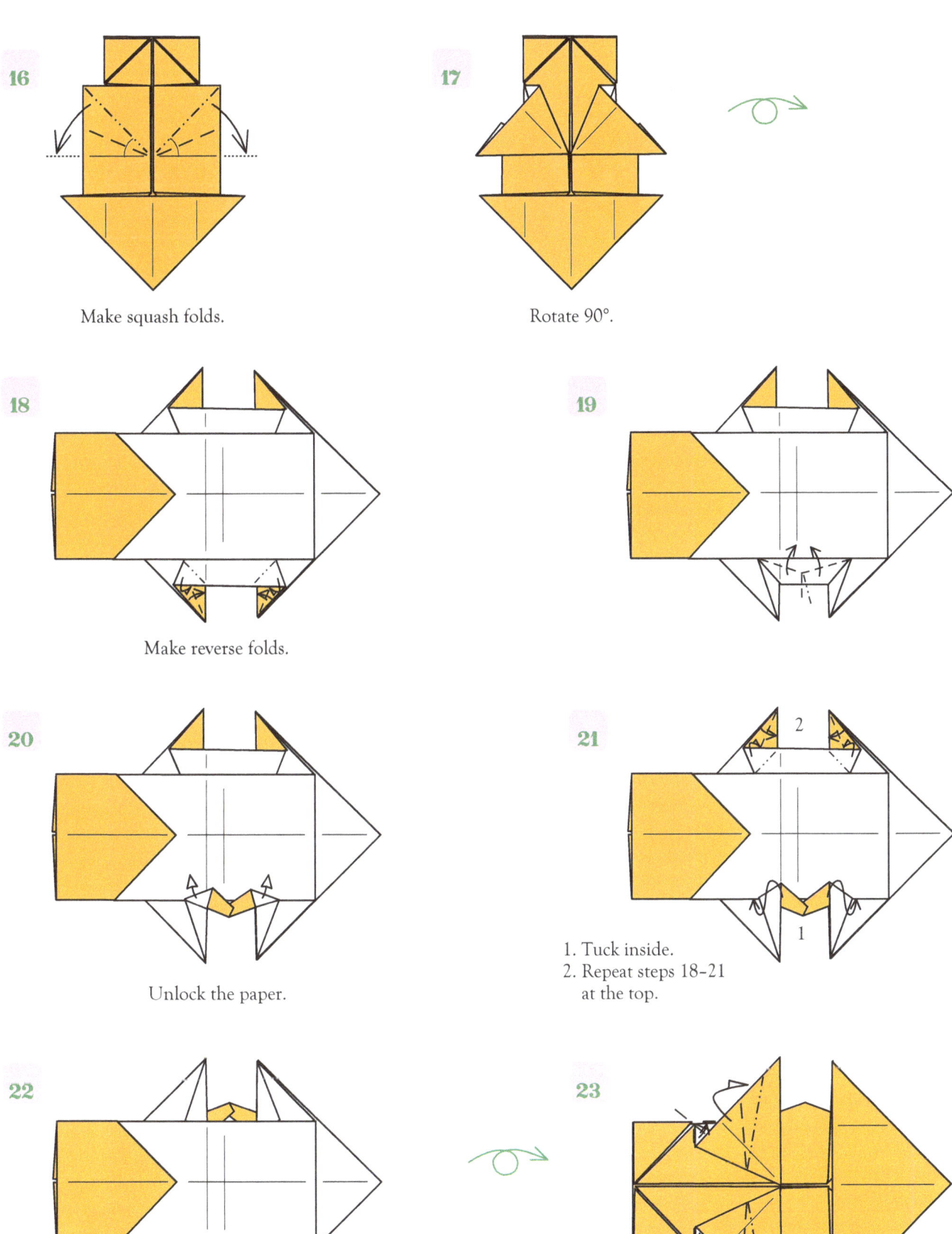

24

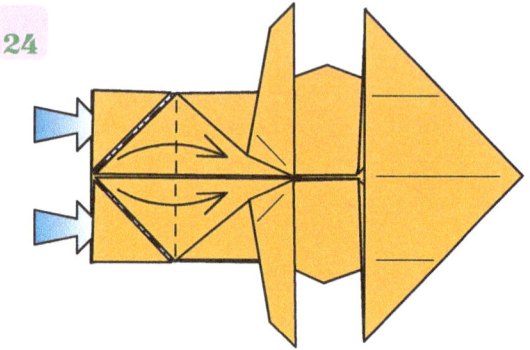

Make squash folds. Rotate 90°.

25

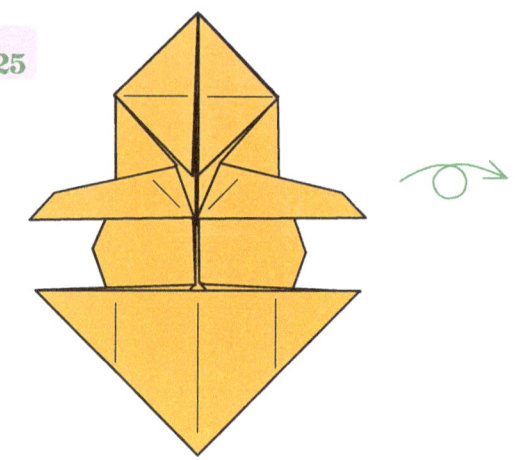

26

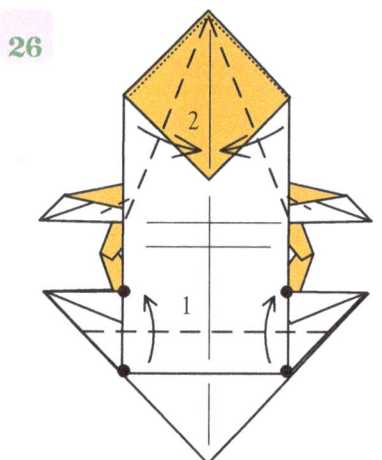

1. Fold up.
2. Fold the inner layers to the center and make small squash folds at the front legs.

27

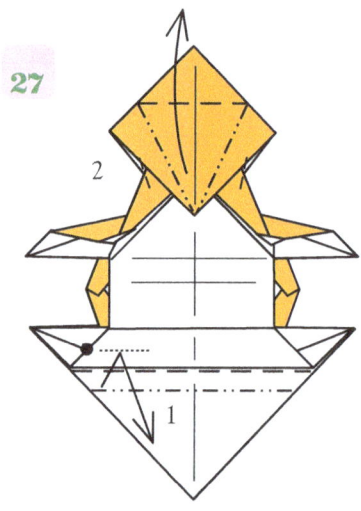

1. Pleat-fold, using the dotted line as a guide.
2. Petal-fold.

28

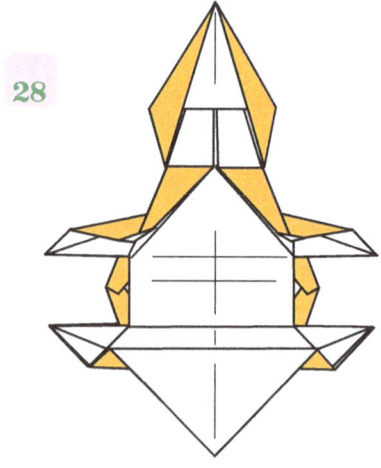

29

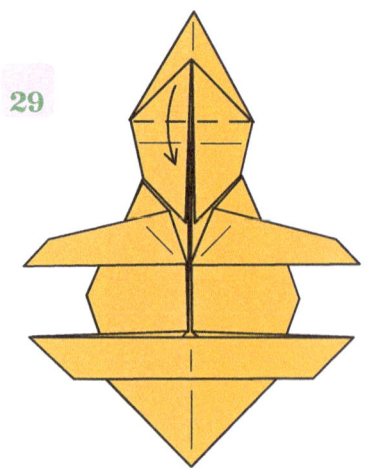

102   *Origami Symphony No. 1*

30

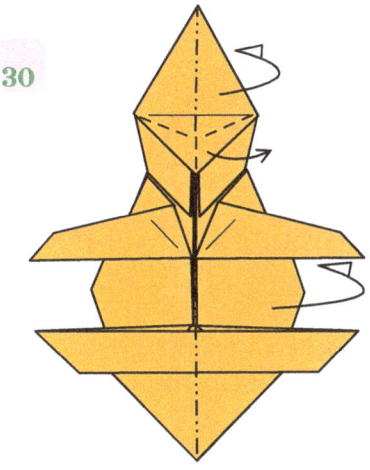

Fold the horn up while folding in half. Rotate 90°.

31

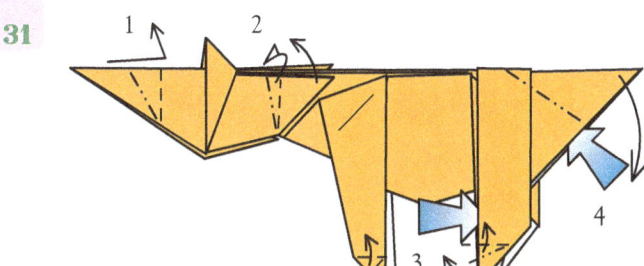

1. Crimp-fold.
2. Crimp-fold, repeat behind.
3. Make crimp folds, repeat behind.
4. Reverse-fold.

32

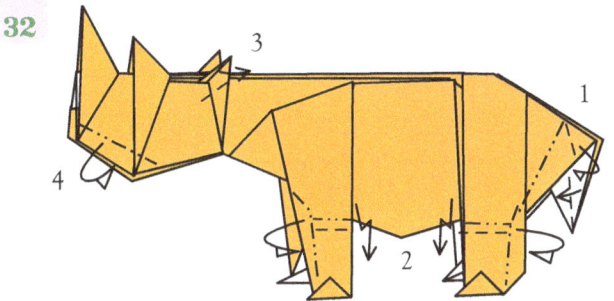

1. Reverse-fold.
2. Shape and pleat the legs.
3. Open the ears.
4. Fold inside.
Repeat behind.

33

1. Shape the horns.
2. Crimp-fold.
3. Shape the back.

34

Rhinoceros

Rhinoceros **103**

Hippopotamus

One might think Hippos would be sluggish on land due to their size, but in addition to being graceful under water, Hippos can run rather fast on land when needed. Hippos spend much of their time in rivers and lakes to stay cool, but do not swim well in deep waters. Hippos come on land for a few hours each day to graze on grasses, their primary food source.

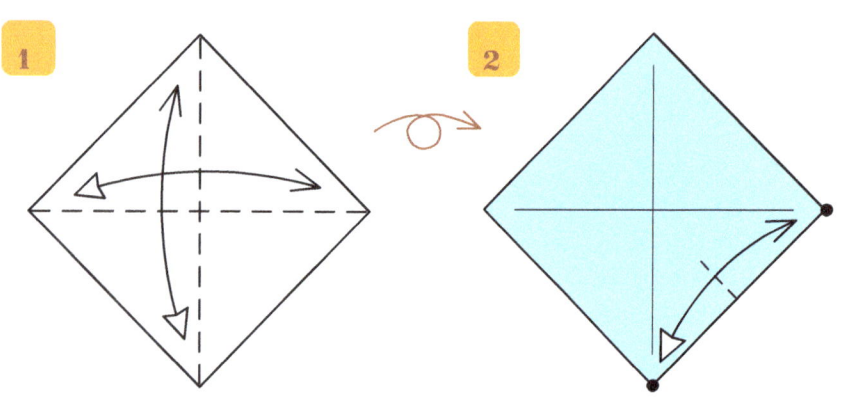
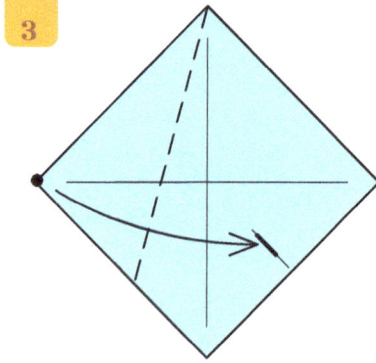

1. Fold and unfold.
2. Fold and unfold on the edge.
3. Bring the dot to the line.

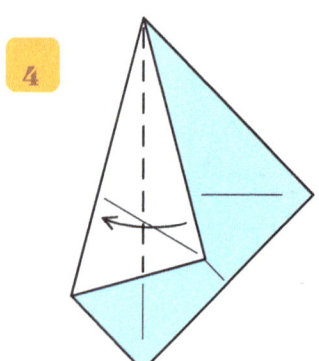
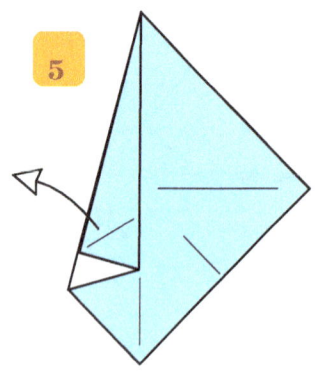
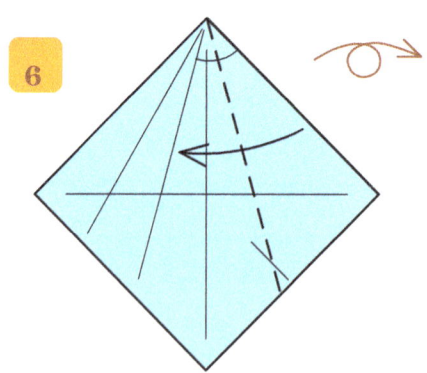

5. Unfold.
6. Repeat steps 3–5 on the right.

104 *Origami Symphony No. 1*

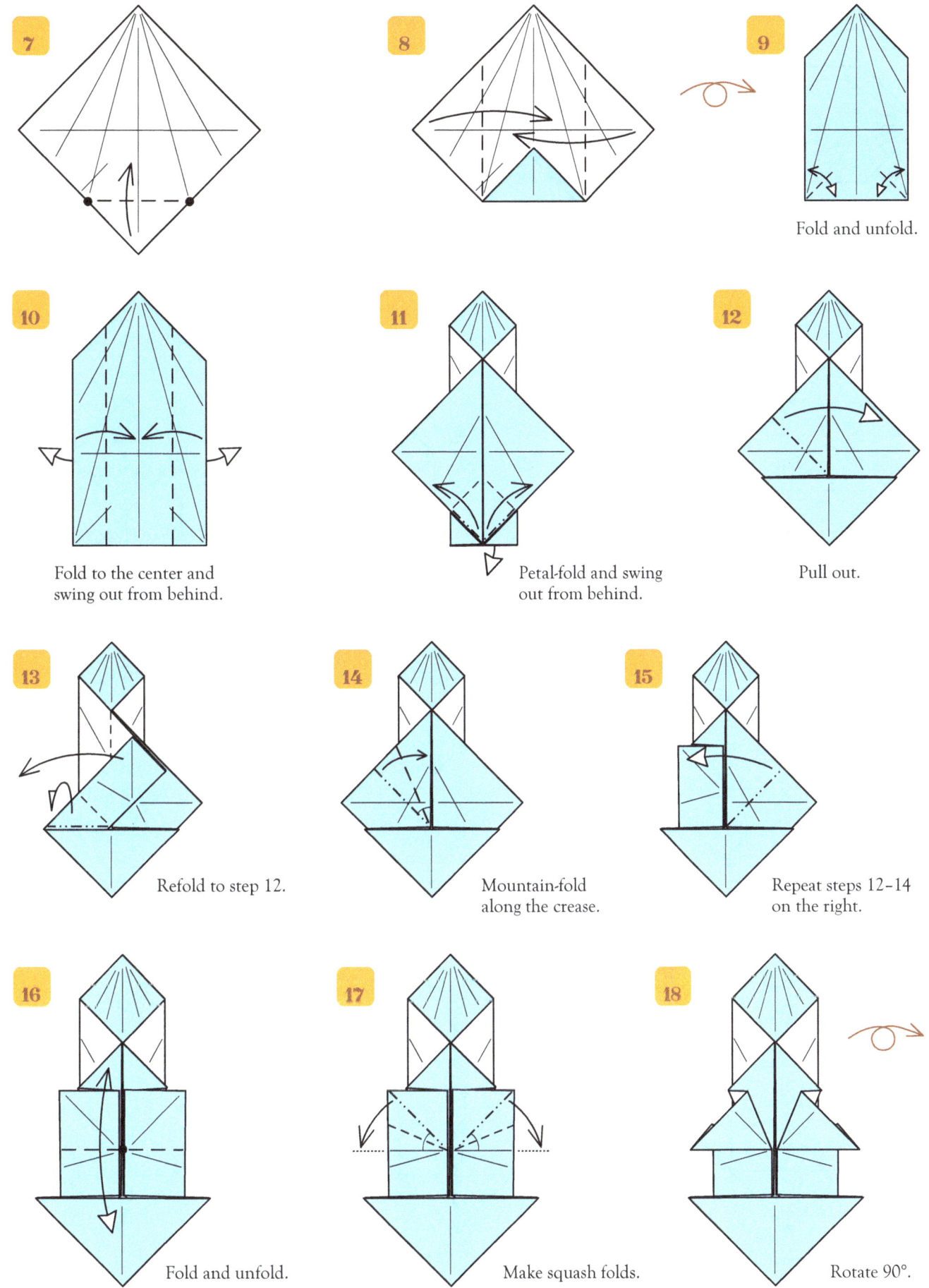

19

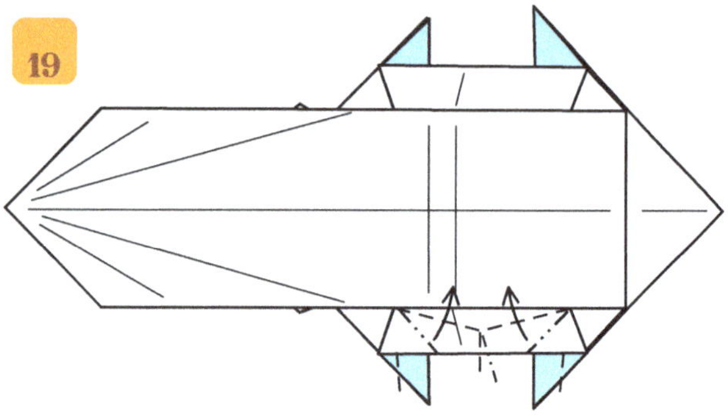

This is a combination of squash folds.

20

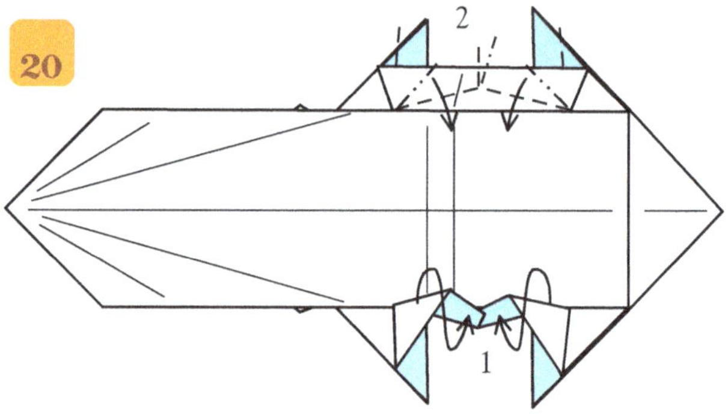

1. Tuck inside.
2. Repeat steps 19–20 on the top.

21

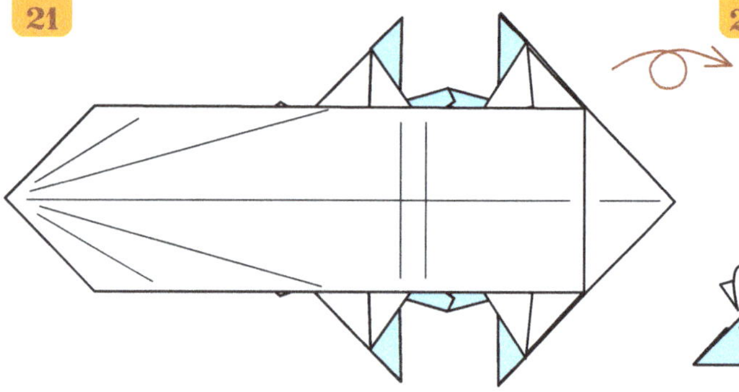

Rotate 90°.

22

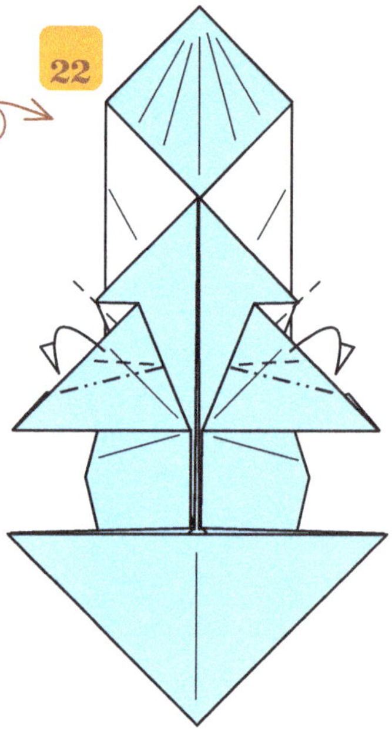

23

24

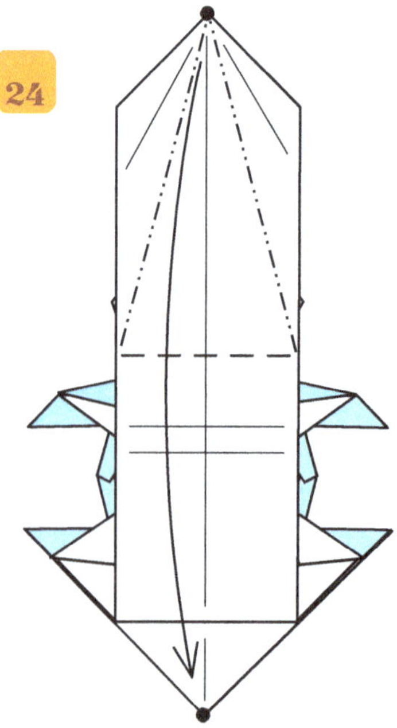

Mountain-fold along the creases.

25

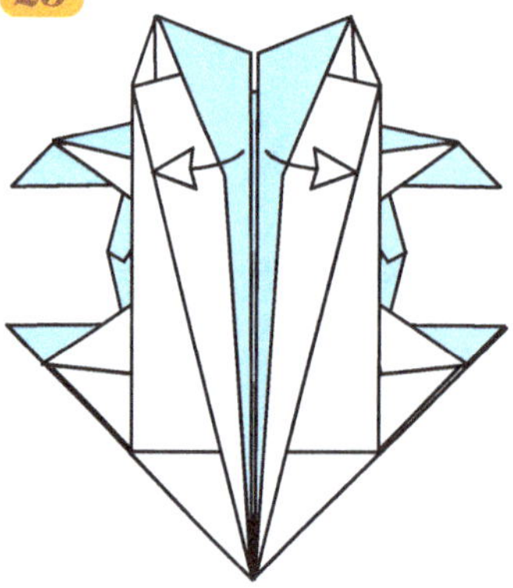

This is 3D. Flatten.

26

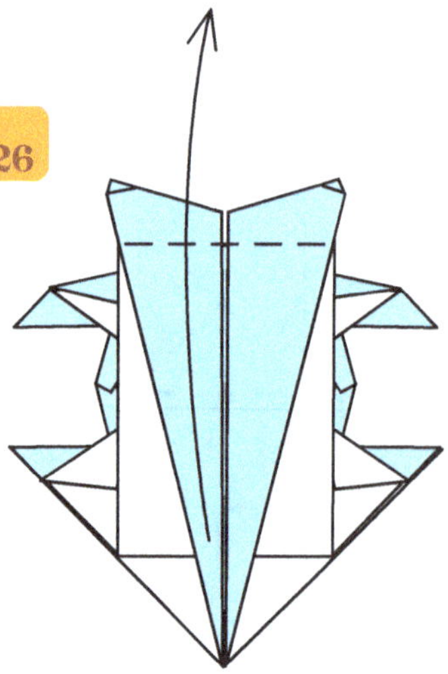

106 *Origami Symphony No. 1*

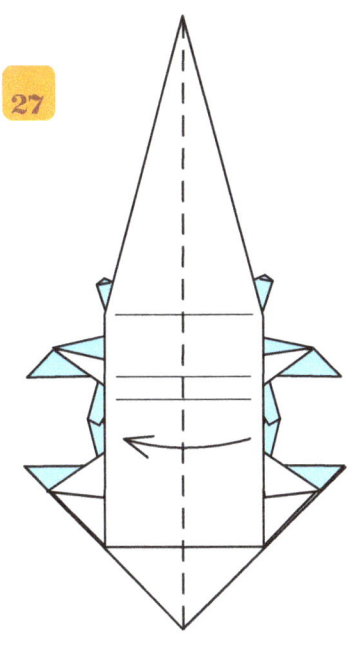

Fold in half and rotate 90°.

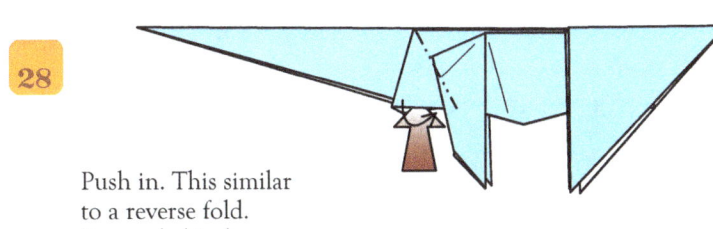

Push in. This similar to a reverse fold. Repeat behind.

1. Crimp-fold.
2. Reverse-fold.

1. Reverse-fold the hidden layers to form the eye.
2. Reverse-fold.
Repeat behind.

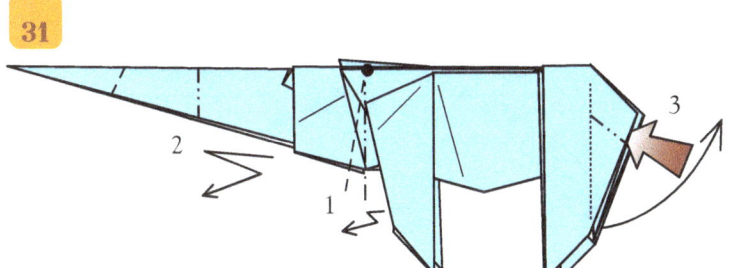

1. Pivot at the dot for this crimp fold.
2. Crimp-fold.
3. Reverse-fold.

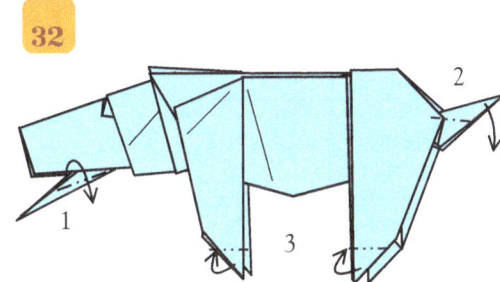

1. Spread the upper layer, repeat behind.
2. Reverse-fold.
3. Reverse folds, repeat behind.

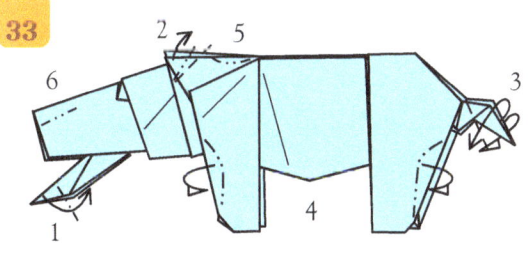

1. Reverse-fold.
2. Pleat-fold the ear, repeat behind.
3. Outside-reverse-fold.
4. Shape the legs, repeat behind.
5. Shape the neck.
6. Shape the head.

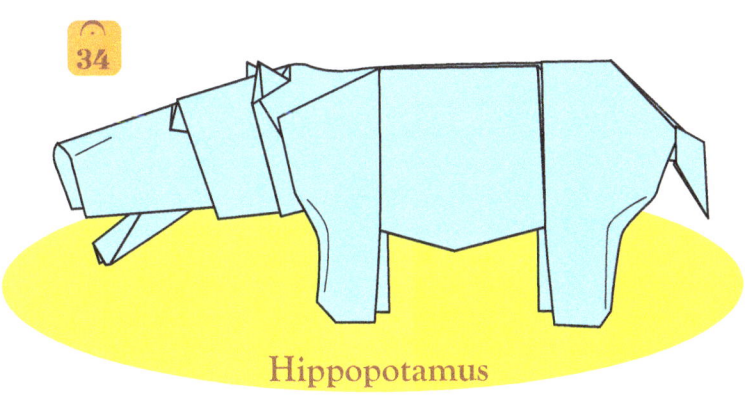

Hippopotamus

Hippopotamus **107**

Baby Elephant

A Baby Elephant, or calf, stands at three feet tall. These cute animals do not yet know what to do with their trunks. A Baby Elephant is raised by the mother and the herd.

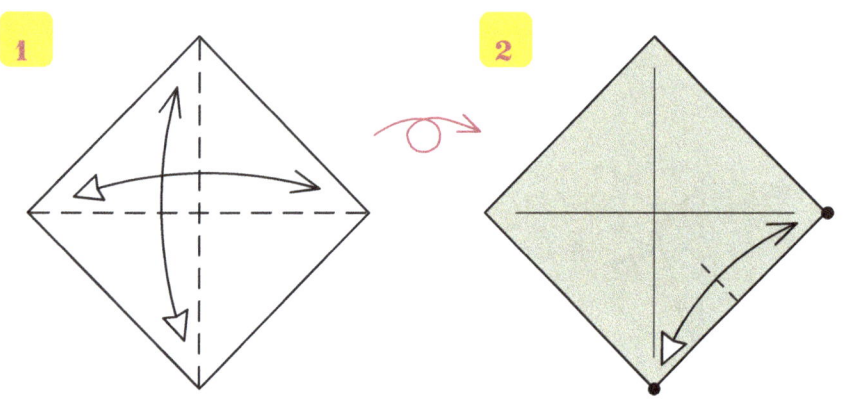
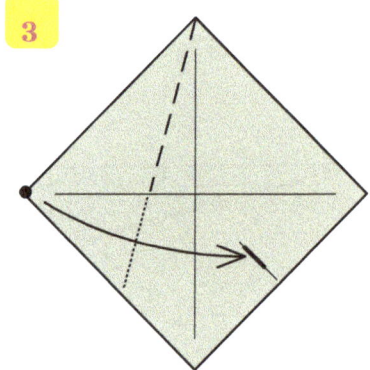

1. Fold and unfold.
2. Fold and unfold on the edge.
3. Bring the dot to the line. Crease on the top half.

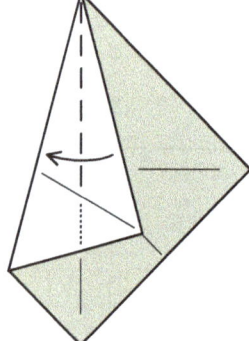
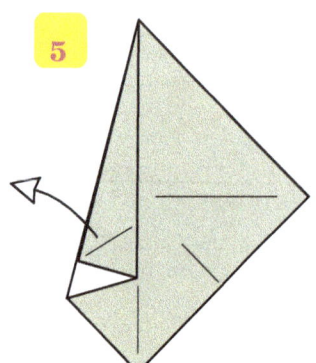
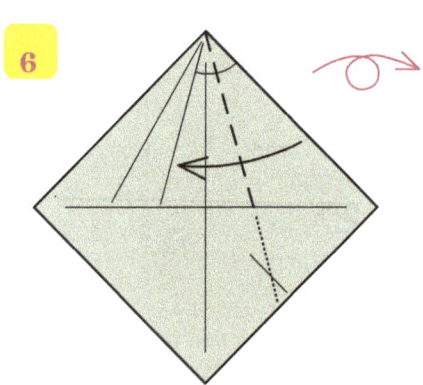

4. Crease on the upper part.
5. Unfold.
6. Repeat steps 3–5 on the right.

108   *Origami Symphony No. 1*

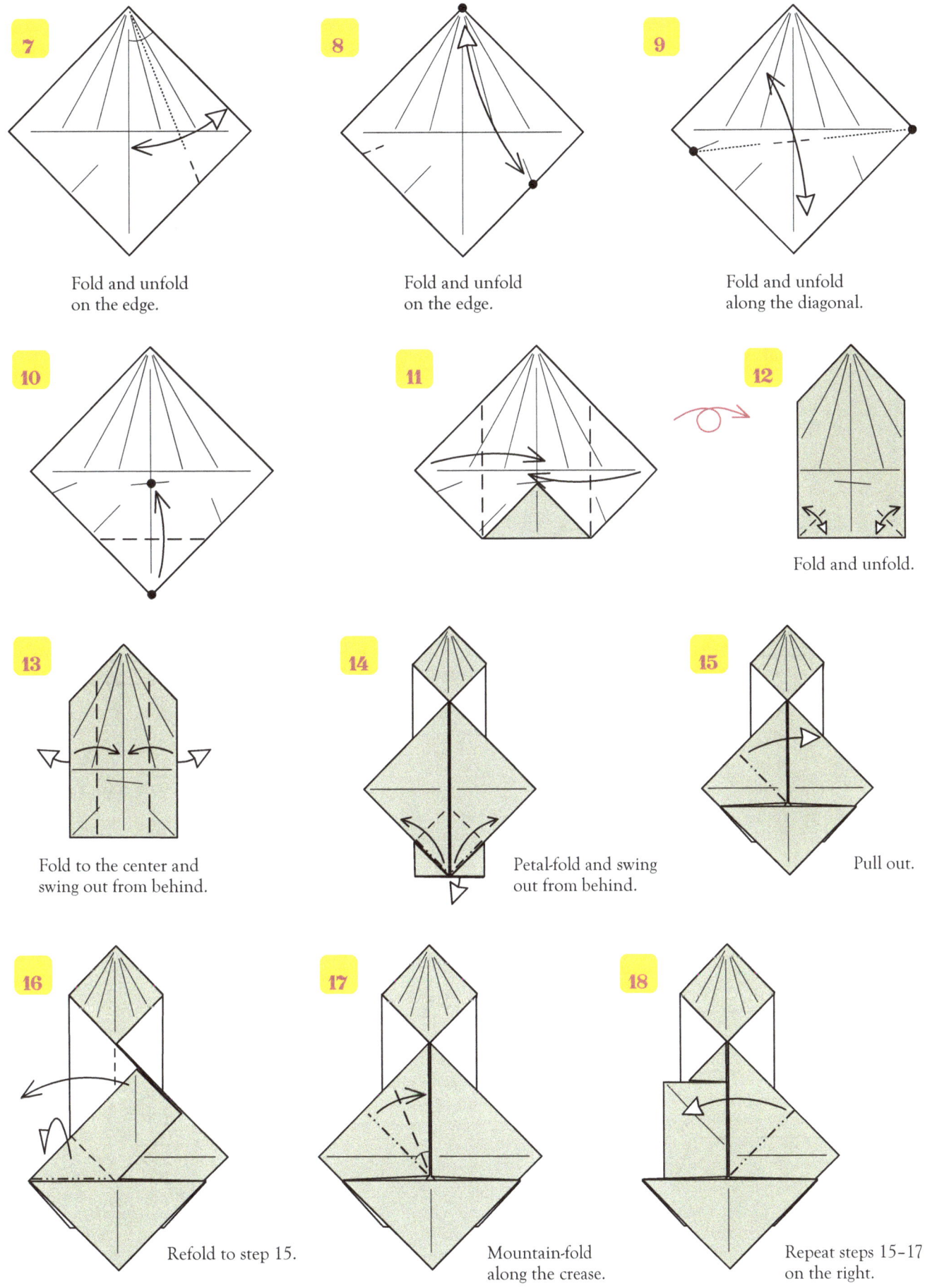

Baby Elephant 109

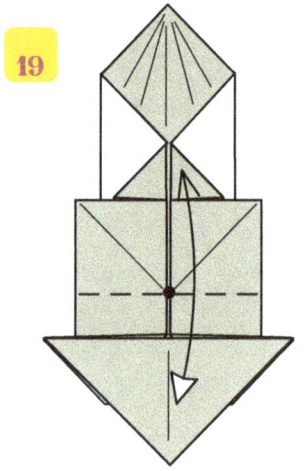

Fold and unfold.

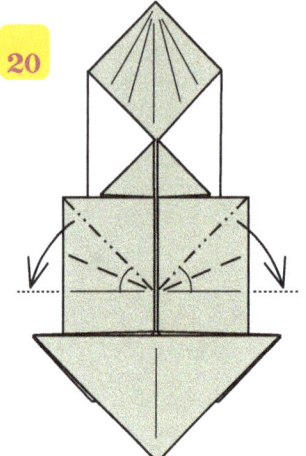

Make squash folds.

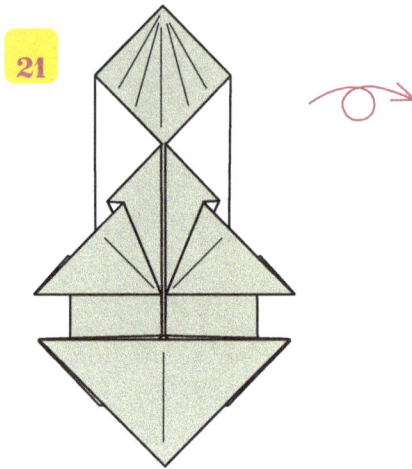

Rotate 90°.

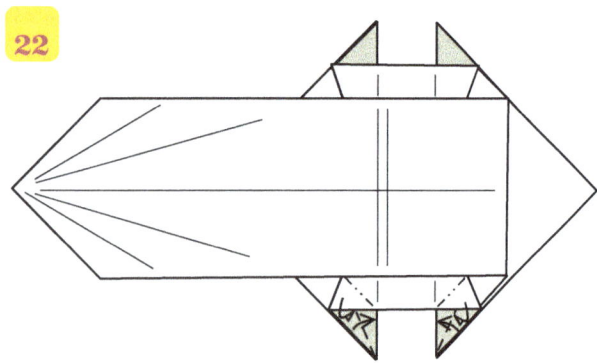

Make reverse folds.

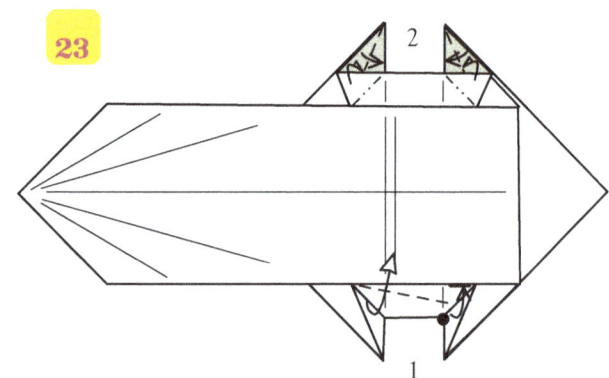

1. The dot will meet the line, spread on the left.
2. Repeat steps 22–23 on the top.

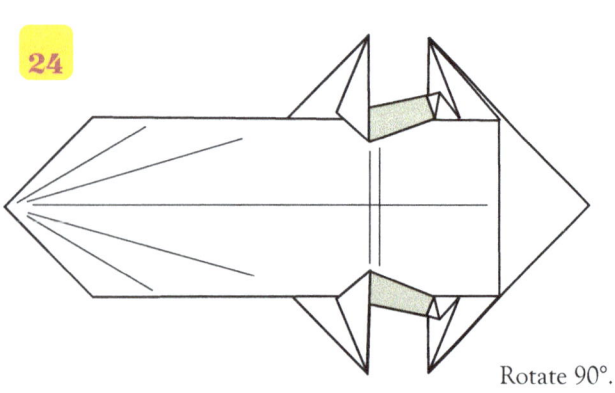

Rotate 90°.

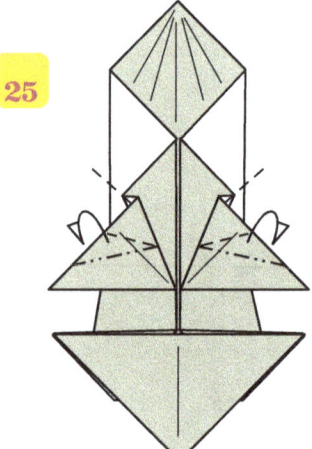

110 *Origami Symphony No. 1*

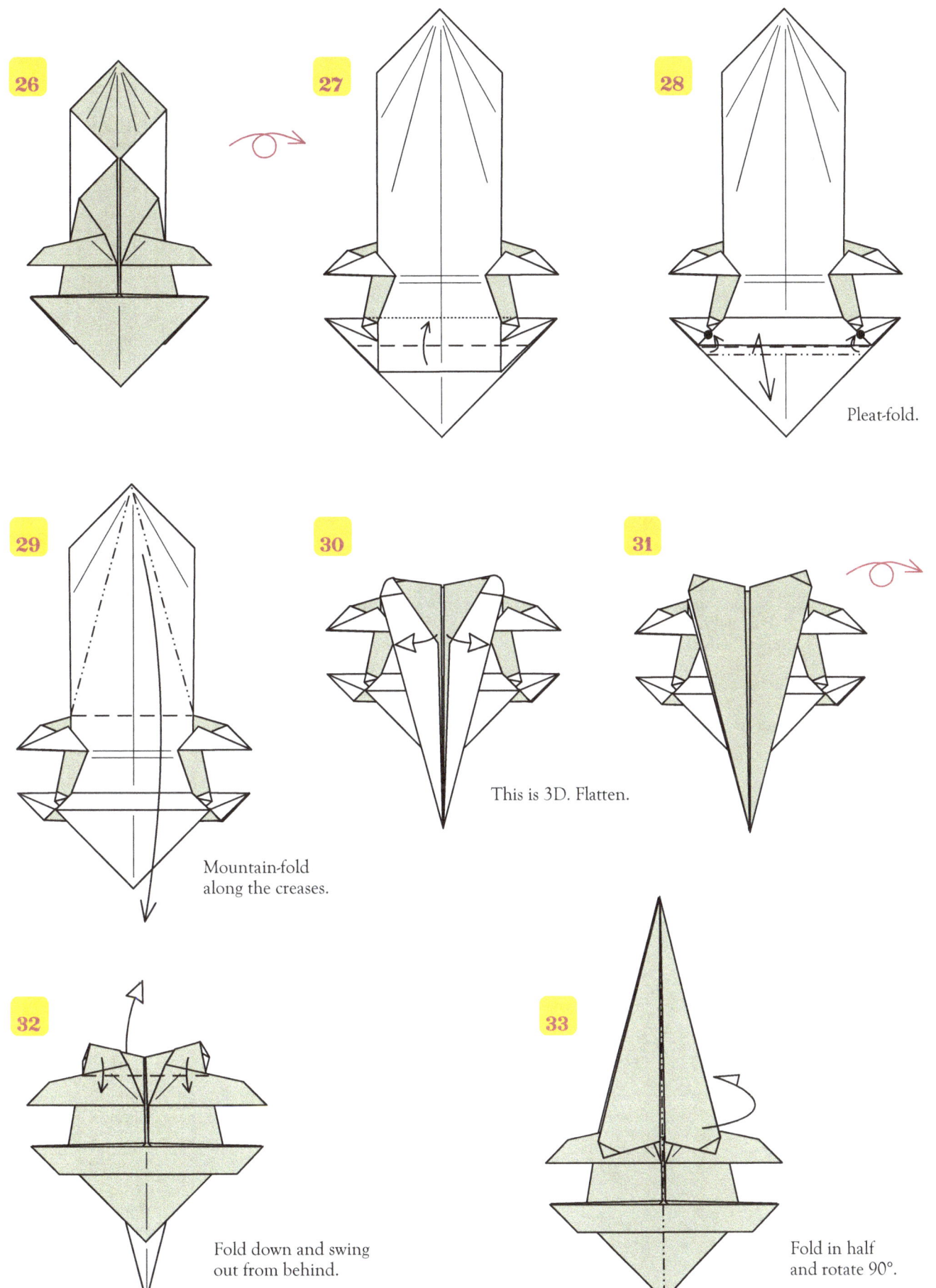

Baby Elephant

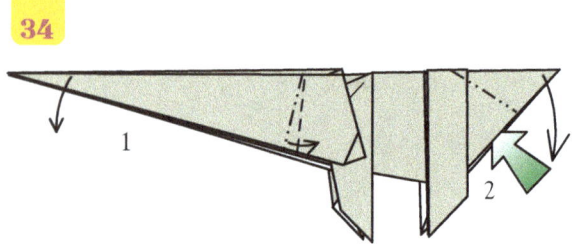

1. Crimp-fold.
2. Reverse-fold.

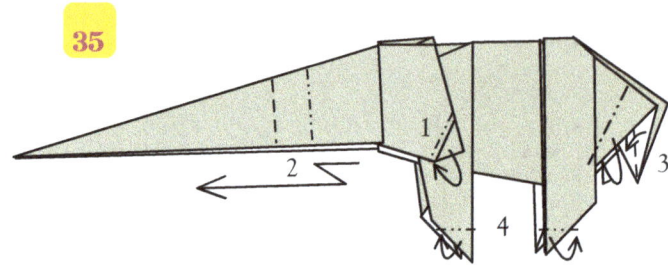

1. Reverse-fold.
2. Crimp-fold.
3. Thin the tail.
4. Make reverse folds.
Repeat behind.

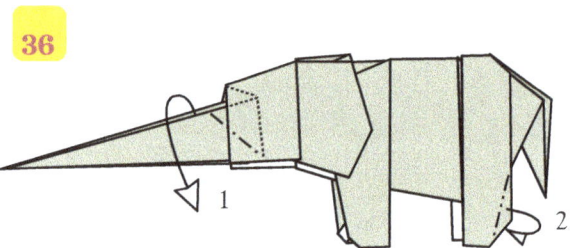

1. Spread the trunk.
2. Fold behind.
Repeat behind.

1. Fold inside, repeat behind.
2. Reverse-fold.

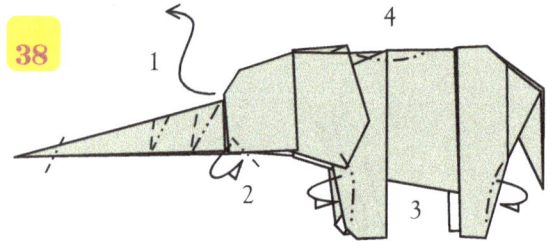

1. Bend the trunk with crimp and reverse folds.
2. Fold behind.
3. Shape the legs.
4. Shape the back.
Repeat behind.

Baby Elephant

112 Origami Symphony No. 1

Elephant

The largest living land animal, the Elephant has no natural predators, though their young and the sick in their herd can be vulnerable to such animals as lions and hyenas. Elephants form deep, lifelong bonds, and are a matriarchal society. The trunk is formed from the nose and upper lip. It is used in several ways to perform complex tasks. Their sense of smell is the best of all animals, and they can smell water twenty miles away.

1. Fold and unfold.

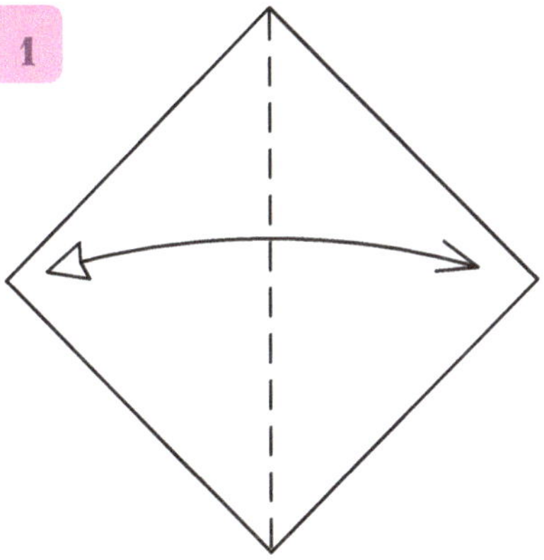

2. Fold to the center and unfold.

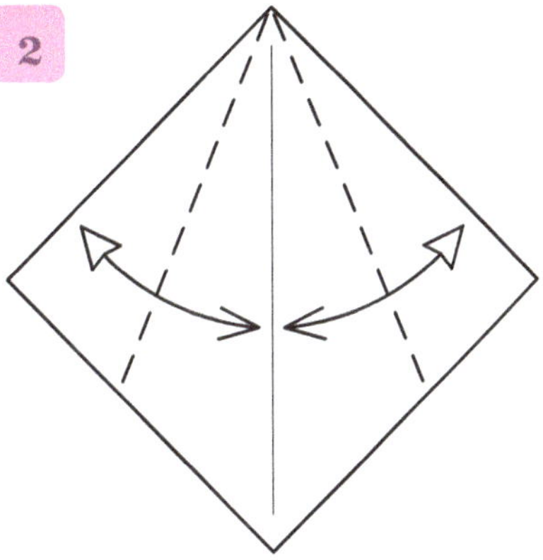

3.

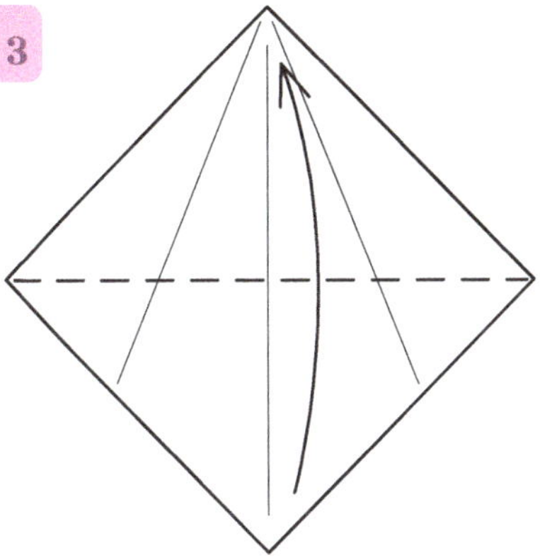

4.

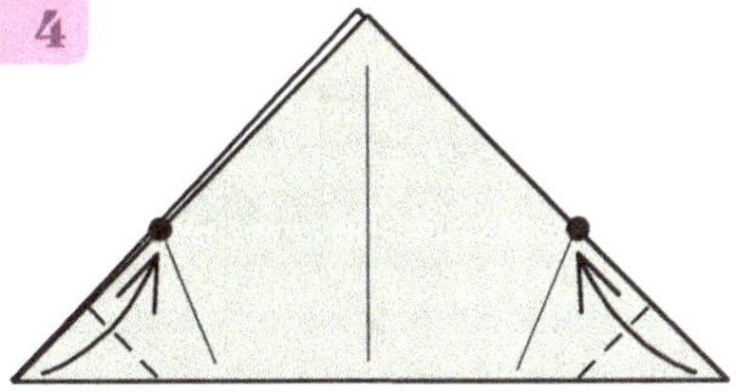

5. 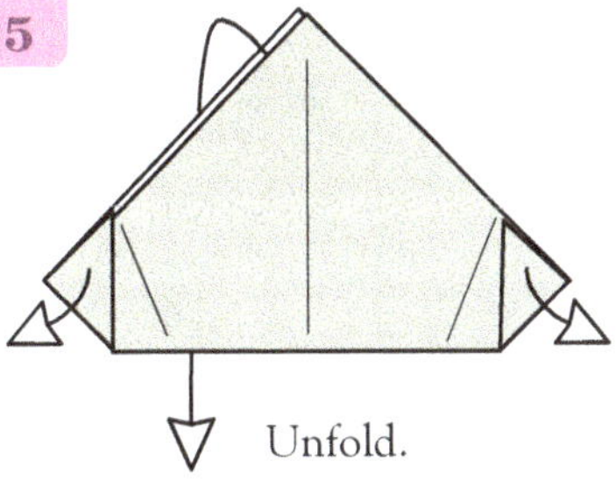 Unfold.

6. Fold and unfold. Rotate 180°.

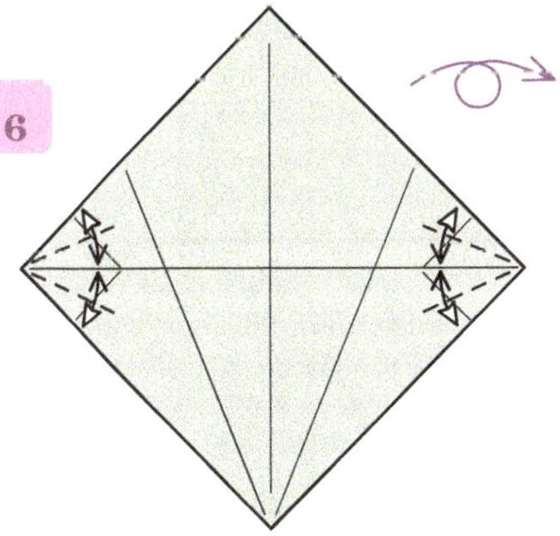

Elephant 113

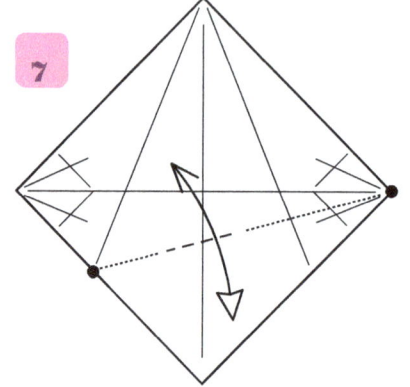

Fold and unfold on the diagonal.

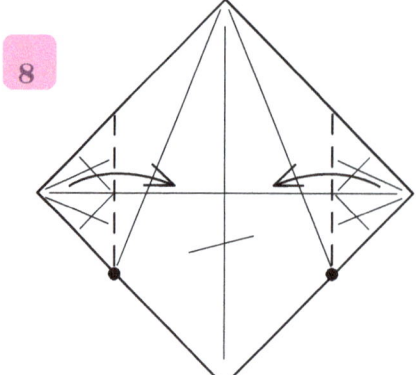

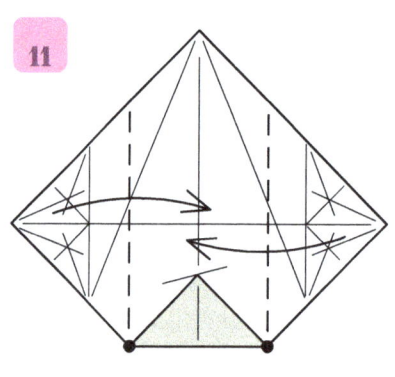

Fold and unfold.

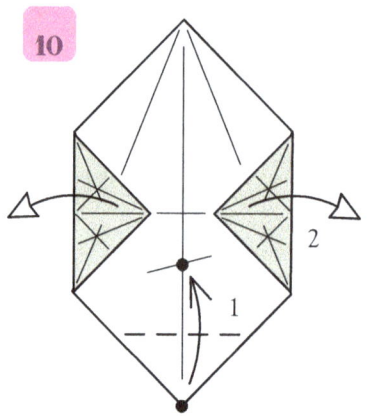

1. Fold up.
2. Unfold.

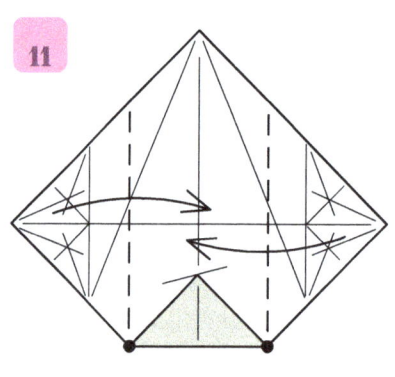

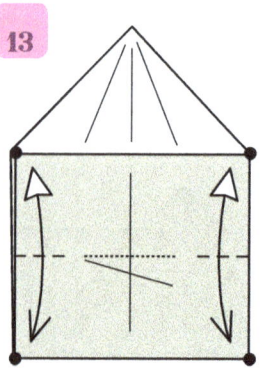

Fold up at the bottom while folding the corners in the middle.

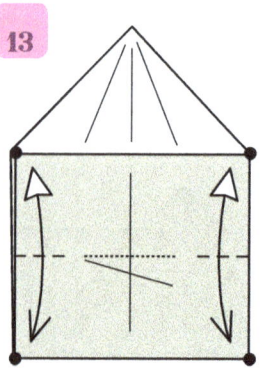

Fold and unfold the top layer.

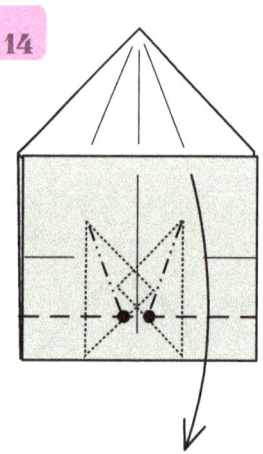

Valley-fold the top layer. Make squash folds on the inner layers.

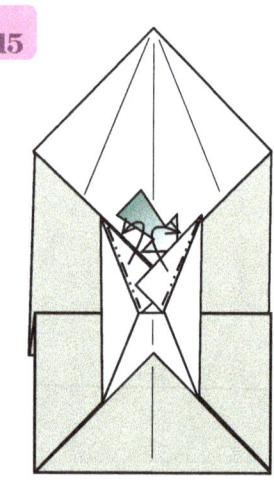

Make two reverse folds.

114   Origami Symphony No. 1

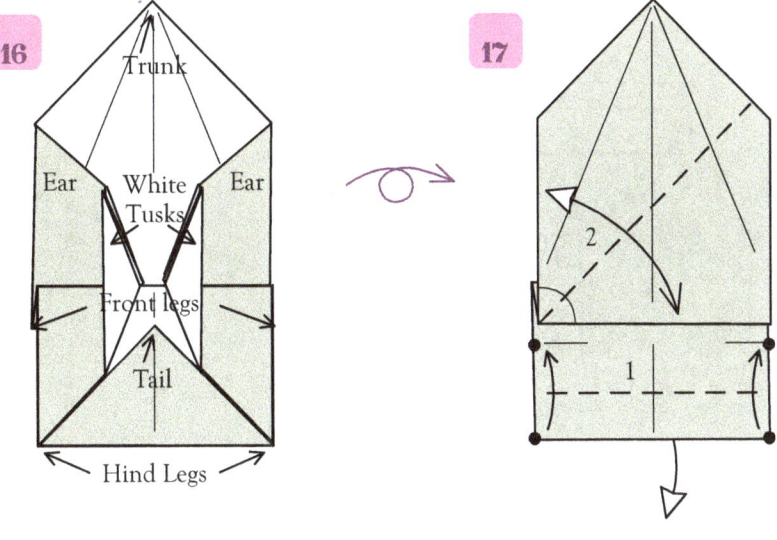
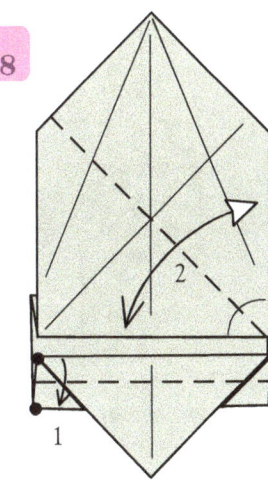

1. Fold up and swing out from behind.
2. Fold and unfold.

1. Fold down.
2. Fold and unfold.
Rotate 180°.

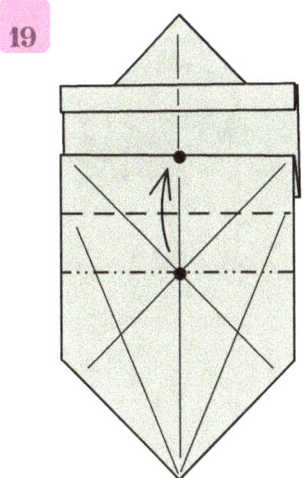
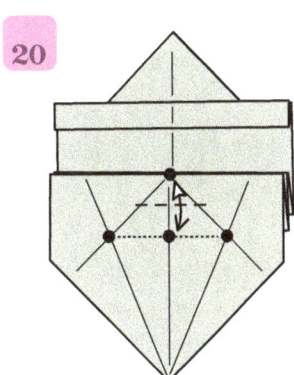
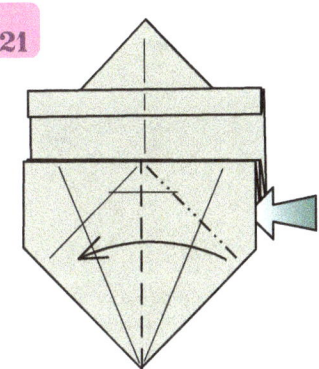

Pleat-fold the top layers.

Fold and unfold the top layers.

This begins a combination of squash folds.

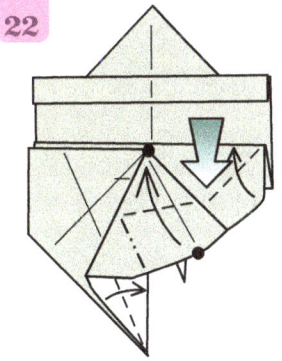
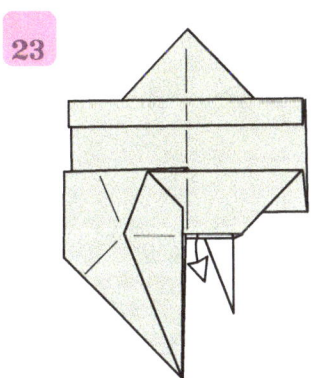
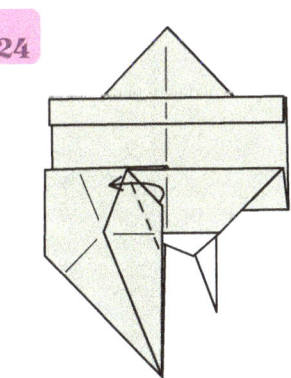

This is 3D. Continue with more squash folds to flatten the model.

Pull out.

Spread the paper.

Elephant **115**

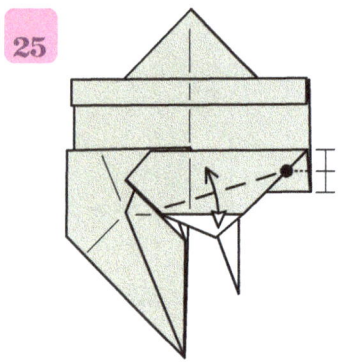

Fold and unfold so the dot is in the middle.

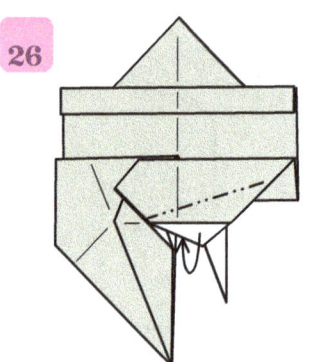

Reverse-fold.

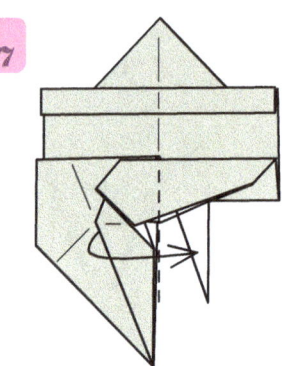

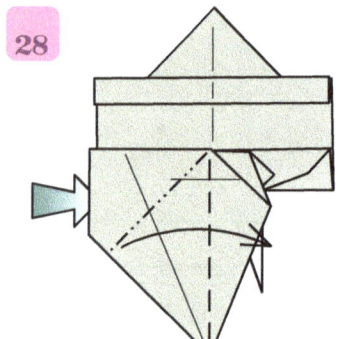

Repeat steps 21–27 in the opposite direction.

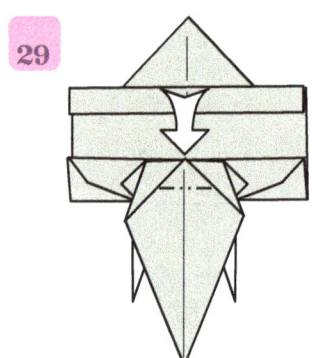

Sink. Spread at the head and ears to sink.

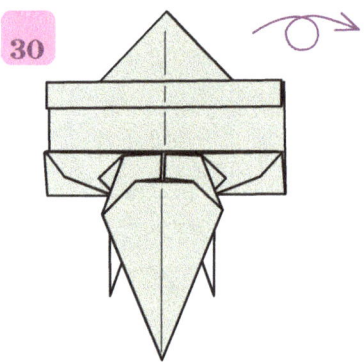

Rotate 90°.

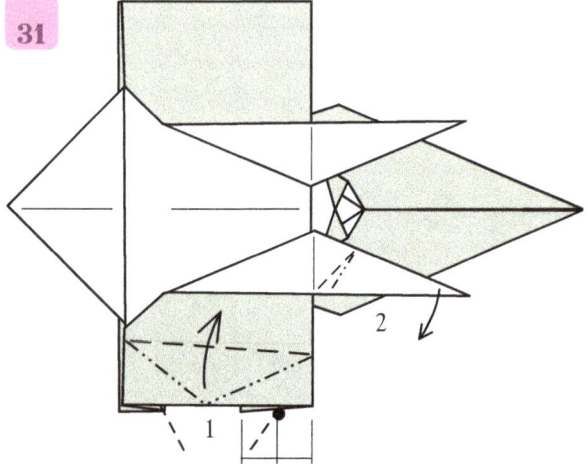

1. Petal-fold. The dot is in the middle of the flap.
2. Pleat-fold.

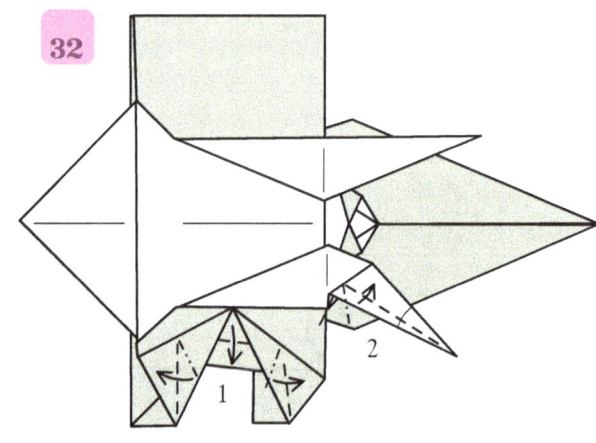

1. Petal-fold.
2. Squash-fold one-third of the angle.

116 *Origami Symphony No. 1*

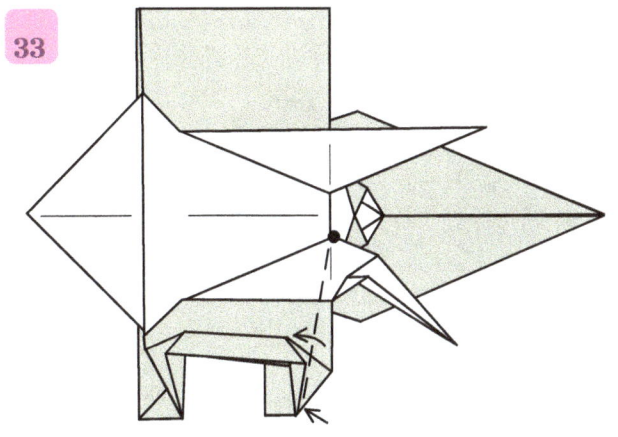

Valley-fold but quite to a point at the bottom, by the arrow. Repeat steps 31–33 at the top.

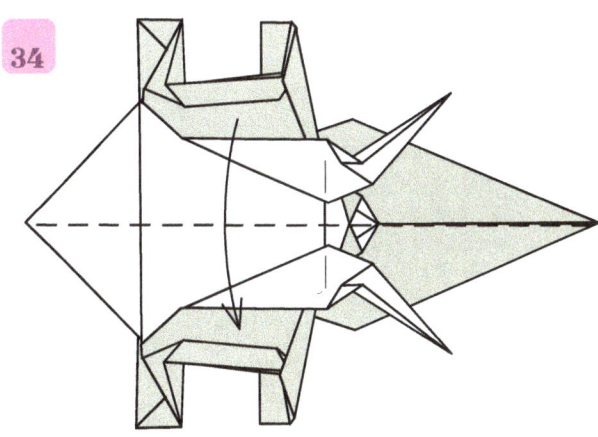

1. Reverse-fold.
2. Reverse-fold, repeat behind.
3. Reverse-fold.

1. Reverse-fold.
2. Reverse-fold.
Repeat behind.

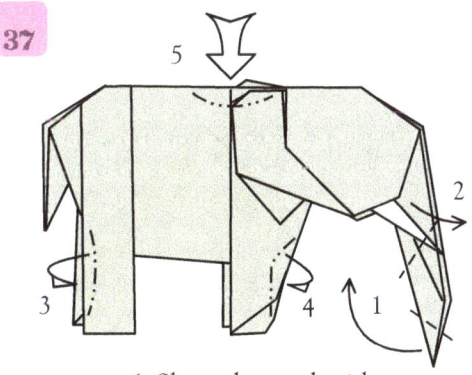

1. Shape the trunk with outside reverse folds.
2. Curl the tusks.
3, 4. Shape the legs.
5. Shape the body.
Repeat behind.

Elephant

Lion

Both male and female Lions possess stealth and cunning, and the male lion is instantly recognized by its large shaggy mane. A Lion's roar is so powerful that it can be heard several miles away.

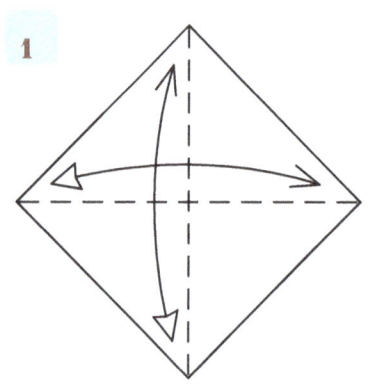

1. Fold and unfold.

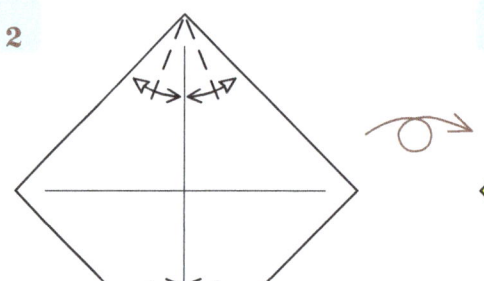

2. Fold to the center and unfold.

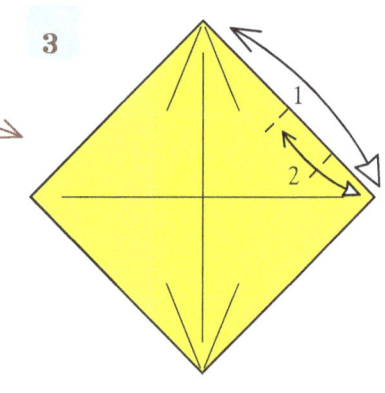

3. Fold and unfold to find the quarter mark.

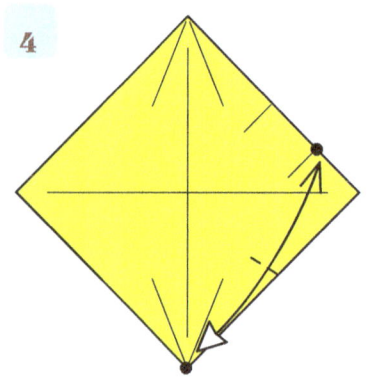

4. Fold and unfold on the edge.

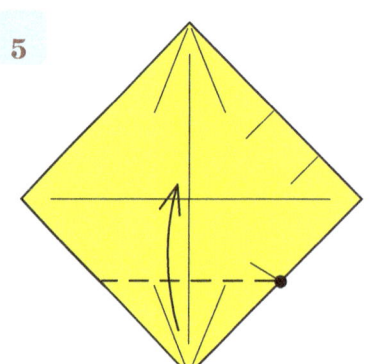

5.

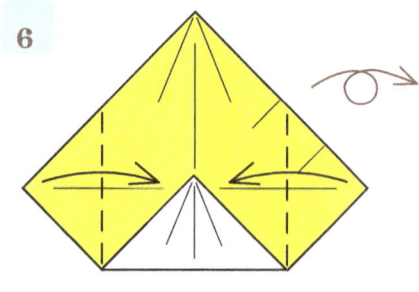

6.

118 *Origami Symphony No. 1*

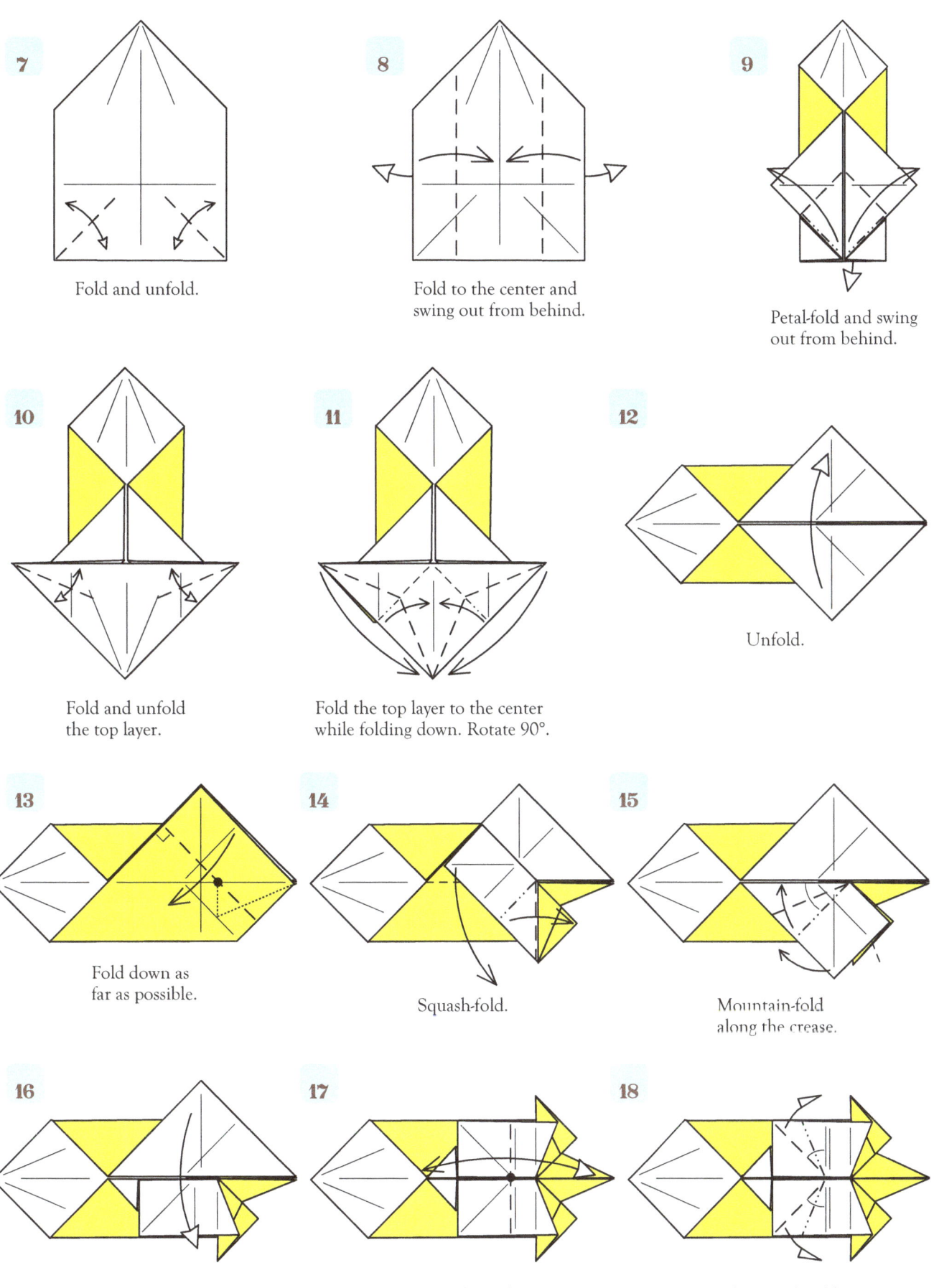

Lion 119

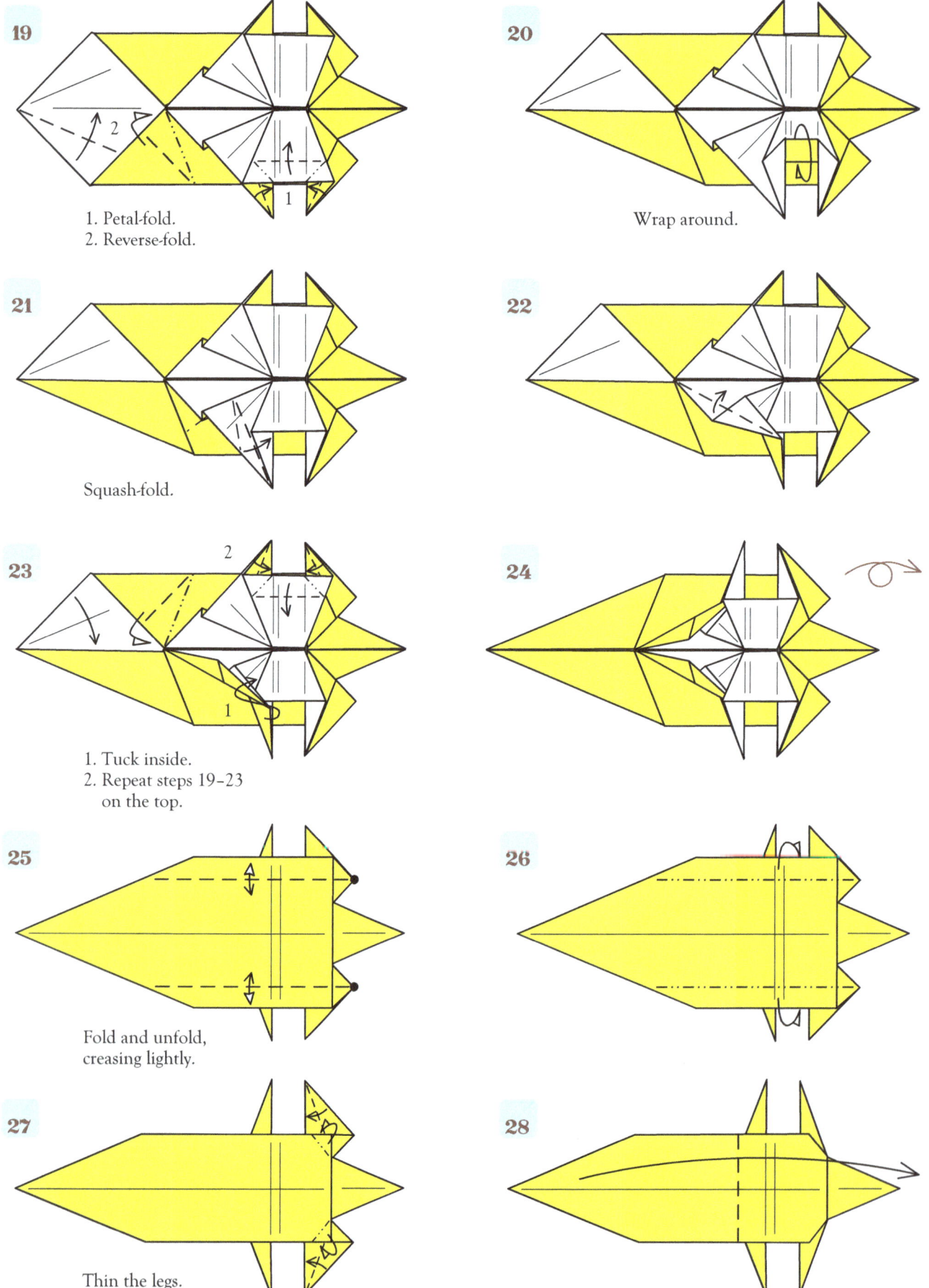

120 Origami Symphony No. 1

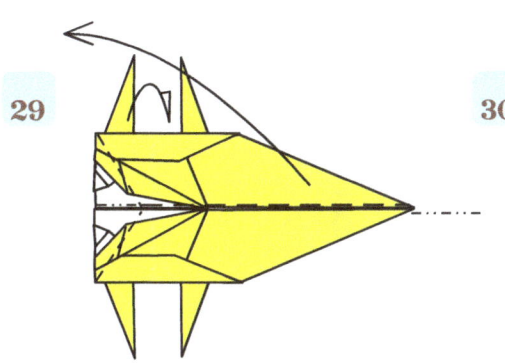

Fold the head up while folding the body in half.

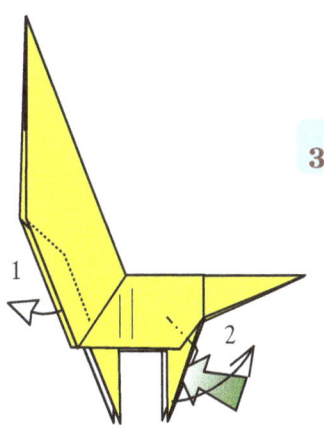

Note the bold line (on the left) is vertical.
1. Pull out.
2. Reverse-fold. Repeat behind.

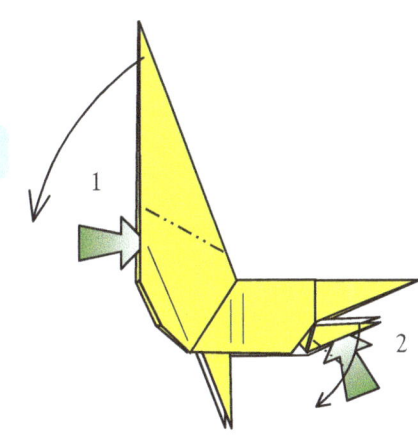

1. Reverse-fold.
2. Reverse-fold, repeat behind.

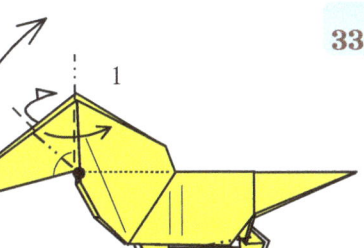

The head is folded down so the dot intersects the head and top line of the back.
1. Crimp-fold.
2. Fold the white paper inside, repeat behind.

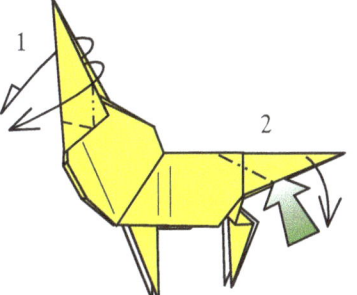

1. This is a combination of an outside-reverse fold with squash folds on the front and behind.
2. Reverse-fold.

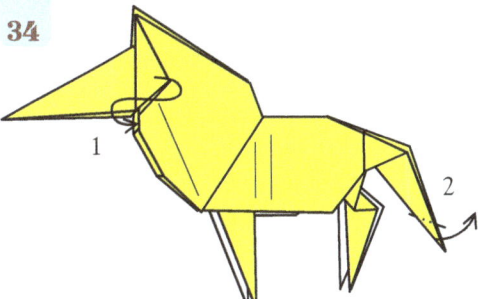

1. Tuck inside, repeat behind.
2. Reverse-fold.

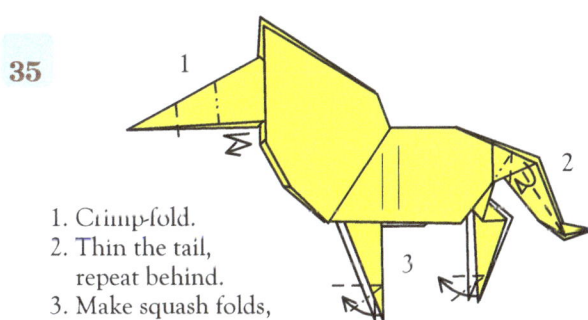

1. Crimp-fold.
2. Thin the tail, repeat behind.
3. Make squash folds, repeat behind.

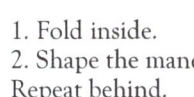

1. Fold inside.
2. Shape the mane. Repeat behind.

Lion

Giraffe

The tallest land animals, Giraffes have very long necks as well as very long tongues, both of which allow them to reach leaves and fruit in high trees. Giraffes sleep throughout the day for several minutes at a time rather than for a long stretch at night because they are prey animals and this is a way they can keep themselves safe and on guard. Once believed to be silent, Giraffes actually hum, but at so low a frequency that the human ear can barely hear them.

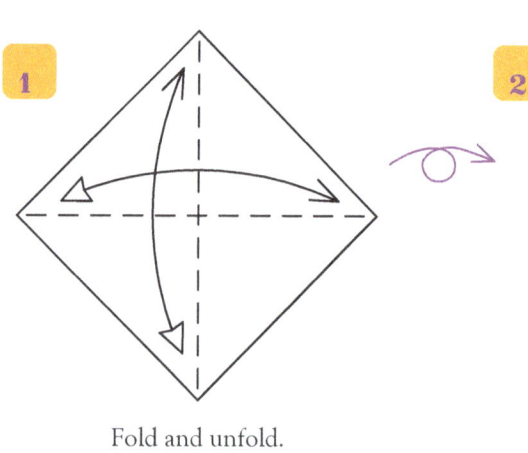

Fold and unfold. Rotate 45°.

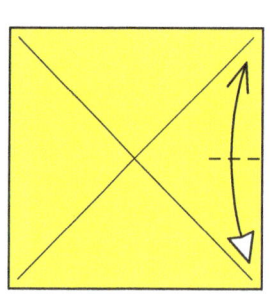

Fold and unfold on the right.

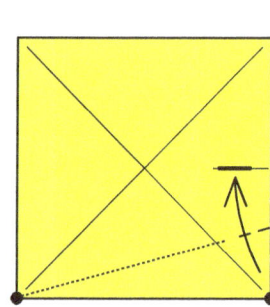

Bring the right dot to the line. Crease on the right.

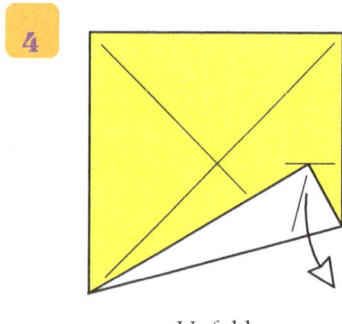

Unfold.

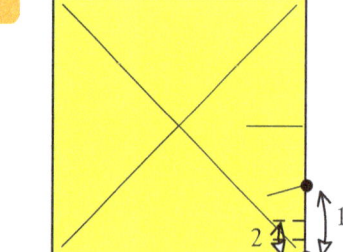

Fold and unfold on the right. Rotate 45°.

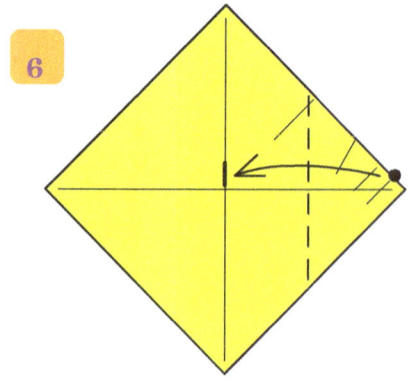

122   Origami Symphony No. 1

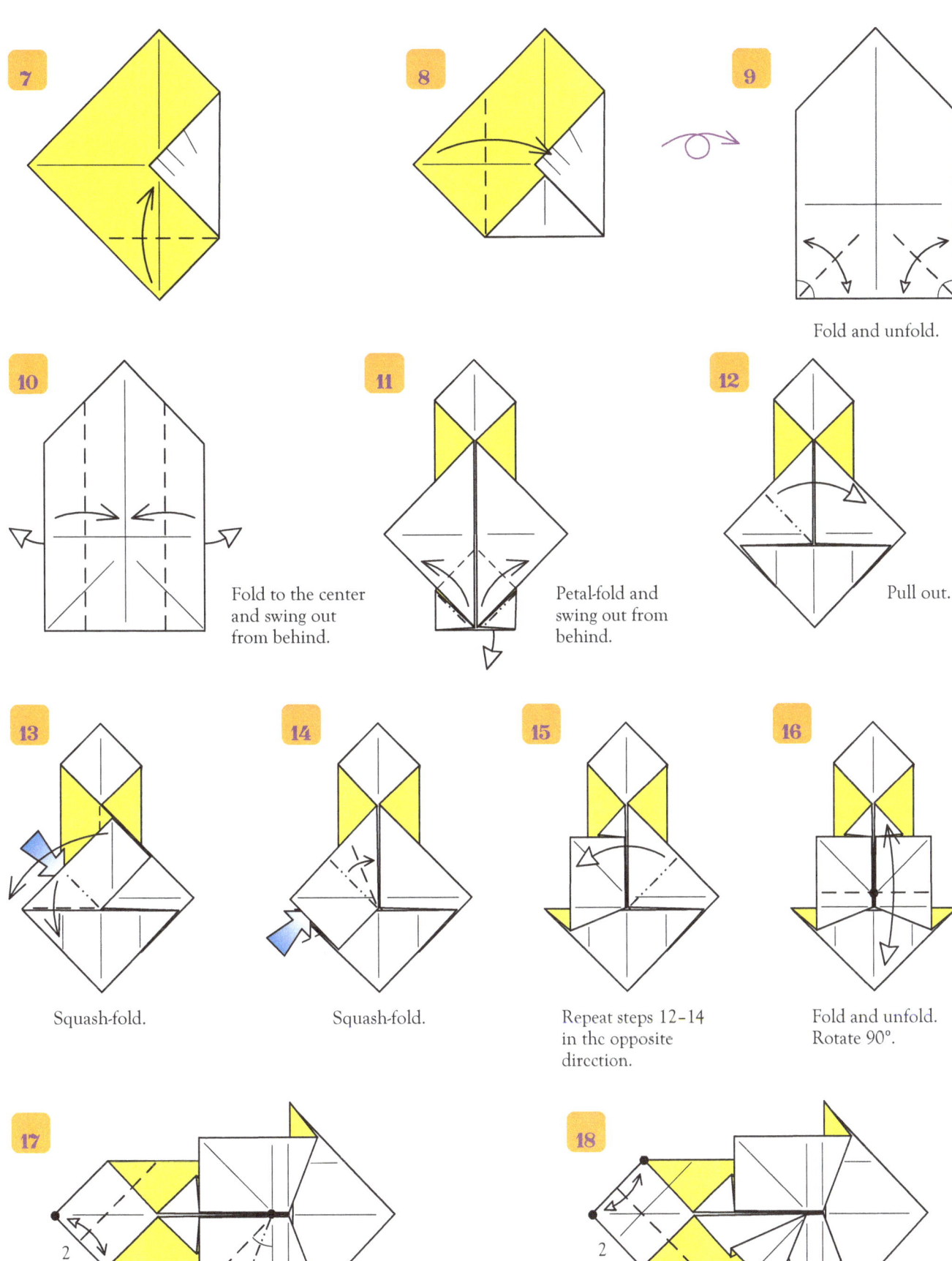

Giraffe 123

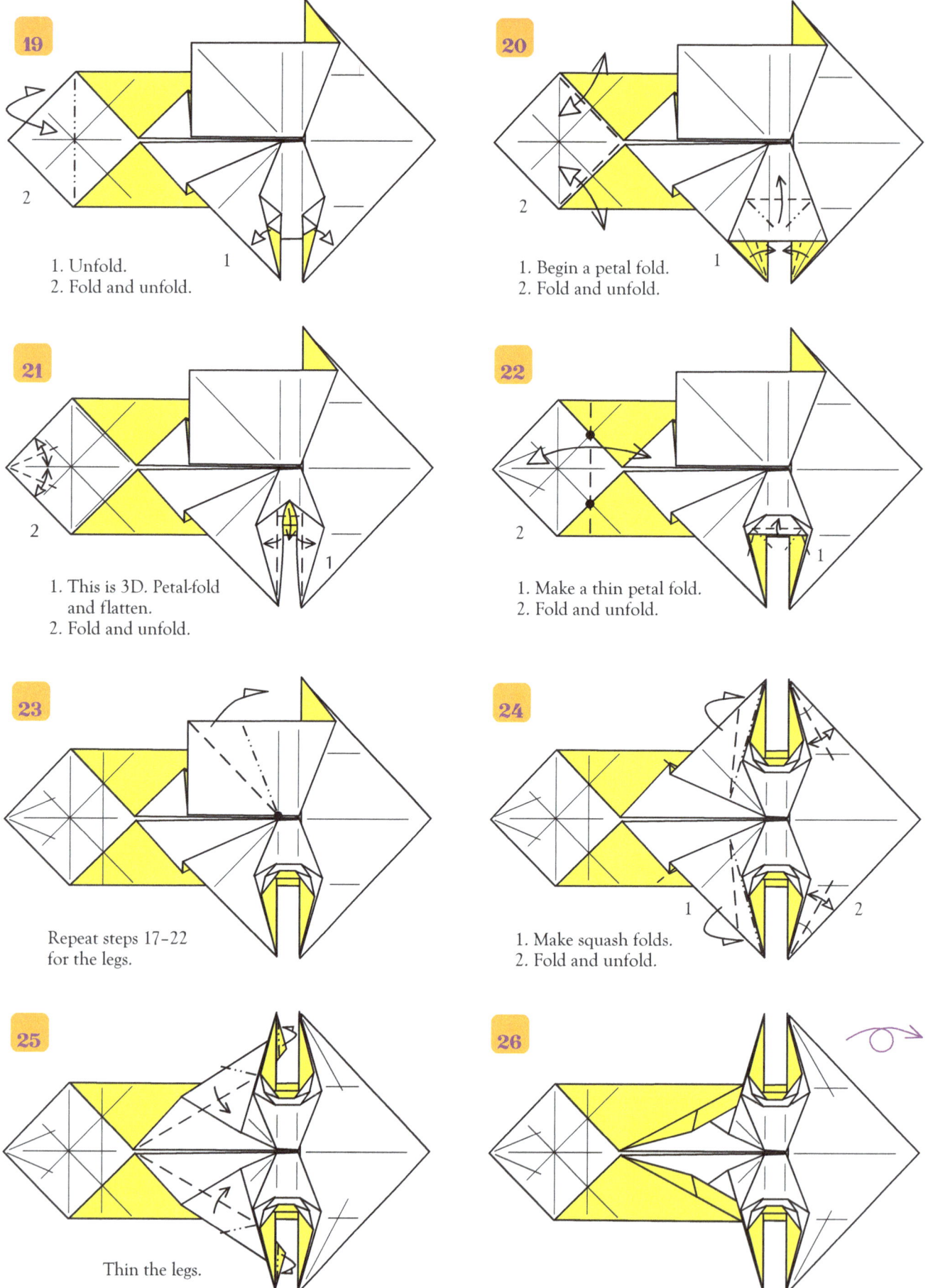

124 Origami Symphony No. 1

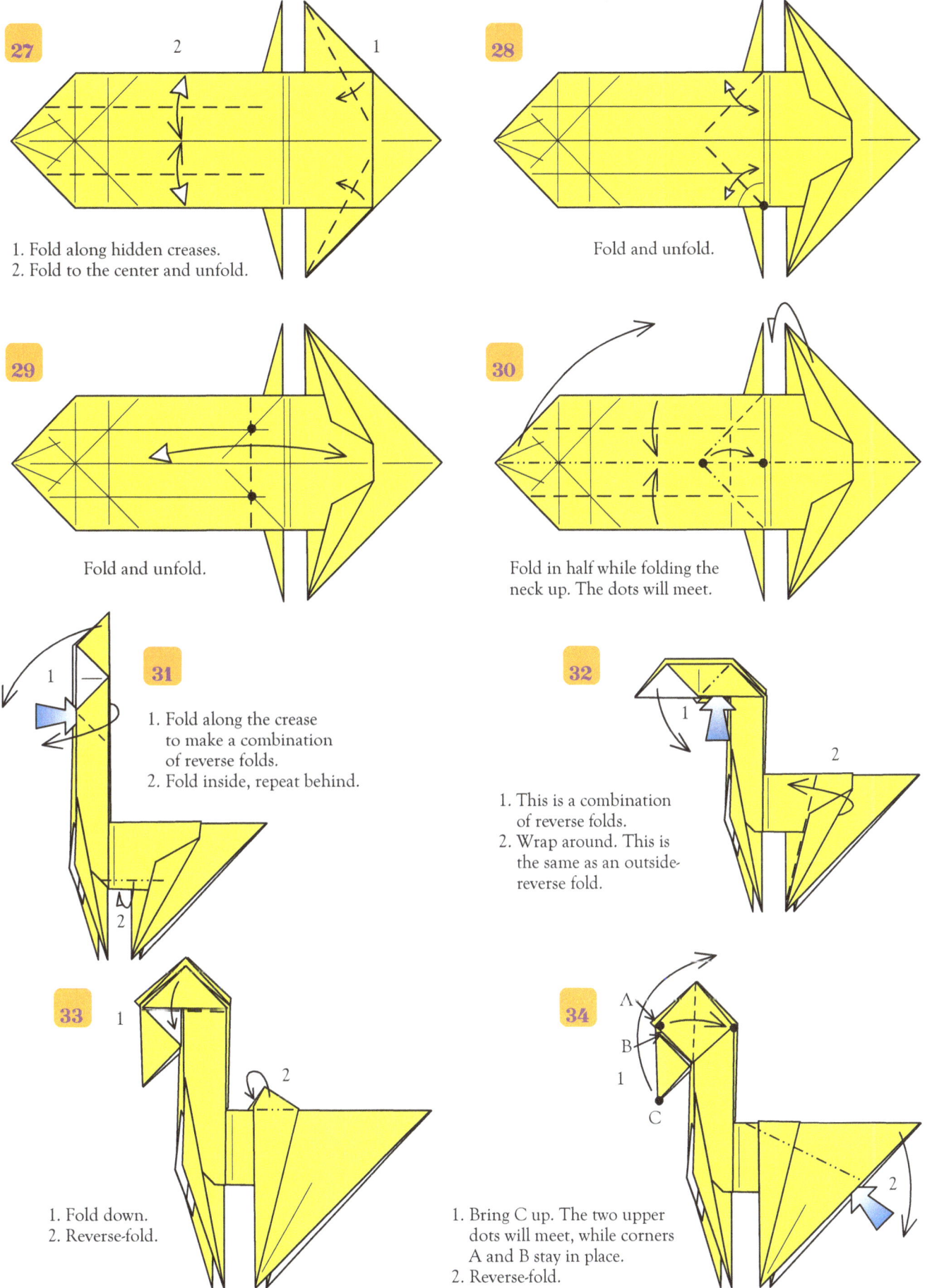

27
1. Fold along hidden creases.
2. Fold to the center and unfold.

28
Fold and unfold.

29
Fold and unfold.

30
Fold in half while folding the neck up. The dots will meet.

31
1. Fold along the crease to make a combination of reverse folds.
2. Fold inside, repeat behind.

32
1. This is a combination of reverse folds.
2. Wrap around. This is the same as an outside-reverse fold.

33
1. Fold down.
2. Reverse-fold.

34
1. Bring C up. The two upper dots will meet, while corners A and B stay in place.
2. Reverse-fold.

Giraffe **125**

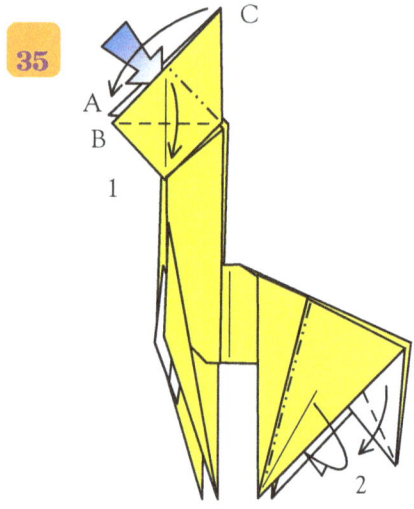

1. Squash-fold.
2. Thin the leg and tail, repeat behind.

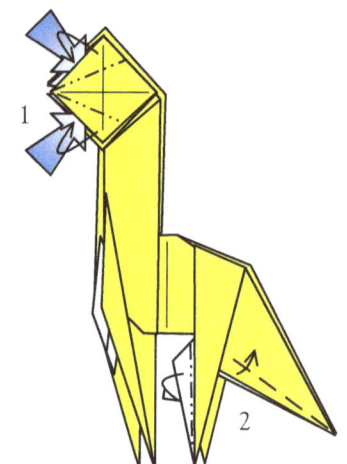

1. Make reverse folds.
2. Thin the leg and tail, repeat behind.

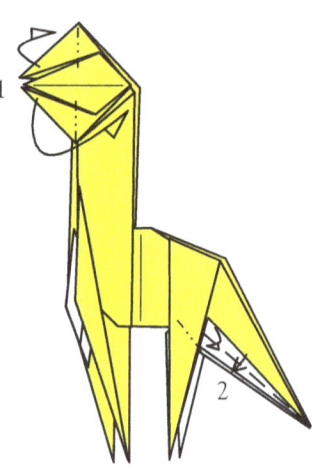

1. Fold behind.
2. Thin the white paper, repeat behind.

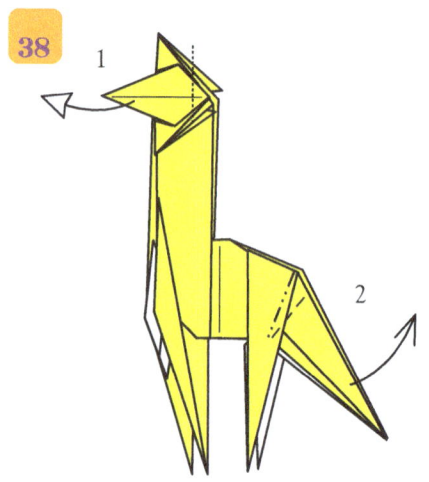

1. Stretch and fold along the dotted line.
2. Crimp-fold.

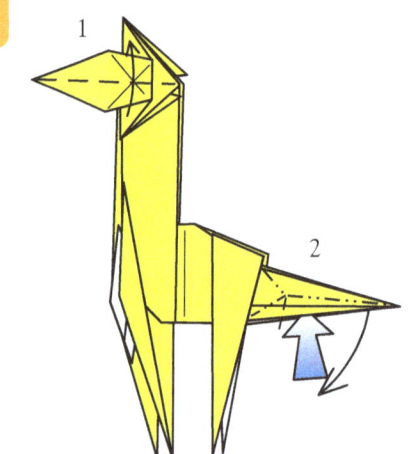

1. Fold up.
2. Double-rabbit-ear.

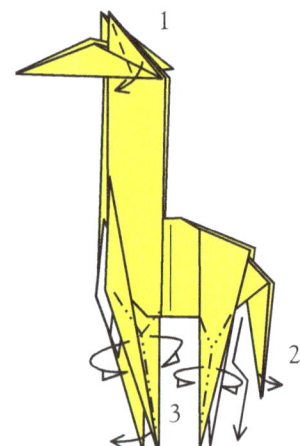

1. Fold the ears down.
2. Shape the tail.
3. Thin and shape the legs.
Repeat behind.

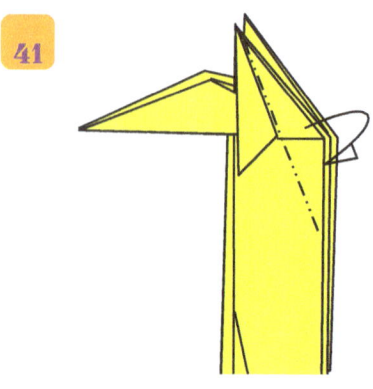

Fold inside and repeat behind.

Fold and unfold.

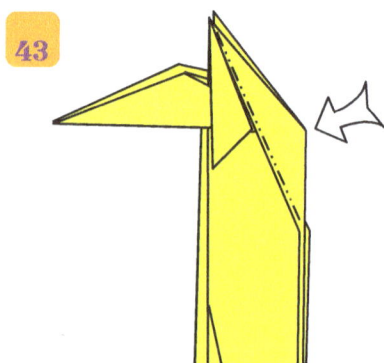

Sink.

126   Origami Symphony No. 1

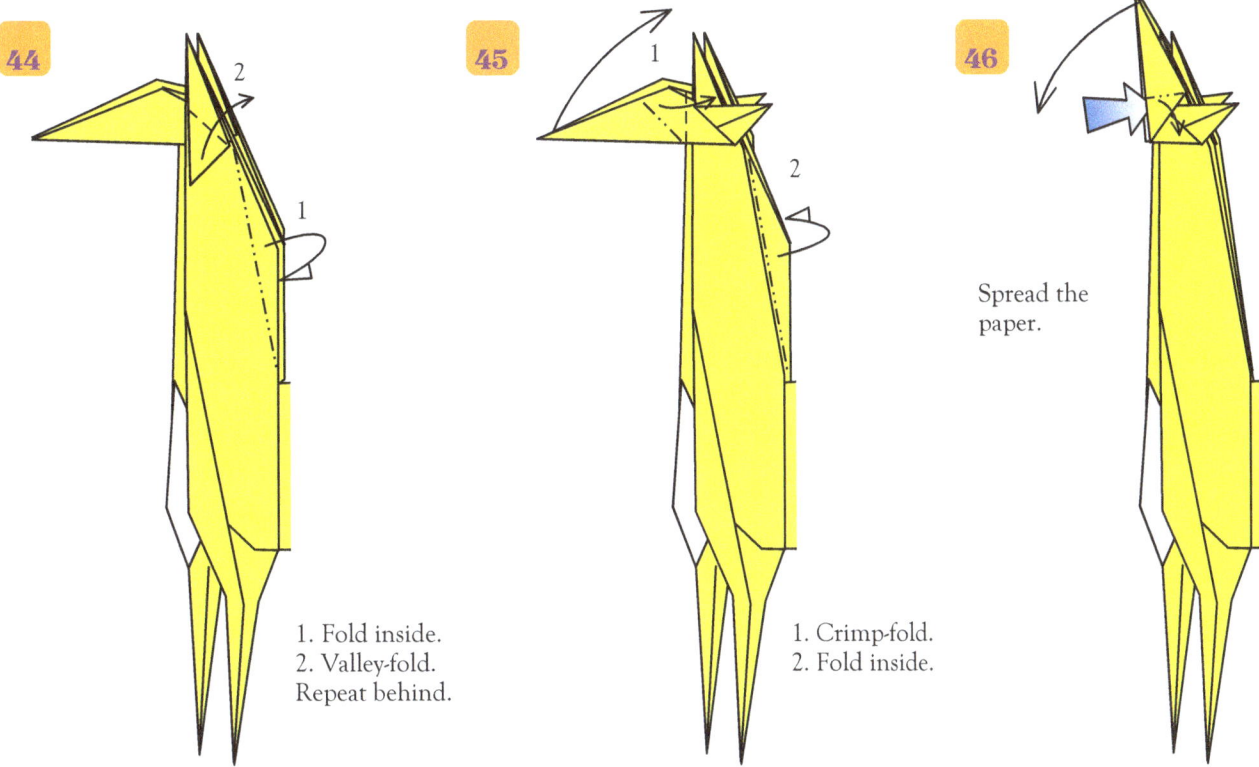

44
1. Fold inside.
2. Valley-fold.
Repeat behind.

45
1. Crimp-fold.
2. Fold inside.

46
Spread the paper.

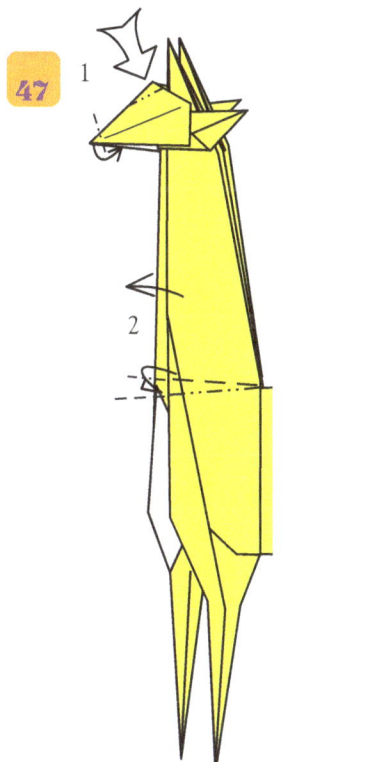

47
1. Reverse-fold and shape the head.
2. Crimp-fold.

48

Giraffe

www.ingramcontent.com/pod-product-compliance
Lightning Source LLC
Chambersburg PA
CBHW081115080526
44587CB00021B/3606